THE PUBLIC SECTOR
in the Mixed Economy

THE PUBLIC SECTOR
in the Mixed Economy

Merlyn Rees

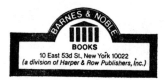
BOOKS
10 East 53d St., New York 10022
(a division of Harper & Row Publishers, Inc.)

© Merlyn Rees

Published in the U.S.A. 1973 by:
HARPER & ROW PUBLISHERS, INC.
BARNES & NOBLE IMPORT DIVISION

ISBN 06-495810-8

Printed in Great Britain

Contents

Contents

14

Preface

During the last twenty years I have worked with students preparing for A level, first-degree, and professional examinations in economics—also with a variety of groups in adult education. From this experience I learned that while there is much scattered material available on the public sector, most textbooks dismiss it in a single and short chapter. On the nature of the mixed economy which is a fact of modern industrial life there is equal paucity of information. I became convinced of the need to correct this imbalance with a book that described the current situation in these fields. This book is the result—in essence descriptive but discussing also the problems that abound.

This need has been reinforced by my experience as a Member of Parliament since 1963, and between 1964 and 1970 as Parliamentary Private Secretary to the then Chancellor of the Exchequer, the Rt. Hon. J. C. Callaghan, and then as a Minister at the Ministry of Defence and the Home Office. In these roles I discovered in practice more of the real extent, depth and diversity of the public sector.

On the political front this experience also reinforced my belief in the irrelevance of much political discussion on both the public sector and the mixed economy. The pretence, for example, that the Labour Party is only for the public sector and the Conservative Party against it and working for a return to some mythical free market economy, just does not in practice stand up to examination. The events of 1972 when the Conservative government 'stole Labour's economic clothes' with interventionist policies, taken with the public ownership of Rolls-Royce, should help to kill the myth. The slowly dawning realisation that a change of government cannot end the mixed economy makes it even more necessary that the informed general public—let alone the student—should be aware of the facts of economic life. There are real problems to solve in the mixed economy and they need political discussion. This is not easy when at each General Election one is led to believe that it is a struggle between the followers of two classical economists, Adam Smith and Karl Marx.

As far as the real issues are concerned the chapter on State Shareholdings is particularly relevant. The growth of state involvement in the private sector in this fashion is not well known. It is a developing field, and yet in the face of it industrialists, civil servants and politicians are floundering. The political cry of 'lame duck' indicates the point. In my view such development gives modern relevance to public ownership: a different species from that of the natural monopolies in the late 1940s.

In the preparation of the book I kept in mind the needs of students working on their own. To this end I have provided many references and a further reading list for the main chapters.

I acknowledge the information provided for me by government departments and by organisations in all parts of the public sector.

I must acknowledge also the stimulus I have received over the years from students in the Sixth Form of Harrow Weald County Grammar School, at the Luton College of Technology, from those following correspondence courses at the College of Estate Management—now of Reading University—and from students of Antioch College, Ohio, U.S.A., at their London Centre. The American mixed economy takes a different form from ours, but a public sector is becoming increasingly more meaningful there. I also owe much to the influence of discussion classes in the W.E.A. and in the Labour movement itself—where the best wards and constituency parties thrive on real political discussion. Those who actually work in the public and private sectors have a different view of these than do some of their advocates. In this respect also there is a difference between theory and practice.

Above all I thank my wife who assisted me with the research and typed innumerable drafts before finality.

1 The Mixed Economy

1 The Mixed Economy

In every type of economic society there are economic problems that have to be solved. There is a basic 'scarcity' of resources which is overcome by the production of goods and services which are exchanged as part of a system of specialisation.

These problems form the basis of enquiry in the study of economics and it is usually thought useful to aid the consequent analysis with two mutually exclusive, and non-existent, forms of society. One labelled 'capitalism'—the other 'socialism'.

Under 'capitalism' the factors of production—land, labour and capital—are allocated by a pricing system operated by the money-backed demand of consumers, and based on competition and laissez-faire in a society where the individual capitalist owns the resources.

Under 'socialism' the same factors are allocated by 'planning committees' or 'boards' operated by the needs of the state in a society in which it owns all the resources.

These definitions are designed to clarify objective analysis but, apart from the fact that they are often counter-productive to this aim because of the motivation of students for or against this or that form of society, such analysis ignores the economic facts of the real world.

Developments in Advanced Economies

In the 'West' consumer sovereignty is an over-simplification, for the producer in fact develops products and persuades the consumer to purchase; for many years the state has played a growing part in economic life. It was Harold Macmillan, not Karl Marx, who wrote: 'The Socialist remedy should ... be accepted in regard to industries and services ... where it is obvious that private enterprise has exhausted its social usefulness, or where the general welfare of the economy requires that certain basic industries and services need now to be conducted in the light of broader social considerations than the profit motive provides.'[1]

[1] Harold Macmillan, *The Middle Way*, Macmillan, 1937, p. 239.

Increasingly this remedy has been adopted; but private ownership predominates.

The European communist states since 1917 or 1945 have never been completely centrally planned—as late as the mid-1960s about half the milk and meat, like most of the fruit, vegetables and eggs produced in Russia, came from private plots.[1] In the last decade the criteria of profitability and interest, albeit in an accounting sense, have become part of managerial life; centralisation of decision taking is no longer completely typical; in some sectors advertising is to be found. A pricing system, within a planned economy, is emerging clearly in Poland and Hungary; it has been part of a conscious new 'socialist' development in Yugoslavia since 1948.[2] Here state ownership of resources predominates.

All the individual economic systems operating under the umbrella descriptions of 'capitalist' or 'socialist' have to be qualified with words of varying degree; there is 'mixed capitalist' and 'mixed socialist'. Changes are constantly taking place, forced by the facts of technology and by the needs and aspirations of emerging social classes. Scandinavia and the United Kingdom show one type of development; Central Europe another and the U.S.A. yet another. The under-developed peasant areas of the world show different trends.

There is, of course, far more philosophically and historically to both capitalism and socialism than their forms of economic organisation would alone imply, but nevertheless economic similarities are constantly emerging. The leader's speech on economic problems at the individual communist party congresses bears a striking resemblance to a presidential State of the Union address, or that of a British prime minister after a general election.

The Private Sector

The private sector itself in the U.K. has not been immune from change. There has been an increase in the size of the firm by growth and merger, and the 500 largest make some 50 per cent of all the profits of private industry. The large firms dominate

[1] E. Crankshaw, Khrushchev, Collins, 1966, p. 304.
[2] (i) See M. C. Kayser (ed.), Economic Development for Eastern Europe, Macmillan, 1968; (ii) P. J. D. Wiles, 'Fifty Years After: What Future for Communism?', Lloyds Bank Review, Oct. 1967, p. 36.

and within the modern managed economy, funds invested with them bear far less risk than in the rest of the private sector. The planning operations involved in the working of these firms have been used to justify planning by the state in the public sector; their very existence casts doubts on another textbook assumption that individual firms cannot grow beyond a certain point without decreasing returns to scale setting in.

The individual shareholder within the joint stock firm is not as collectively important as in the past. The institutional shareholders—insurance companies and investment trusts—are important, but nevertheless, overall there has been a growing separation between ownership of capital and control of the actual running of the firm.

The complexities of modern industry have meant the growth in power and social significance of the manager, the technical specialist, the organisation man. These managers have a different outlook and motivation from that of the old-style capitalist. This is equally true of the trade union official, whose own organisation has changed with its more institutionalised role.

The ploughing back of profits has always been the major source of capital for industry. Since the war a smaller proportion of profits has been distributed to the shareholder, which has further strengthened the managerial position against that of the outside provider of capital.

The profit motive is still dominant but its role has changed, particularly in the large firms.[1] Profits are no longer personal to the manager and this change makes the situation within the firm similar to that in a nationalised industry, or even to industry in Eastern Europe.

The growth in the power of the large manager-controlled corporation is a feature of modern capitalism which has had a profound impact on social and political life, particularly in the U.S.A. where the concentration of such power is much more clearly seen.[2]

[1] See Expenditure Committee (House of Commons) Minutes of Evidence, 28 Feb. 1972, Further and Higher Education—where a company director complained that too many graduate recruits were out of sympathy with the idea of profit-making.
[2] In this whole field of changes within capitalism, see C. A. R. Crosland, *The Future of Socialism*, Cape, 1956, chapter I, and particularly pp. 33-8, and for the American scene, Charles Reich, *The Greening of America*, Allen Lane: The Penguin Press, 1971.

International Companies

The growth in the international power of the large corporations
is also a feature of modern economic life. From a monetary point
of view the U.K. is more important as a parent of international
companies than as a host, e.g. British Leyland with manufactur-
ing/assembly facilities in 60 countries.[1] The most important
progenitor of international companies is nevertheless the U.S.A.,
and companies from that country predominate in the foreign
capital which controls 58 per cent of U.K. motor car production;
50 per cent of electronics; 65 per cent of pharmaceuticals; and
80 per cent of office machinery.[2]

Increasingly the ownership of industry by international companies is raising problems which are becoming a matter of political
urgency. 'They can dodge taxes and exchange controls.' Their
methods of achieving this 'increased the strain on sterling in
1967 and the companies gained from devaluation itself'.[3] There
are new problems for trade unions emerging which will give
new importance to regional and international trade union organisations.

Factors Influencing Government Involvement

In the United Kingdom, the first country to be industrialised,
the nature of the capitalist system has altered. Not only has the
private sector itself changed but the state has become involved
in the management of the economy. Overall it has also become
a mixed economy, part public, part private, the proportions of
which have changed under the influence of unemployment, technology and war.

The influence of those pre-war years of unemployment, particularly in the 'distressed areas', on government policy was
enormous. It was the driving force behind government intervention to break the business cycle, and behind government
intervention against the market forces which were siting new

[1] *International Companies*, Report of a Trade Union Congress Conference on International Companies, see p. 4 and table IV, p. 86.
[2] *Ibid.*, table VI, p. 87.
[3] Nicholas Faith, 'Squaring up to Yankee Imperialism', *Sunday Times*,
25 April 1971.

and expanding industries in the South of England.[1]

'The war was a prolonged exercise in central planning and control',[2] and whether it was for the armed forces, civil defence, or the allocation of manpower; in agriculture, industry, science; or in the effect it had on ideas about social security or the functions of the state, its effect was traumatic.[3] It was the world not only of Churchill but of Bevin and Beveridge. The development of technology in the service of the armed forces was one aspect of the war effort. Its momentum has carried on in the same field and for civil purposes. New technological techniques have brought new forms of industrial organisation in both the private and public sector, and indeed changed the proportions of each.

For many reasons, there has developed over the years a mixed economy in which the government intervenes in a variety of ways.

ECONOMIC POLICY

Fiscal and Monetary Policy

A major sign of the departure from the prevailing free market philosophy of the 1930s is in the extension of budgetary policy.

Large sums of money are raised by taxation to pay for expenditure on defence, education, social security, housing and the health service.[4] There is current discussion about the machinery of government both local and national and also about the methods

[1] See D. H. Aldcroft, *The Inter-War Economy: Britain 1919–1939*, Batsford, 1970, p. 80, for unemployment in the regions 1912–36; p. 81, for numbers of factories opened in Greater London between 1932 and 1937.

[2] Sir Oliver Franks, *Central Planning and Control in War and Peace*, lectures delivered at the London School of Economics and Political Science, 1947, p. 8.

[3] Angus Calder, *The People's War, Britain 1939–45*, Cape, 1969, which not only re-creates the wartime situation but provides a full book list for each aspect of the war discussed.

[4] The Expenditure Estimates for 1971–2 were as follows (£m):

Defence	2,545
Trade and Industry and Employment	2,394
Environmental Services	3,643
Social Services	3,481

of raising revenue but, despite the private sector that exists in
the civil fields, there is little strength in any argument for moving
back to the free market forces of the past. In 1968 Mr Reginald
Maudling expressed the belief that 'There is no more reality in
a concept of a perfect market that operated before socialism was
invented than there is in the concept of a golden age of man
... to return to nineteenth-century laissez-faire would drive us
back to the days of the great depression.'[1] Mr Edward Heath
early in the life of his administration expressed his philosophy as
'We agree that in many of these matters the State does have a
necessary part to play, though the exact nature of the State's role
changes from time to time. But we are also convinced that in
recent years the balance has gone too far in favour of the State.'[2]
The main political argument is about balance not absolutes,
despite the 'new style' and attitude that Mr Heath brought to
economic policy, and despite the fundamentalist belief of Mr
Enoch Powell in the virtues of free market forces.

The nature of the argument is the same in the developing
aims of fiscal policy based on the 'macro-economic revolution'
of the pre-war years—the counter-cyclical policy for ironing out
the boom and slump of trade cycles by budget deficits and surpluses, by public works and other government investment
policies;[3] based also on policies to redistribute incomes by direct
taxation and the consequent transfer payments of tax reliefs and
payments of social security.

The same type of political argument is found in discussions of
monetary policy, i.e. the control of economic activity by raising
and lowering interest rates, adjusting hire purchase regulations,
and restricting or increasing bank credit.

In the 1960s there was a return of academic support for
monetary policy, particularly for the money supply theory
advocated by Professor Milton Friedman of Chicago. It was the
movement of opinion against monetary policy in the late 1950s

[1] *Sunday Times*, 15 Sept. 1968.
[2] Speaking at the Annual Conservative Local Government Conference,
13 March 1971.
[3] There are many eminent economists whose names are associated with
this development in economic thought, e.g. D. H. Robertson and J. M.
Keynes in Britain, Ohlin in Sweden, Mitchell and Schumpeter in the
U.S.A. The original ideas of J. A. Hobson earlier in the century are too
often forgotten.

which had led to the new policies of indicative planning by the Macmillan government.

Planning

In 1962 there was created the National Economic Development Council (Neddy) with the following terms of reference:

(a) To examine the economic performance of the nation with particular concern for plans for the future in both the private and public sectors of industry.
(b) To consider together what are the obstacles to quicker growth, what can be done to improve efficiency and whether the best use is being made of our resources.
(c) To seek agreement upon ways of improving economic performance, competitive power and efficiency; in other words to increase the rate of sound growth.

The Council sits under the chairmanship of the Chancellor of the Exchequer and consists of leaders of industry, the trade unions and government. It is an independent but publicly financed forum for the debate on economic matters of national importance. It is aided in its work by the National Economic Development Office, as are the Economic Development Committees which are similarly independent representative committees to examine the needs and growth objectives of key individual industries. The long list of N.E.D.O. publications, *Investment Appraisal*; *Value Added Tax*; *Economic Assessments to 1972*—forecasts of economic patterns and trends to 1972 from 13 E.D.C.s—Agriculture, Chemicals, Electrical Engineering, Electronics, Food Manufacturing, Hosiery and Knitwear, Hotels and Catering, Machine Tools, Mechanical Engineering, Motor Manufacturing, Paper and Board, Rubber, Pan-Textiles (Clothing, Hosiery and Knitwear, and Wool Industry, etc.)—shows the nature and extent of their work.

There are those who question the efficacy of consultative planning in general and Neddy in particular, but in the long run it has become clear that there is value in the meeting together of both sides of industry and the provision of information. Neddy's job is to influence the climate of opinion, to put together the great knowledge and experience of industry in a form in which it can be used for the management of the economy. This type of planning is, in retrospect, not deep involvement in industry but it is another move away from the economy of the free market with its two mutually exclusive sides.[1]

Incomes Policy

Another such move may be observed in the field of 'incomes policy'. Discussion of such a policy is not new, for its need became apparent as the disciplines of the pre-war mass unemployment were perceived after 1950 to be historical.[2] It is seen in the National Incomes Commission set up in 1962 to consider and make recommendations on claims for improvement in pay or working conditions. The failure of this body led to further developments under the Wilson administration.

There was the 'Joint Statement of Intent' signed in 1965 by employers, trade unions and government, together with the establishment of the National Board for Prices and Incomes. There followed 'norms' and a freeze; restraints in prices, dividends and rents. There was devaluation which, though a response to much deeper economic problems, could in absolute terms be seen as a failure for incomes policy. Nevertheless, in relative terms there were aspects of success. The policy was educative, for certainly by the middle of the period discussions of productivity were no longer simply academic. More generally there grew a realisation that there was a problem of income determination in our society.

The greatest practical success was the work of the National Board for Prices and Incomes. Its objective reports on a wide variety of matters in the field of prices and incomes influenced employers and unions alike.[3] It did much to modernise the archaic pay structures of British industry and, although it was dismantled by the Heath Government there had to be set up a series of Courts of Enquiry, which were, in effect, ad-hoc N.B.P.I.s, to deal with particular problems as they arose. There is a logic which

[1] Basil Taylor, 'The N.E.D.C. After Six Years', *Westminster Bank Review*, Feb. 1968, p. 16: 'The idea that an economy grows and can be made to grow faster without loss of important freedoms for any, has reached public consciousness mainly through Neddy's activity.'
[2] See Ian Mikardo, *Trade Unions in a Full Employment Economy*, New Fabian Essays, Turnstile Press, 1952.
[3] The N.B.P.I. published 170 reports. The Final General Report of April 1971 is an admirable summing-up.

eventually comes to all parties in government, brought about by
the hard facts of reality. There seems every likelihood of a
return one day to the N.B.P.I. or something very like it.[1]

The discussion and arguments that accompanied the introduction of an 'incomes policy' revealed something of the nature of
the Labour Party, as did the emotional trauma during the later
passage of the Industrial Relations Bill through Parliament. During this period one noted also the emergence at national level of
a type of Toryism based on the ideas of middle management and
lower-middle-class concepts. In so far as these attitudes in both
parties are typical of the facts of industrial life it may well all be
more realistic, but it does more to pose the problem rather than
suggest a solution.

Perhaps the greatest difficulty is that there are no signposts
to the future in this field, and certainly the tied-state unions of
Soviet Russia have little appeal. The Industrial Relations Act
is seen by some as an attempt to oil the wheels of a free-market
wage-negotiating system by strengthening the hand of the
employers and trade union leaders against unofficial strike leaders.
It could be marginally advantageous if this proves to be the result,
but it will not remove the trends of half a century which have
brought social and economic value judgments into the determination of incomes. In any event the fundamental defects of the
Act will be altered either before or after repeal.

There are factors in the day-to-day running of industry; pensions, grievance procedure, collection of union dues, health and
safety, paid leave provisions, holiday rosters, etc., which require
the voluntary cooperation of both sides of industry. This is
basically true of wage determination itself, but the continued
existence of a large force of low-paid workers and of excessive
overtime, together with the constant need to change pay structures especially in the public sector, will necessitate continued
government intervention.[2] This is reinforced by the need of
government to consider the overall aggregate effect of changes in
purchasing power on the economy.[1]

[1] As early as November 1970 the government set up the non-statutory
and independent Office of Manpower Economics, which provides a
secretariat for certain public pay enquiries; services ad-hoc pay
enquiries; and researches into pay and manpower. See below, p. 39.
[2] See Professor Hugh Clegg, How to Run an Incomes Policy and Why
We Made Such a Mess of the Last One, Heinemann Educational, 1971.

The incomes policies of the 1960s may not have found final solutions but they are part of a long-term trend. Indeed by late 1972 the Heath government was even further up against the 'logic of reality' and the country was back to the Prime Ministerial meetings with the T.U.C. and C.B.I. and to the inevitable 'wages freeze'. As with central planning itself, an incomes policy is going to take long to evolve.

Regional Policy

The interwar depression, in the U.K., caused more perhaps by structural rather than cyclical unemployment, has bitten deeply into our economic and social thinking.

Counter-cyclical investment policy has been one reaction. The other has been direct government intervention to affect the location of industry. The correction of regional imbalance is an aspect of planning that has driven even non-interventionist governments to resist market forces.

Regional policy in the U.K. is based on the Special Areas legislation of the 1930s with its grants and 'trading estates'. The Barlow Commission of 1940 rationalised the anti-unemployment philosophy of the 1930s at a time when planning for the war effort made it inevitable. In 1945 came the Distribution of Industry Act; Industrial Development Certificates which prevent factory growth in the prosperous areas; and the beginning of the new and expanded towns.

There was legislation in the early 1960s by the Conservative Government; Local Employment Acts and the concept of small growth points. After 1964 the Wilson government introduced direct investment grants and the discrimination of the Regional Employment Premiums. The Hunt Committee was appointed to look at the economic prospects in certain areas where the general economic prospects were bleak. As a consequence, a number of areas in the North-east, Yorkshire and Humberside, Notts and Derbyshire, South-east Wales, Leith and Plymouth, were designated 'intermediate areas' and given economic aid, but to a lesser degree than in the development areas. One indication of the change is that aid to industry in 1963–4 had been £30m; by 1969–70 it had increased to £314m.

[1] For an interesting article on the anti-inflationary argument for an incomes policy, see Sidney Weintraub, 'An Incomes Policy to Stop Inflation', *Lloyds Bank Review*, Jan. 1971, p. 1.

The Heath administration returned to investment tax allowances and ended the system of direct grants. There was a division of opinion about the effect of this change which enabled tax reductions to be made in the country as a whole but, on the other hand, resulted in a smaller number of industrial firms moving to both the development and intermediate areas. There remained, however, a state-backed incentive for industry to expand in these areas—with building grants, rent-free periods for factories; assistance towards the movement of key workers. There are training grants and other forms of training assistance at Government Training Centres.

Eventually in the 1972 Budget, in the face of growing unemployment of over 1,000,000 people, the Conservative Government announced major changes in policy.[1] Improved tax allowances for investment in plant, machinery and buildings were instituted for the country as a whole, with a return to cash development grants in the regions. The intermediate areas were extended and regional development grants in respect of buildings were made available.

A Minister for Industrial Development was appointed to the Department for Trade and Industry to take charge of a new Industrial Development Executive and be advised by an Industrial Development Board consisting of prominent persons in industry, banking, accounting and finance.

The logic of market forces is not allowed to work itself out completely in the regions. The eight planned regions designated in 1964 for England[2]—apart from those in Wales, Scotland and Northern Ireland—are another development of planning which is complementary to the N.E.D.C. and the Industrial E.D.C.s and another move away from free market forces.

[1] 'Industrial and Regional Development', Cmnd 4942, March 1972. See also the Industry Act 1972, in which there was not only the legislative form for changes in regional policy but also fundamental changes in the form of government financial assistance for industry.
[2] Northern, North West, Yorkshire and Humberside, East Midlands, West Midlands, South West, South East, and East Anglia, with (i) a regional economic planning council with members from industry, commerce, trade unions, local authorities and universities—with the task of collecting information, researching into trends, investigating particular problems and generally advising the central government; (ii) a regional economic planning board of the regional chief officers of government departments, in effect a little Whitehall, to coordinate regional government policy.

REGULATION AND INVOLVEMENT IN AGRICULTURE AND INDUSTRY

Regulation

Modern budgetary policies and planning, whether national or regional, may be twentieth-century concepts but the intervention of the state as a referee was seen early on in the industrial revolution. At the least the state provided laws of commerce, justice in the courts and a police force. This type of intervention has grown and developed.

At first the state looked after safety on the railways, then on the roads, now in the air. The Secretary for Trade and Industry has wide responsibility in these respects and, for example, spends large sums of money on a radar system to allocate air space to aircraft over the United Kingdom. The same department administers legislation affecting commercial arrangements which act in restraint of trade. It is also responsible for the Monopolies Commission which itself seeks to prevent the full effect of free market forces.

The Home Office is responsible for the police force and the fire service. There are compendious health regulations administered by local authorities which have a long history, for even in the heyday of laissez-faire recurrent epidemics affected those who did not themselves live in the poorer areas of the growing urban districts.

There is a Central Health Services Council, General Nursing Council, British Pharmacopoeia Committee, Committee on Safety of Medicines, and a Medicines Commission which report to the Secretary of State for Health and Social Security.

There are Traffic Commissioners in respect of Public Service Vehicle Licensing, and Licensing Authorities in road haulage, which report to the Secretary of State for the Environment.

The list of regulatory powers of the Department of the Environment is long for it has great responsibilities in Housing, Local Government and, as its new title affirmed, with the whole question of pollution which modern technology is forcing on to the public mind. A typical example of the many quasi-judicial decisions that this department makes is that of October 1970 when under Town and Country Planning legislation the Minister decided that the runway at the municipally-owned Leeds–Bradford Airport could not be extended. Increased noise outweighed economic advantage.

In this and many other ways the state plays a major part in regulating industry and commerce.

Agriculture

Over the years regulation has given way to greater involvement, and this is clearly seen in agriculture, which is firmly a privately owned sector of the economy but which, particularly since 1939, has received large sums of money from the state.

Since the war there has been a system of agricultural support which consisted in 1971–2 of guaranteed prices for wheat, barley, oats, rye, potatoes, sugar beet, fat cattle, fat sheep and lambs, fat pigs, milk, eggs and wool; with production grants for hill sheep, and brucellosis incentives for dairy and beef herds. Other grants and subsidies are paid for field drainage, water supply and farm improvements, etc. The total estimates for 1971–2 were originally £296·8m and after the March 1971 annual review a further £46·6m was added.

'Annual Review and Determination of Guarantees', *Cmnd* 4623, 1971.

(£m)

	1971–2 (original estimates)	Effects on original 1971–2 estimates of 1971 review determinations
I Implementation of price guarantees		
Cereal		
Wheat	22.8	+ 5.2
Barley	10.5	+ 6.9
Oats and mixed corn	5.6	+ 1.3
	—— 38.9	——+13.4
Potatoes	6.0	
Fatstock		
Cattle	23.1	+18.9
Sheep	7.0	+ 8.2
Pigs	29.0	+ 7.3
	—— 59.1	——+34.4
Eggs, hen and duck	8.9	− 3.1
Wool	6.4	+ 0.3
Total I	**119.3**	**+45.0**

	1971-2 (original estimates)	Effect on original 1971-2 estimates of 1971 review determinations
II Relevant production grants		
Calves	29.9	—
Beef cows	6.2	—
Hill cows	14.3	—
Hill sheep	9.3	+ 0.4
Winter keep	5.1	— 0.1
Brucellosis eradication incentives	0.6	+ 1.3
Fertilisers	33.3	—
Lime	4.8	—
Ploughing	0.2	—
Field beans	—	—
Field drainage (except tiling)	0.6	—
Small farmers	0.8	—
Farm business records	1.2	—
Crofting (cropping, etc.)	0.5	—
Other	1.4	—
Total II	108.2	+ 1.6
III Other grants and subsidies		
Field drainage (tiling)	6.0	—
Water supply	0.3	—
Livestock rearing land	0.5	—
Hill land	1.9	—
Farm capital grants	11.1	—
Farm improvements	14.6	—
Farm structure	1.4	—
Investment incentives	14.7	—
Crofting improvements	0.4	—
Other	0.2	—
Total III	51.1	—
Totals I, II, and III	278.6	+46.6
Administrative expenses estimate	14.1	—
IV Other services		
Payment from U.K. Government for the benefit of agricultural producers in Northern Ireland	2.1	—
Payments in respect of agricultural training	2.0	—
Total estimated cost of agricultural support	296.8	+46.6

Significant changes in this system of support are to be made, but it is unlikely that this private sector of the economy will move away from dependence on the state.

Industry

The involvement of the government in industry is much greater both in the amount of finance and in form.

Government has long given advice and information to industry. In 1971–2[1] it was expected that about £8m would be spent on activities designed to promote exports; commercial intelligence, participation in trade fairs, etc.

The Department of Trade and Industry which superseded the Ministry of Technology is 'responsible' for industry in this way. It concerns itself also with standards and quality; consequently it provides grants to the British Standards Institution and for the authentication of the quality of British products, e.g. electronic components.

This Department itself provides research facilities (£13m) and also makes grants to private industrial research associations (£3·5m). It finances general productivity and specialist advisory services to industry provided by itself, universities, Industrial Liaison Centres; by the National Computing Centre and the Computer-aided Design Centre (£3m).

The need to modernise and restructure older industries and to promote new technological industries has led to even greater involvement. The shipbuilding industry has for long faced state-subsidised foreign competition: it has many problems, not the least of which is obsolete equipment and yards, accompanied by bad employer/labour relationships. In 1966, after the Geddes Report on the Ship Building Industry, funds were made available through the Ship Building Industry Board to promote the regrouping and re-equipment of the industry. These were limited to £20m for grants and £32·5m for loans and purchase of shares, e.g. Upper Clyde Shipbuilders (U.C.S.).[2]

[1] See 'Supply Estimates 1971–2', HC 302, 1971, 'Class IV Trade, Industry and Employment', where the breakdown of the total sums spent by the Department of Trade and Industry may be seen.

Where approximate figures are given they are, unless otherwise stated, rounded figures from this source.

[2] For full details see chapter 5.

The estimates of expenditure by the Board for 1971–2 showed a decline from approximately £9m to £7·5m. This reflected the optimistic assumption of the Geddes Report that support would end, and the government did not renew the life of the Ship Building Board after the end of 1971.

Guarantees by the government of up to £1,000m are available to back the purchase of British ships by British ship-owners, while relief from certain import duties and indirect taxes was arranged through the Treasury.

In the early days of the Conservative government in 1970 there was undoubtedly a reappraisal made of this credit system. Credits were held up late in that year and in the early months of the next, with a resulting profound effect on shipbuilding orders; the removal of the investment grants had a similar effect.

As a result of this it was announced in August 1971, in the midst of the U.C.S. crisis that the limit on credit was to be raised from £700m to £1,000m from the beginning of 1972 but that, as the Ship Building Industry Board was to end, such credit was no longer to be issued on the recommendation of the Board on condition that reorganisation has taken or is to take place.

State intervention matters to the ship-building industry. Despite the 'lame duck' philosophy which guided Conservative government policy, and spotlighted by the story of U.C.S., the history of the last 50 years would indicate that the more direct Geddes-type support will return. As a representative of the ship-builders has said, 'Industry must also be able to rely upon the active support of the Government, for while shipbuilders would prefer to operate freely, it is unrealistic to think that any country without official help can compete with those nations where State aid in various forms is available.'[1]

The government has aided the computer industry, not only through the advice centres but with expenditure for research and development. The major involvement came in 1968 when with the assistance of the Ministry of Technology the three major British computer companies were brought together to form Inter-

[1] Quoted in *House of Commons Official Report*, vol. 822, no. 192, 2 August 1971, col. 1137. In fact, by Part III of the Industry Act of 1972 the 'home credit scheme' for shipbuilding was reframed in view of the demise of the Shipbuilding Agency Board and a temporary construction grant scheme set up. The new Industrial Development Executive was also to turn its attention to this industry.

national Computers Ltd (I.C.L.)—with a 10·5 per cent government holding.[1] In 1971–2 £2·25m was estimated for the Computers Merger Scheme. The Conservative government, giving
evidence to the Parliamentary Select Committee on Science and
Technology, made it clear that they regarded a British-owned
computer manufacturing capability as essential to the national
economic welfare, and that it intended to achieve this by appropriate procurement policies. By August 1971 it became apparent
that the government meant this and that they were not prepared
to treat I.C.L. as they did Rolls-Royce.

Financial support was made available through the cooperative
advanced computer technology project; one example of the work
done under the Science and Technology Act of 1965 whereby
financial support for the practical application of the results of
scientific research may be given. In some projects a return to
the taxpayer is sought by a levy on commercial sales and share
in licensing royalties. The government has also continued the
previous practice of guaranteeing orders from the public sector
and ensuring that the banks back with credit the leasing operations of I.C.L.

Under the Industrial Expansion Act loans of over £60m were
made available towards the capital cost of electricity generating
capacity for the aluminium smelter projects in Anglesey and
Invergordon. These projects are not only examples of development that would not have taken place without the state but they
are another example of regional policy. In 1971–2 £8·75m was
estimated for this purpose.

The same concern for regional development is seen from the
financial aid given to the individual Tourist Boards in Great
Britain and to the British Tourist Authority itself. In 1971–2
some £12m was estimated for expenditure in this field together
with the once-for-all grants for improvement and extension of
hotels under the Development of Tourism Act of 1969.

Under the Science and Technology Act of 1965 purchases are
made by the government Preproduction Order Support (£1m)
scheme to speed up the use of new equipment. This is loaned
free to industry for evaluation and sold, if required, at a low
price to the evaluer.

This scheme has been used in machine tools, textiles, plastics,

[1] See chapter 5.

printing, fish processing machinery, mechanical handling and construction equipment, and scientific instruments.

Another aspect of this development work is seen in the work of the National Research Development Corporation, a statutory corporation whose main function is to develop and exploit inventions resulting from publicly financed research.[1] The full extent of the work of this body is not revealed by the £2·25m estimates for 1971–2. The work of this organisation typifies the growing mix of the two sectors of the economy.

The grants made to private industry illustrate the nature of the involvement of the state in British industry. The Wilson government concentrated the machinery for this involvement in a Ministry of Technology; under the Heath government this was transmogrified into a Department of Trade and Industry. The instruments for Min-Tech involvement were the Science and Technology Act; the Industrial Expansion Act of 1968, and the Industrial Reconstruction Corporation (I.R.C.) of 1966. The purpose of this body was 'To provide for the establishment of a public corporation with the functions of promoting or assisting the re-organisation or development of any industry or section of an industry and establishing or developing or promoting the establishment or development of any industrial enterprise, and for matters relating to the corporation and its functions.' It was, in effect a state merchant bank, to advise firms how to regroup, how to rationalise, how to make the most of large-scale operations; sometimes advisory, sometimes acquiring a stake in ownership. Its whole philosophy epitomises that of the mixed economy, with the state trying to achieve what the free market forces had failed to do; to face foreign competition and to take full advantage of the pace of technological change.

The total investments of the I.R.C. by January 1971 were £122m, of which £87m went into loans, £22m into loans convertible into equity, and £13m in equity. It had been involved in about 100 mergers, which were four per cent of all those that took place; but they were significant mergers—Leylands, Chrysler, I.C.L., etc. In 1971 the I.R.C., together with most of the powers of the Industrial Expansion Act, was ended by the Conservative government.[2]

[1] See chapter 4.
[2] See chapter 5.

The Secretary of State for Trade and Industry made it clear,
however, that despite the policy of disengagement there would
continue to be an active interest in the reorganisation and restructuring of industry but that industry would be assisted to do
'what industry wishes'.[1] This phrase might explain the greater
emphasis being put on the work of the Industrial and Commercial Finance Corporation (I.C.F.C.) which had been set up in
1945 by the Bank of England, the London Clearing Banks and
the Scottish Banks to provide credit for industrial and commercial businesses in Great Britain, particularly in cases where the
facilities of banking institutions and the Stock Exchange were
not readily available.

However, the I.C.F.C. is independent; it operates in the field
of small and medium-sized companies; it has not the specified
function of the I.R.C.—'to promote the greater efficiency and
international competitiveness of British industry with specific
regard to regional policy'.[2] For these reasons neither the I.C.F.C.,
nor its wholly-owned subsidiary Industrial Mergers Ltd, whose
principal activity is to collect a list of merger-potential companies, could be used to replace I.R.C.

The dissolution of I.R.C. might have been a balanced judgment—unlike that against the Industrial Expansion Act which
had been absolute[3]—but, given the growing mix of the economy,
something very like it will have to be recreated.

Involvement by the government itself was not to end but
would be more *ad hoc* rather than systematic. Given that the time
span of such involvement lasts for periods of years rather than
months this is perhaps surprising.

Indeed, involvement there still was after the departmental
changes and the repeal of legislation and after the policy of disengagement; the story of Rolls-Royce revealed this daily. The
taking into public ownership of this company was perhaps the
most politically traumatic experience ever faced by the Heath
government. In the light of the industrial involvement of government in the U.K., as in other parts of the world, the actual event

[1] *Official Report*, 30 Oct. 1970, vol. 815, col. 568.
[2] 'Industrial Reorganisation Corporation', *Cmnd* 2889, pp. 2, 3, Jan.
1966.
[3] The Industry Act of 1972 recreated in almost identical words the purposes of the Industrial Expansion Act—but with greater powers and
more money.

should have surprised no one. It arises from the nature of industrial development in the western capitalist world.

Whatever form the involvement of the state may take, private industry will continue to receive large sums from the Exchequer. The following figures of the total sums of money advanced to private firms over a period are indicative of a trend.[1]

	£m
1965–66	47
1966–67	9
1967–68	320
1968–69	509
1969–70	605

The change to investment allowances will change the amount of money involved and the mode of involvement—but in this respect, as in others, involvement by the state in industry will continue to modify market forces.

GOVERNMENT EXPENDITURE IN THE PRIVATE SECTOR

Extent and Public purchasing policy

The extent of the involvement of government with industry would not be fully comprehended without some analysis of the vast expenditures by the government for the goods and service of firms in the private sector.

For example, in the financial year 1971–2 it was estimated that some £490m would be spent in Great Britain on housing,[2] on roads £400m, on the health service over £1,600m, on education at school over £440m.

[1] Written Parliamentary Answer, 15 March 1971. N.B. These figures comprise subsidies, current grants to private bodies, capital grants and net lending to the private sector under the Trade, Industry and Employment programme and part of the Transport programme. They exclude R.E.P., Selective Employment Tax, additional payments, expenditure on employment services and promotion of local employment, and loans to the Highlands and Islands Development Board. The whole of expenditure on investment grants is included although these grants had a regional differential.

[2] In 1970, 145,182 houses were completed in the public sector. See *Local Housing Statistics England and Wales*, no. 17, Feb. 1971, Department of the Environment, Welsh Office.

To varying degrees these sums are spent through local
authorities, but the same Civil Estimates for 1971–2 give many
examples of direct expenditure by the central government, e.g.
on actual building by the Department of Environment. It was
estimated in the White Paper on Public Purchasing and Industrial Efficiency 1967 that 'the Central Government buys about
5 per cent of the total output of all manufacturing and construction industries'.[1]

It continued,

It has long been recognised that the Government has special
influence and responsibility in relation to the efficiency and
progress of its supplying industries and their export performance. At the same time, the influence the Government can
exert, as a purchaser, on any particular industry must depend
to a significant extent on the proportion of the total output
of the industry which it takes, or at least on the proportion
relative to that of any other major purchasers. This influence
has been exercised, as with the aircraft industry, in promoting
the reorganisation of the supplying industry. In the field of
management, purchasing authorities encourage contractors to
use, where appropriate, techniques conducive to efficiency such
as budgetary control, critical path analysis, value engineering
and quality control. Regional development is assisted by
arrangements which give some measure of preference in
Government purchasing to suppliers in Development Areas.[2]

The primary objective of government purchasing policy was
laid down as 'to obtain what is needed, at the right time and in
such a way as to secure the best value for money spent. But there
is much that can be done to ensure that public purchasing provides positive encouragement to British industry to make itself
efficient and competitive both at home and in markets overseas.'[3]
Examples were given of the Department of Education and
Science, the Ministry of Health, the Ministry of Housing and
Local Government and the Ministry of Public Building and
Works cooperating to promote dimensional coordination in
building, the development and standardisation of building components and industrialised methods of building 'which should

[1] 'Public Purchasing and Industrial Efficiency', Cmnd 3291, 1967, p. 3.
[2] Ibid., p. 3, section 2.
[3] Ibid., p. 3, section 4.

lead to all-round economy and a market which goes far wider than Government needs'.[1]

The White Paper was concerned with the central government purchasing but it concluded: 'The total value of purchases by the rest of the public sector is substantially greater than that of purchases by the Central Government. Much has already been done in this field. The Government propose therefore to invite the cooperation of local authorities, the nationalised industries and other public bodies in a review of the ways in which the Government's objectives in the field of public purchasing can best be developed in the rest of the public sector.'[2] It is an example of the transference of business planning ideas to government, as is the report in the Conservative government's White Paper on Government Organisation for Defence Procurement and Civil Aerospace.[3] It is another aspect of government involvement with the private sector.

Effect on the Firm

Part of the private sector, supplying everything from bricks and computers to cotton wool swabs and surgical instruments, is heavily dependent upon government expenditure. It alters the outlook of the firms concerned. It modifies at least the 'merchant adventuring' spirit said once to be prevalent; it removes an element of risk from the results of boardroom decision taking.

In the field of civil aircraft procurement, the saga of the RB211 engine showed a government trying to reinstate a contract for a technically efficient project which was not 'commercially viable'.

Whether this phrase has any real meaning in this type of operation and on this scale is questionable. Dr Robin Marris has expressed the view that 'the private profit criterion is almost useless for most of the important decisions in a modern economy; how and where to develop regions, how to help the poor, whether

---

[1] *Ibid.*, p. 3, section 5.
[2] *Ibid.*, p. 8, section 28.
[3] *Cmnd* 4641, 1971. See also *H.C. Official Report*, vol. 836, cols. 217-8, 5 May 1972, in which the government announced that 'The Property Services Agency and HM Stationery Office will keep the possibility of extending their purchases from the private sector under continuous review with the aim of securing the best value for money.'

to build Concorde ...'.[1] Mr Enoch Powell, M.P., has confirmed
that Concorde was 'politics from the start' and profitability not
a factor.

Large sums were made available for launching the Concorde
in the first instance and it is doubtful if private industry could
have raised the risk capital involved. 'Launching aid' to aerospace
firms has been a growing feature of the last decade; without it
many projects would never have begun development.[2]

Sir George Edwards of the British Aircraft Corporation has
said of such aid, 'This has proved to be an example of the
government doing a "pump priming" operation and taking a
share of the risks which an individual Company could not support.' He continues, 'It is probably the only way to ensure that
we, as a nation, get our share of the massive rewards in world
markets while at the same time keeping advanced industry
efficiency sharp, because potentially crippling sums of its own
money are equally involved.'[3]

Defence

The government purchases goods and services in the private
sector for defence. For 1971–2 there were estimates of over £20m
expenditure for 'accommodation stores' and services including

[1] Taken from an article in the *Guardian*, 13 April 1971, 'Government
Suffering from Ignorance'.
[2] Government Lauching Aid for Civil Aircraft and Engines

	£m
1960–61	6.05
1961–62	7.25
1962–63	9.86
1963–64	8.43
1964–65	6.07
1965–66	3.01
1966–67	2.30
1967–68	12.10
1968–69	18.96
1969–70	33.70

H.C. Official Report, vol. 813, 10 March 1971, col. 125. These figures
do not include expenditure on Concorde or on the A300 project study
costs.
[3] Sir George Edwards, *Partnership in Major Technological Projects*,
7th Maurice Lubbock Memorial Lecture, 14 May 1970, Oxford University Press, 1970, pp. 15, 16; see also p. 225, below.

furniture; of over £20m for clothing; and a similar sum for provisions. This type of procurement has long gone with defence expenditure, but with the purchase of sophisticated aircraft and ships, together with their associated electronic equipment, there has come a far more profound effect on modern industry.

One result of this has been the development of a system of 'quality assurance', now centred in the Procurement Executive at the Ministry of Defence, which ends up with stage-by-stage inspection by resident civil servants of equipment as it is produced in the factories concerned.[1]

Another aspect of such development was expressed revealingly by President Eisenhower in a speech at the end of his years in the White House.

Our military organization today bears little relation to that known by any of my predecessors in peacetime, or indeed by the fighting men of World War II or Korea.

Until the latest of our world conflicts, the United States had no armaments industry. American makers of plowshares could, with time and as required, make swords as well. But now we can no longer risk emergency improvisation of national defense; we have been compelled to create a permanent armaments industry of vast proportions. Added to this, three and a half million men and women are directly engaged in the defense establishment. We annually spend on military security more than the net income of all United States corporations.

This conjunction of an immense military establishment and a large arms industry is new in the American experience. The total influence—economic, political, even spiritual—is felt in every city, every state house, every office of the federal government. We recognize the imperative need for this development. Yet we must not fail to comprehend its grave implications. Our toil, resources, and livelihood are all involved; so is the very structure of our society.

In the councils of government we must guard against the acquisition of unwarranted influence, whether sought or unsought, by the military-industrial complex. The potential for the disastrous rise of misplaced power exists and will persist.

We must never let the weight of this combination endanger

[1] See page 44, below.

our liberties or democratic processes. We should take nothing
for granted. Only an alert and knowledgeable citizenry can
compel the proper meshing of the huge industrial and military
machinery of defense with our peaceful methods and goals, so
that security and liberty may prosper together.

The President wrote of this speech that it was 'the most
challenging message I could leave with the people of this
country'.[1]

The political problem of the industrial/military complex has
not been solved and Professor Galbraith could write in 1971 a
disturbing account of the enmeshed relationships between the
armed services and the specialised defence contractors.[2] The
Eisenhower challenge still faces the U.S.A.

I have been a British defence minister, and for many reasons
—historical, procedural and constitutional—this precise challenge is not ours. Nevertheless, it is something to be watched.

One aspect of the industrial involvement is, however, relevant
in the U.K. Wherever defence expenditure is cut or a particular
project cancelled, the issue is blown up politically by the producers, both employer and employed, who for obvious reasons
are heavily committed to continued expenditure. Such commitment is rarely objective.

Another similarly relevant aspect is the heavy involvement in
defence contracting by individual firms who become dependent
on the state for their capital provision.[3] The added problem to
individual countries in Europe of the small size of the national
markets, leads to international cooperation as with the Italian-
German-U.K. consortium for the multi-role combat aircraft. This
type of development may be one part of a solution to another
problem—the overcommitment of scarce sophisticated resources
within one country to defence requirements, to the detriment of
civilian research and development.

The defence industry consists of large units which sub-
contract down the line to smaller firms, producing a final pro-

[1] Dwight Eisenhower, *The White House Years. Waging Peace 1956-61*,
Heinemann, 1966, p. 616.
[2] J. K. Galbraith, *How to Control the Military*, N.C.L.C. Publishing
Society.
[3] *Ibid.*, pp. 7, 8. N.B. In the U.S.A. not only does the government supply
much of the working capital, but also owns much of the plant of the
specialised defence contractors.

duct for which there is only one buyer. There is extra gain if packaged projects can be sold overseas—providing also sophisticated defence equipment and staff to operate it. The industry accordingly develops a philosophy and organisation different from that found in the usual joint stock public company. In the case of Rolls-Royce, which is heavily dependent on government contracts and support, in both the civil and military aircraft fields, the stresses and strains of the joint stock organisation caused a British Conservative government in 1971 to take parts of the firm into public ownership. The balance had been further tilted within the mixed economy.

The public sector is thought by some to be a temporary bureaucratic nightmare built on the aberation of mind of an ill-informed welfare-dominated electorate; by others without much joy it is thought to be technologically inevitable. By others it is seen to be the most significant political development in a technological world because of the fact that ownership is taken out of the hands of the capitalist.

Whatever the attitude to it might be, the public sector shows no sign of decline and, indeed, employs a growing proportion of the resources of the country.

The public sector is an important part of the mixed economy. It consists of the activities of Central Government, of Local Authorities, of Public Corporations, and of a growing sector of state shareholding in the 'private' sector.

Further Reading

Graham Bannock, *The Juggernauts*, Weidenfeld, 1971.
Sir Edward Boyle, 'Conservatives and Economic Planning', Lecture of 14 Oct. 1965 to C.P.C.; pamphlet printed 1966.
Sir Alexander Cairncross, *Essays in Economic Management*, Allen & Unwin, 1971.
T. E. Chester, 'Mergers and Opportunities for Managers', *National Westminster Bank Quarterly Review*, May 1969.
T. E. Chester, 'Large Organisations—their Role in the U.K. Economy', Aug. 1971, p. 24.
J. C. R. Dow, *The Management of the British Economy 1945–60*, Cambridge University Press, 1964.
Peter F. Drucker, 'The New Capitalism', *Dialogue*, vol. 4, no. 3, 1971, p. c.
J. K. Galbraith, *The New Industrial State*, Hamish Hamilton, 1967.
Aubrey Jones, 'A Policy for Prices and Incomes Now', *Lloyds Bank Review*, no. 103, Jan. 1972, p. 1.
Wayland Kennet, Larry Whitty and Stuart Holland, *Sovereignty and Multinational Companies*, Fabian Tract 409, July 1971.
Michael Kidron, *Western Capitalism Since the War*, Penguin Books, 1970.
Charles Levinson, *Capital, Inflation and the Multinational*, Allen & Unwin, 1971.
J. Mitchell, *Groundwork to Economic Planning*, Secker & Warburg, 1966.
J. Mitchell, *National Board for Prices and Incomes*, Secker & Warburg, 1972.
H. Schoeck and J. W. Wiggins (eds.), *The New Argument in Economics. The Public versus the Private Sector*, Van Nostrand, 1963.
A. Shonfield, *Modern Capitalism*, Oxford University Press, 1966.
A. Shonfield, *Modern Capitalism—the Changing Balance of Public and Private Power*, Oxford University Press, 1968.
R. Skidelsky, *Competition and the Corporative Society*, Methuen, 1972.
Christopher Tugendhat, *The Multinationals*, Eyre & Spottiswoode, 1971.
John Vaizey, *Capitalism*, Weidenfeld, 1971.
Mira Wilkins, *The Emergence of Multinational Enterprise*, Oxford University Press, 1971.
'French Planning: Some Lessons for Britain', *Political and Economic Planning*, vol. XXIX, no. 475, 9 Sept. 1963.
'Inquest on Planning in Britain', *ibid.*, vol. XXXIII, no. 499, Jan. 1967.
'Public Sector Purchasing', a report to the Economic Group of the Parliamentary Labour Party by R. Maxwell.

2 Central Government

2 Central Government

The activities of the central government through control and regulation are an important part of the mixed economy; it also engages in activities itself.

Government Expenditure and Total Employed

The total expenditure by government in 1971–2 was estimated to be over £14,000m and when transfer payments, etc., are taken into account the actual public expenditure remaining totals some £10,000m.[1]

The total number of people employed by the central government was 1,907,000 or 7.6 per cent of the entire labour force.[2]

Definition

The central government sector of the economy is defined by the Central Statistical Office to embrace all bodies for whose activities a Minister of the Crown, or other responsible person is accountable to Parliament.[3] It contains two main groups: first, government departments and other bodies coming under its aegis—including the armed forces—whose expenditure is charged directly to supply votes; and second, other organisations which are grant-aided and responsible in various ways to the department but are not administered by them.

GOVERNMENT DEPARTMENTS AND ASSOCIATED ORGANISATIONS

The government departments concerned, including those of the Northern Ireland government,[4] are the Treasury, Home Office;

[1] 'Estimates for 1971–2', Memorandum by the Chief Secretary, March 1971, tables I and II, pp. 2, 3. See also 'Public Expenditure 1969–70 to 1974–5', *Cmnd* 4578, 1971.
[2] *Economic Trends*, no. 212, June 1971, p. xlvi.
[3] *National Accounts Statistics. Sources and Methods*, ed. R. Maurice, C.S.O., 1968, p. 251.
[4] In 1972 provision was made temporarily for a Secretary of State in the government of the United Kingdom to act as chief executive officer

Department of Trade and Industry; Department of the Environment; Ministry of Defence; Foreign and Commonwealth Office; Scottish Office; Welsh Office; Ministry of Posts and Telecommunications; Ministry of Agriculture, Fisheries and Food; Department of Education and Science, etc.

The associated organisations include such bodies as:

	No. of non-industrials at 1 April 1971
The Charity Commission	313
Commission on Industrial Relations	125
Countryside Commission	85
Court of Protection	145
Crown Estate Office	131
Decimal Currency Board	28
Exchequer and Audit Department	580
Export Credits Guarantee Department	1,570
Registry of Friendly Societies	100
Land Registry	4,100
Office of Manpower Economics	45
Metrication Board	60
Office of the National Insurance Commissioners	42
National Savings Committees	647
Office of the Parliamentary Commissioner for Administration	57
Public Record Office	318
Public Trustee Office	565
Public Works Loans Commission	47
Office of Registrar of Restrictive Trading Agreements	72
Rating of Government Property Department	47
Water Resources Board	156
Office of the Umpire (National Service and Re-instatement in Civil Employment)	1

The nature of the work of these bodies is revealed in their titles, and their size by their numbers employed.

Annual Reports are issued in most instances.[2] One example is the Countryside Commission, with 12 members and responsible to the Department of the Environment and the Welsh Office,

as respects Irish services. The functioning of the individual government departments in Northern Ireland was not affected.

[2] See Further Reading, p. 80, below. N.B. In March 1972 it was announced that the Public Trustee Office was to be wound up because of declining business (see 'The Public Trustee Office', *Cmnd* 4193, 1972).

which replaced the National Parks Commission in 1968.[1] Its function is to encourage the provision and development of recreational facilities in the countryside. These include the creation of country parks, the establishment of camping sites and picnic areas, and the increased use of reservoirs and waterways for bathing and sailing—with an additional responsibility for conservation.

All those employed by the departments and organisations are classified as civil servants. The total employed in April 1971 was estimated to be 703,105—consisting of 501,095 non-industrials and 202,010 industrial employees.[2]

This classification between industrials and non-industrials in this post-Fulton period will undoubtedly have to change—but it serves to illustrate the nature of the work carried out by the State.

Non-Industrial Civil Service

Range of occupations
The non-industrial civil servants consist of the following groups:[3]

	Functional Analysis	1971–2
(i)	Administrative	1,587
(ii)	Executive	39,434
(iii)	General Category	
	Administration Group	203,613
	Economist Group	230
	Statistician Group	323
(vi)	Professional, Scientific and Technical	96,448
(v)	Clerical	50,414
(vi)	Typing, Machine Operating, etc.	41,555
(vii)	Office Keepers, Messengerial, etc.	20,810

[1] Fourth Report of the Countryside Commission for the Year Ended 30 Sept. 1971', H.C. 38, 1971. N.B. There is a separate commission for Scotland.

[2] Memorandum by the Chief Secretary, *op. cit.*, table XII, p. 52.

[3] The general category was established on 1 Jan. 1971, comprising initially three groups—the Administration, the Economist and Statistician Groups. Staff in certain other General Service and Departmental Classes are to be considered for inclusion in the new General Category.

Arising also out of the recommendations of the Fulton Report, arrangements are being made for senior posts in the administrative and other classes, to be merged into an open structure at the top levels of the Civil Service.

(viii) Other staff detailed in schedules	36,655
(ix) Staff in Departmental Classes of less than 100 (not detailed in schedules)	10,026
	501,095

It covers a wide variety of occupations[1] carried out by people operating in a service still based on the principles and philosophy of the Northcote–Trevelyan Report of 1854. It is motivated by a basic attitude of service to the community which it would be impossible to measure by a profit-and-loss account. The question of efficiency and lack of management techniques, etc., are different matters which do need change, but the standards of the Civil Service are high. Nowhere is this more clearly seen than in the ranks of the small administrative grade.

This consists of the Permanent Secretaries who head the great departments of state, and who remain when their political chiefs leave for a variety of reasons; together with the Deputy Secretaries and Under-Secretaries. It includes also some senior statisticians and economists.

The Executive grade illustrates the wide range of occupations required by the state. In the Customs and Excise branch, for example, there are 5,448 outdoor grades who are inspectors, collectors and surveyors, with 3,339 in the waterguard service (concerned with the prevention of smuggling) and 1,317 watchers (employed on the quayside, at airports, in warehouses and at distilleries to see that goods are not improperly removed). In the Home Office are 1,004 in the immigration service and 488 prison governors. In the Inland Revenue there are 4,968 tax inspectors, and in the Exchequer and Audit Department 485 Auditors. The Department of the Environment employs 440 District Auditors.

The General Category consists of those top-level civil servants not classified in the Administrative group—Assistant Secretaries and below, and includes the young and mainly ex-university principals, various executive groups and also some clerical officers. Economists and statisticians are separately classified under this heading.

The Clerical group itself is self-explanatory but includes some employed as Collectors of Taxes and others in the Lord Chan-

[1] The following figures to illustrate the range of occupations are taken from the Memorandum by the Chief Secretary, *op. cit.*

cellor's department. Group (vi) of 41,555 Typing, Machine Operators, etc., includes 3,853 classified as personal secretaries, 24,308 typists, 7,787 machine operators and 2,400 photoprinters. This is an extraordinarily large labour force. In the private sector it would be remarkable; in the public sector it is taken for granted.

Group (vii) includes—amongst its nearly 21,000 staff—3,764 cleaners, 309 laboratory attendants, 1,490 museum warders and 10,891 offce keepers and messengers. Group (viii) includes 4,016 departmental police, 160 fire officers, 1,292 information officers, 4,070 instructional officers, 3,680 supervising in stores, 2,190 telephonists, 10,685 prison officers, and 518 coastguards.

The group classified as Professional, Scientific and Technical of nearly 100,000 people illustrates the growth of governmental activities in the twentieth century. What private firm employs professional staff in such numbers and with such diversity? There are, for example, 359 accountants, 30 actuaries, 104 conservation officers, 7,518 architectural and engineering draughtsmen, 4,634 cartographic and recording draughtsmen.

There are 7,682 experimental officers who work in a variety of scientific establishments; as do 4,559 scientific officers and 5,406 scientific assistants. There are 811 solicitors and legal assistants, 292 librarians, 700 medical officers, 593 nursing staff, 203 psychologists and 763 photographers. There are 1,595 radio technicians, 2,073 telecommunications technical officers and 2,897 wireless staff. There are 482 wireless technicians in the Home Office which, together with the large number of prison officers and immigration officers mentioned earlier, reveals it as not only a policy-making department. It is also the employer of 119 nursing staff, mainly in the prison service.

There are 25,761 clerks of works and quantity surveying assistants, most of whom are employed by the old Ministry of Public Building and Works sector of the new Department of the Environment; as are the 5,049 'Professional Classes' in Works Groups (i.e. surveyors, civil engineers, etc.) and 394 student draughtsmen.

Amongst the Ministry of Agriculture staff there are 109 calf certifying officers, 343 in drainage and water supply, 148 horticultural marketing inspectors and 828 national agricultural advisory service officers.

The Ministry of Defence employs 2,478 engineers and industrial chemists, 491 lecturers and 2,083 teachers, 94 civilian medical practitioners and 1,533 officers in the Royal Fleet Auxiliary.

The Department of Education and Science directly employs 477 inspectors of schools—with their expertise, enough to staff many schools. The Department of Employment employs 721 factory inspectors, while the Department of Trade and Industry employs 133 inspectors of mines and quarries. The Department of Health and Social Security at the special hospitals such as Broadmoor has on its staff 935 male nurses. The Board of Inland Revenue employs 6,427 valuation officers.

The Department of Trade and Industry has a wide range of activities. It is the employer of 1,325 Air Traffic Control Officers, 154 Communications Officers, 186 operations officers and 190 signals officers. They work at highly complex radar operating institutions in all parts of the country but particularly near London Airport. The same department has on its roll 622 staff at the Patent Office and 389 marine surveyors.

The government directly employs this large number of highly skilled professional, scientific and technical staff. Nowhere is this more important than in the specialised complex field of Research and Development.

Research and Development

Research and Development is vital to the modern complex technological economy. In the absence of government intervention it is argued that 'the market process is likely to result in both and under-allocation of resources to R. & D. and a maldistribution of these resources between basic research and applied research and development, because the private return on R. & D. may well be less than the social return'.[1] The central government consequently directly involves itself in the field of basic research and development.[2]

Pure research is carried out by the Research Councils which are the responsibility of the Department of Education and Science; their employees are not civil servants.[3]

[1] Hill Samuel, 'The Role of the Government in Research and Development', Occasional Paper no. 4, Oct. 1969, p. 21.
[2] See, 'Framework for Government Research Development', *Cmnd* 5046, 1972, 'III The Organisation of Research and Development in Government Departments'.
[3] See p. 69, below.

In the field of R. & D. there has been much discussion over the years about the division between research and development and also about the appropriate government department to control such activities. From 1916 to 1965 when the Ministry of Technology came into existence the organising government body was the Department of Scientific and Industrial Research.[1]

It is no accident that it came into being in 1916 under the impetus of war; the theme of the white Paper of 1915,[2] which preceded the birth, has a modern ring:

> A special need exists at the present time for new machinery and for additional State assistance in order to promote and organize scientific research with a view especially to its application to trade and industry.... If we are to advance or even maintain our industrial position we must, as a Nation, aim at such a development of scientific and industrial research as will place us in a position to expand and strengthen our industry and to compete successfully with the most highly organized of our rivals.

There were further changes; the Ministry of Technology gave way to the Department of Trade and Industry in 1970. The resulting temporary Ministry of Aviation Supply ended after a short life. Research and Development is split between the Department of Trade and Industry, the Ministry of Defence and the Department of the Environment.[3]

[1] See N. Vig, *Science and Technology in British Politics*, Pergamon, 1968, for a full discussion of this aspect.

[2] 'Scheme for the Organisation of and the Development of Scientific Research, *Cmnd* 8005, 1915.

[3] In 'Reorganisation of Central Government', *Cmnd* 4506, Oct. 1970 it was announced that Ministry of Technology responsibility for aerospace, research and procurement would not form part of the new Department of Trade and Industry but that as a temporary measure the aviation group of MinTech would pass to a separate Ministry of Aviation Supply.

In April 1971 there was published 'Government Organisation for Defence Procurement and Civil Aerospace', *Cmnd* 4641. In this it was announced that there was to be set up a single procurement organisation responsible to the Secretary of State for Defence and combining the existing responsibilities of the Ministry of Defence and of Aviation Supply.

This organisation is responsible for the management of all defence research and development establishments.

The Department of Trade and Industry now has within it six Industrial Research Establishments.

The Laboratory of the Government Chemist in London grew out of the laboratory created by the Revenue Department of the Treasury in 1842. It provides a wide variety of analytical and advisory services to all Government departments and over 40 per cent of its work is for H.M. Customs and Excise. It carries out no direct work for industry but, because of its import and export responsibilities, there is close liaison between the laboratory and major British industries. It employs a total staff of 393: 315 Professional, Scientific and Technical; 75 Administrative Support Staff; and three Industrials.

The National Engineering Laboratory (N.E.L.)[1] at East Kilbride, Glasgow, carries out research in selected fields of mechanical engineering to provide industry with new ideas and detailed technical information that will help to improve designs and production processes.

Current work provides many examples of innovations of profit to industry, particularly in the fields of fluid power, machine tools, metal forming and the design of pumps and fans. It employs a total staff of 964: 516 Professional, Scientific and Technical; 129 Administrative Support Staff; and 319 Industrials.

The National Physical Laboratory (N.P.L.) at Teddington was established in 1900 to provide a national centre for measurement and standards and to bring scientific knowledge to bear practically upon everyday industry and commercial life. N.P.L. is a world-leading laboratory in the field of accurate measurement; it also carries out applied research programmes in materials, in air and sea transport and in computer use. The majority of all new British merchant ships are based on hull designs tested and developed in model form by its Ship Division. In industrial aerodynamics, N.P.L.'s work has led to improved designs of civil engineering works, for example the Severn Bridge, the funnel of the Queen Elizabeth II, the Drax power station and Corby New Town. It employs a total staff of 1,589: 954 Professional,

---

[1] On the N.E.L. campus is also the Birniehill Institute; it provides postgraduate courses and training for staff from industry in the latest design techniques, particularly those using computers.

N.B. See New Technology, no. 47, June 1971, D.T.I.: 'N.E.L. knows the Ropes' by G. R. Borwick, for one example of the work carried out at this establishment.

Scientific and Technical; 215 Administrative Support Staff; and 420 Industrials.

The Safety of Mines Research Establishment at Sheffield is basically concerned with fundamental research into mining hazards, e.g. explosions, fires, mechanical failures, pneumoconiosis. Research is also carried out to improve the design and materials of mining equipment where its performance affects the safety of mineworkers, e.g. methods of gas detection; electrical apparatus for use in potentially inflammable atmospheres; breathing apparatus; airborne-dust sampling; design and materials of haulage, cage-suspension and roof-support equipment for use in mines. It employs a total staff of 389: 238 Professional, Scientific and Technical; 85 Administrative Support Staff; and 66 Industrials.

The Torry Research Station at Aberdeen is concerned with the handling and processing of fish at all stages from capture to consumption and is concerned with improving quality at every stage. It played a major part in the development of freezing fish at sea. It employs a total staff of 211; 102 Professional, Scientific and Technical; 25 Administrative Support Staff; and 84 Industrials.

The Warren Spring Laboratory at Stevenage, undertakes applied research for industry, mainly in the fields of chemical engineering and mineral science and technology, and investigates atmospheric pollution mainly on behalf of the Department of the Environment. It operates an R. & D. consultancy and advisory service for the mining and metallurgical industries. It employs a total staff of 421: 245 Professional, Scientific and Technical; 67 Administrative Support Staff; and 109 Industrials.

The Department of the Environment is responsible for four departments.

The Fire Research Station at Boreham Wood conducts research into all aspects of fire, including fire detection and extinction, safety and plant protection and structural fire standards. It employs a total staff of 189: 102 Professional, Scientific and Technical; 49 Administrative Support Staff; and 38 Industrials.

The Forest Products Research Laboratory at Aylesbury studies timber utilisation as an aid to the proper exploitation of British and Commonwealth forest resources. It carries out work on the preservation of timber, mechanical and chemical processing, including development of new processing methods and machinery, and tests on the strength of timber, timber structures and joints. It employs a total staff of 197: 110 Professional, Scientific and Technical; 23 Administrative Support Staff; and 64 Industrials.

The Water Pollution Research Laboratory at Stevenage is concerned with studying the effects of pollution on natural waters in order to develop scientific systems of water resource management and to improve the efficiency of methods for treatment of the domestic and industrial waste waters that cause pollution. The work is undertaken also for industry, river and local authorities: It employs a total staff of 299: 139 Professional, Scientific and Technical; 25 Administrative Support Staff; and 66 Industrials.

The Hydraulics Research Station at Wallingford provides a service for the civil engineering profession. The field of work embraces all aspects of civil engineering hydraulics including flow over weirs and spillways, the design of flood protection schemes, the silting of rivers, estuaries and harbours, sea defences and the design of harbours. It employs a total staff of 241: 137 Professional, Scientific and Technical; 28 Administrative Support Staff; and 76 Industrials.

The Building Research Station at Garston, Watford, is concerned with almost the whole field of building: for example, all building materials except wood; the design and performance of structures; constructional techniques, including mechanical aids; the efficiency of building in respect of heating, lighting, sound insulation, etc.; and the organisation, productivity and economics of building work. The results of much of its work are incorporated in Codes of Practice and British Standards. It employs a total staff of 935: 505 Professional, Scientific and Technical;[1] 178 Administrative Support Staff; and 252 Industrials.

The work of the Department of the Environment in all these fields is not simply through a responsibility for its research organisations. There is, for example, a section responsible for building

---

[1] The scientific and professional staff cover a wide range of disciplines, including mechanical engineers, civil engineers, electrical engineers, physicists, chemists, psychologists, mathematicians, statisticians, economists and medically qualified personnel.

research in the Department itself. Research is an important aspect of the wider concern for the environment.

The Ministry of Defence now controls the following establishments.

The Royal Aircraft Establishment (R.A.E.) at Farnborough was founded in 1905. Its responsibility is for aircraft and missile research and development. It is the largest research and engineering unit of its kind in western Europe. An Industrial Applications Unit has been set up to maintain liaison between industry and the establishment and to identify industrial research problems outside its main field of aerospace. The Central Unit for Scientific Photography has also been set up to assist industry and others to apply scientific photographic techniques to the solution of research and development problems.

There are a number of satellite establishments, notably R.A.E. Bedford, the home of the Aerodynamics Department's modern wind tunnels and also the base for R.A.E.'s work on blind landing and naval air work. At Aberporth in Wales and at West Freugh in Scotland the establishment runs guided weapon ranges. It employs a non-industrial staff of 3,830.

The Aeroplane and Armament Experimental Establishment at Boscombe Down, Wilts, has as its primary task the assessment by flight testing and other means of military aircraft, armament and equipment before delivery to the Services. There is an aeromedical school which provides a service to test pilots and observers, while the Empire Test Pilots' School trains test pilots both from the U.K. and overseas.

The National Gas Turbine Establishment at Farnborough is the government centre for research into the problems of gas turbine engines and related systems for land, sea and air use. It employs a total non-industrial staff of 571.

The Royal Radar Establishment at Malvern is primarily concerned with defence radar. The establishment's guided weapons work is mainly in electronics. The second main activity is R. & D. for Air Traffic Control (A.T.C.) on behalf of the Department of Trade and Industry. This includes system coordination for combined military and civil A.T.C. There is also an Industrial Applications Unit which aims to exploit for industrial purposes the results of defence R. & D., including the hire of special facilities to industry. It employs a total non-industrial staff of 1,424.

The Signals Research and Development Establishment at Christchurch provides R. & D. support in meeting the telecommunications needs of the services. Some of this work is done within the establishment but a very large part is carried out in the telecommunications industry and universities by contracts.

The Explosives Research and Development Establishment at Waltham Abbey, Essex, is a centre for chemical research. Its primary function is to undertake research on, and the development of, explosives and propellents.

The Rocket Propulsion Establishment at Aylesbury, is almost wholly engaged on R. & D. directed to rocket propulsion.

The Aircraft Torpedo Development Unit at Helston, is responsible for the development of fight-in-air materials for torpedoes, mines and pyrotechnics.

It is not the policy of the government to release details of staff at these establishments and, where they have been made available because of the fact that there is a substantial civil content, no breakdown into types is given. In the Rayner Report[1] it is revealed, however, that professional, scientific and technical staff make up approximately 35 per cent of the total non-industrial staff at these establishments.

The Ministry of Defence is responsible for other establishments, e.g. Admiralty Experimental Works, Admiralty Marine Engineering Establishments, Admiralty Oil Laboratory, Naval Construction Research Establishment, Admiralty Distilling Experimental Station and the R.N. Nuclear Propulsion Test and Training Establishment which also employ a significant number of scientifically trained staff.

The Army has similar organisations, e.g. Army Personnel Research Establishment, Stores and Clothing Research and Development Establishment—and at Porton the Chemical Research Establishment and the Microbiological Research Establishment.[2] Much of the work at the latter is in the field of public health and there is discussion concerning its possible transfer to the Department of Health and Social Security.

Another important scientific organisation, which works to the

[1] 'Government Organisation for Defence Procurement and Civil Aerospace', *Cmnd* 4641, April 1971, p. 55.
[2] C. E. Gordon Smith, *Microbiological Research Establishment, Porton*, 'Research Establishments in Europe', no. 69, *Chemistry and Industry*, 19.

R.A.F. department, is the Meteorological Office at Bracknell. It employs a total staff of 3,567 (which is inclusive of 174 locally engaged overseas)—2,784 Professional, Scientific and Technical, 324 Administrative and 70 Industrial. It also employs 215 staff with a variety of nautical skills aboard the weather ships in the Atlantic.

The 'Met Office' of course makes day-to-day forecasts—with the help now of an advanced computer. It also has responsibilities for pre-flight planning and weather forecasting and more recently for the international World Weather Watch. It is active in research, particularly in the field of cloud and rainfall.[1] It receives many enquiries from the general public and from industry; but the latter makes too little use of the services provided. The experts of the world are more aware of these than are British industry and local authorities.

It was seen earlier than the *Ministry of Agriculture, Fisheries and Food* is an employer of professional and scientific staff. By its very nature it engages in research activities.

It is responsible for two veterinary laboratories at Weybridge and Lasswade, and a Cattle Breeding Centre at Shinfield, near Reading. There are 21 Veterinary Investigation Centres in all parts of the country and a Plant Pathology Laboratory at Harpenden, together with the Royal Botanic Gardens at Kew. At Tolworth, Surrey, there is an Infestation Control Laboratory with units at Worplesdon and Slough. There are Sea Fisheries Laboratories at Lowestoft, Weymouth, Burnham-on-Crouch, Conway, London and the Isle of Man; Salmon and Freshwater Fisheries Laboratories in London and Devon; and for research purposes there are four vessels.

In the name of research there are state farms—13 experimental husbandry farms and 11 experimental horticultural stations totalling 15,000 acres. These employ 246 Professional, Scientific and Technical, 94 Administrative Support Staff and 393 Industrial Staff—which form part of the total staff of 1,735 Professional, Scientific and Technical, 475 Administrative Support Staff and 871 Industrials, who work in the above laboratories, etc.

At the regional centres of the National Agricultural Advisory Centre there are also specialist advisors in bacteriology, entomo-

[1] 'Annual Report of the Meteorological Office', 1970.

logy, nutrition chemistry, plant pathology and soil science.

Similar work is carried out in Scotland where the Department of Agriculture and Fisheries for Scotland maintains a marine research laboratory, six research ships at Aberdeen and a fresh-water research laboratory at Pitlochry.

There are other government departments which are involved in research—for example, the Home Office where the Police Scientific Development Branch is responsible for research into police science and technology. It employs psychologists, scientific officers and experimental officers, together with pathologists, at the Central Research Establishment and at eight regional labora-tories. The Scientific Advisers Branch of the Home Office, which advises over a wide field of scientific research, also employs pro-fessional staff of this kind.

Overall the government is a substantial employer of scientists and technologists without taking into account the indirect em-ployment of such staff through the National Research Develop-ment Corporation and the U.K. Atomic Energy Authority[1] which hived off in 1954 and is the largest government-sponsored organ-isation for research and development.

Problems and the Fulton Report

In recent years there has been much questioning of the role of the Civil Service and as a result, in February 1966, a Royal Com-mission was appointed under the chairmanship of Lord Fulton 'to examine the structure, recruitment and management includ-ing training of the Home Civil Service'. A consideration of the industrial civil service was specifically excluded.

The report appeared in 1968. It criticised both central and personnel management; it questioned whether enough use was being made of accountants as managers rather than as book-keepers. It commented on the lack of opportunity and responsi-bility provided for scientists, engineers and other specialist classes.

It recommended that a Civil Service Department should be set up and a Civil Service College; that the system of classes should be abolished and replaced by a unified grading structure based on job evaluation. Proposals were made for introducing

---

[1] For N.R.D.C. see pp. 167-70 below; and for U.K.A.E.A. see pp. 71-2 below.

accountable management, improved management services and the setting up of planning units in each department.

Further, follow-up enquiries were suggested and of these the most important was that into 'the desirability of "hiving off" activities to non-departmental organisations'.[1] This suggestion has been given added significance by the growth of the large-scale super-department. The case for this development has not yet been proven in practice—except in the case of the Ministry of Defence. The very large department certainly does give rise to problems of ministerial responsibility and managerial diseconomies of scale. Hiving off may well create further problems of parliamentary accountability but this is part of a wider problem that has to be solved in any event.

Hiving off occurred with the Atomic Energy Authority in 1954 and in another fashion with the General Post Office in 1969. In the same year a Green Paper was issued by the then Minister of Technology on the matter of the organisation of government research. In this it was argued that because of the need 'to rationalise programmes in A.E.A. and Ministry of Technology establishments, the need to link government laboratories more closely with industry so they can better understand and more readily help to solve some of its problems and the need for work to be undertaken increasingly on a contractual and commercial basis—the Government is considering setting up a new organization, outside the Civil Service, in which all these research and development resources would be brought together under a single management'.[2] Political events prevented this hiving-off development and, indeed, there has since been a splitting up of responsibility for the establishments. This may well improve line management within the responsible government department; it remains to be seen if it improves research and development.

Nevertheless, hiving off is being considered by the government as was announced in the White Paper on the 'Reorganisation of Central Government', Cmnd 4506. It is part of a review of departmental functions—'both whether they are necessary to central government and whether they might more effectively be

[1] 'The Civil Service', vol. 1, Report of the Committee 1966–68, Cmnd 3638, p. 106.
[2] 'Industrial Research and Development in Government Laboratories. A New Organisation for the Seventies', Ministry of Technology, 1969, pp. 11, 12.

organised in different ways'.[1] As far as the Atomic Weapons
Research Establishment is concerned the government announced
in August 1971 that this part of A.E.A. was to be transferred to
the Ministry of Defence. This was undoubtedly an administrative decision that brought about a rationalisation of function
with those of the other establishments controlled by the Ministry
of Defence; but for the first time it marshalled nuclear weapons
research and production under a Defence Minister. The civil
scientific aspect which is so important is thereby weakened.

Too much concentration on the recommendations of the Fulton
Report would create the impression that nothing is right with
the Home Civil Service. This is not the case as I know from
experience; civil servants were already attending their own Centre
for Administrative Studies and returning to universities and business schools. The supporting volumes of Fulton, which include
statistical and explanatory papers, do not reveal a self-satisfied
organisation.[2]

Indeed, over the years, it has built up a system of relationships between management and staff associations which has been
the envy of other civil services. In 1916 the then government
appointed a committee under the Chairmanship of Mr J. H.
Whitley, M.P. for Halifax and later to be Speaker of the House
of Commons, with terms of reference as follows:

(i) to make and consider suggestions for securing a permanent
improvement in the relations between employers and workmen,
and

(ii) to recommend means for securing that industrial conditions affecting the relations between employers and workmen
shall be systematically reviewed by those concerned, with a view
to improving conditions in the future.

The committee eventually recommended the setting up of
joint councils over industry as a whole. In the Civil Service there
was set up a Whitley Council with the following objects:

To secure the greatest measure of co-operation between the
State in its capacity as employer, and the general body of

[1] *H.C. Official Report*, 18 June 1971, vol. 819, no. 161, col. 145.
[2] See *The Civil Service: Fulton Report*, vol. 2, Report of a Management
Consultancy Group; vol. 3, Surveys and Investigations; vol. 4, Factual,
Statistical and Explanatory Papers; vol. 5, Proposals and Opinions (by
Government Departments, Staff Associations, etc.).

civil servants in matters affecting the Civil Service, with a view to increased efficiency in the public service combined with the well-being of those employed; to provide machinery for dealing with grievances, and generally to bring together the experience and different points of view of representatives of the administrative, clerical and manipulative Civil Service.

Such councils have been set up at national, departmental and local level to discuss everything from pay, equipment of first aid rooms, noise abatement in work places, to the dispersal of office staffs from London. The Whitley concept is one that private industry, for whom is was designed, could well emulate.[1]

Much has been done in the past; there has been a spurt since Fulton as the first reports of the new Civil Service Department show.[2] This department came into existence on 1 November 1968 to take over the Treasury's functions in respect of the pay and management of the Civil Service, together with the coordination of government policy in relation to pay and pensions throughout the public sector. Arrangements were made to ensure the continued independence of the Civil Service Commission in the selection for jobs.

As part of its work in management the department was given the responsibility for the development and dissemination of administrative and managerial techniques; the general overseeing of departmental organisation, together with the provision of central management services, i.e. organisation and methods, computers and operational research, etc. There has been a beginning made in the unification of the classes. Outside management consultants have been used jointly with C.S.D. and the Home Office staff to review the management of the Prison Service. The new department helped in the planning of departmental computer projects, and in the autumn of 1969 about 135 such projects were in progress, e.g. the Police National Record Scheme; the Central Records of Driver and Vehicle Licenses Scheme.

In November 1968 a panel of businessmen, under the chair-

[1] Whitley Councils in the United Kingdom. 'A Study in Staff Relations', given by R. Hayward, then Secretary-General Staff Side to a symposium organised by l'Institut International des Sciences Administratives to study the possibility of a European Civil Service in Brussels, June 1963, p. 3.
[2] C.S.D. Report 1969, 'First Report of the Civil Service Department'. C.S.D. Report 1970–1, 'Second Report of the Civil Service Department'.

manship of Sir Robert Bellinger, was set up to review civil service manpower; it made an interim report in April 1970. It indicated areas in which manpower economy could be achieved by, for example, reducing excessive monitoring and checking of work; increasing delegation of authority, etc. It recommended the introduction of improved internal audit systems and a reappraisal of the tasks of Departments. Its work is still continuing.

Much change is taking place with an emphasis on management and accountability. The Civil Service does need to become a managerial-type organisation. It is in the Industrial Civil Service, operating in industrial/technical units which were not in the remit of Fulton, that improvements in this respect are most necessary.

Industrial Civil Service

Range of Activities

There are over 3,000 separate government establishments or units with 'industrial' manpower. These are widely distributed over the country but with concentrations in the south-west and south-east. They cover many activities, from warship, aircraft and vehicle repair and maintenance to the minting of coins and, until 1971 when the government decided to sell the interests to the private brewers, to the Carlisle, Cromarty Firth and Gretna brewing and public houses.

From an industrial point of view these establishments can be divided into 'some fourteen different functional activities':[1] Engineering Production; Filling Factory; Engineering and Vehicle Repair and Maintenance; Electronic Repair and Maintenance; Aircraft Repair and Maintenance; Works Services Maintenance; Research and Development; Explosives and Gases; Dockyards; Storage; Repair and Maintenance associated with Storage; Administrative and Domestic (Training, Catering, etc.); Headquarters Inspectorates; Field Inspectorates.

The functions which account for the largest total numbers of employees are, in order of size, Administrative and Domestic, Works Services Maintenance, Dockyards, Research and Develop-

[1] 'Pay and Conditions of Industrial Civil Servants', April 1970, Report 146, N.B.P.I. appendix C.

ment, Engineering Production, Storage and Engineering Repair and Maintenance.

The majority work in establishments employing 1,000 or more people; others work in small groups as cooks, domestics, stokers, gardeners and general labourers in non-industrial establishments. Unlike the non-industrials who are represented by unions whose membership has been largely confined to the Civil Service, the industrials are, in general, represented by such unions as the Transport and General Workers Union; the Amalgamated Union of Engineering and Foundryworkers; the National Union of Tailors and Garment Workers; and the National Union of Agricultural and Allied Workers, etc.

On 1 April 1971, the government employed a total of 202,010 industrial civil servants in a wide range of occupations. Most government departments employ some 'industrials'; of the civil departments the largest employer is the Department of the Environment with 32,495.

Department of the Environment
In 1970 the old Department of the Ministry of Public Building and Works was absorbed into the new super-Department of the Environment.[1] It brought with it a substantial number of industrial employees who still operate organisationally through the existing Scottish, Welsh and the English regional arrangements.

The task of this now sub-department is the care and maintenance of government buildings, workshops, plant and installations. It meets the demands of other government departments as, for example, when the Ministry of National Insurance was first set up it had to 'find and equip a network of local offices throughout the country as well as headquarters and regional offices'.[2] In collaboration with scientists it designed the 'novel structures' for the first atomic energy establishments at Harwell and Windscale.[3] Since 1963 it has provided the works services for the armed services: everything from barrack repairs to building runways—at home and abroad.

It maintains the Royal Palaces and Parks and the House of Parliament. Since 1902 it has run a convalescent home at Osborne

[1] 'The Reorganisation of Central Government', *Cmnd* 4506, 1970.
[2] Sir Harold Emmerson, *The Ministry of Works*, Allen & Unwin, 1956. p. 11.
[3] *Ibid.*, p. 11.

in the Isle of Wight, and since 1852 has managed the Brompton Cemetery. It is responsible for monuments and historic buildings. Through its responsibilities for art galleries and for the artistic provisioning of government departments and embassies, etc., it is a substantial owner of works of art.

When the Department of the Environment absorbed the M.P.B.W. it became the sponsoring department for the building and construction industry—with the aim of influencing its operating efficiency. Sponsorship falls far short of control but influence is obtained through informal and committee-type formal contact. Its power is strengthened by the fact that the state is a large spender in the civil engineering and building fields. It acts as building agents for government departments, and for example, it acts for the Ministry of Defence in providing homes for servicemen; it has experimented in the use of industrialised building in a fashion that undoubtedly influenced local authorities.[1]

This department is a large middleman in the provision of household furnishings for government departments. Its influence on design has been large; it has advised Regional Hospital Boards and local authorities on the bulk purchase of furnishings.

Ministry of Defence

Defence activities in the widest sense of the term need the services of more than military personnel, and in all parts of the world where often additional local staff are engaged. The 'Functional Analysis of Civilian Personnel' in the 1971 Defence White Paper shows the extent of these activities (see p. 58 below).[2]

The Ministry of Defence itself employs 141,660 industrial staff to which must now be added most of the 11,273 ex-Ministry of Aviation Supply employees.

The functional breakdown of the occupational figures not only illustrates the wide variety of employment but spotlights again the significance of research and development and also of production facilities.

[1] In May 1972 a Property Services Agency was set up within the Department of the Environment for the provision to other Government Departments of property management services, building construction and maintenance and the appropriate supplies.

[2] 'Statement on the Defence Estimates 1971', *Cmnd* 4592, annex A, table 8. N.B. While these figures include the then Ministry of Aviation Supply Staff, they do not include Ministry of Environment Staff employed on defence work.

FUNCTIONAL ANALYSIS OF CIVILIAN PERSONNEL

Major Programme	Analysis	Total
Nuclear strategic force	Polaris 3,800	3,800
Navy general purpose combat forces	Amphibious forces 300; other ships 4,900; overseas naval bases 5,600	10,800
European theatre ground forces	B.A.O.R. 30,200; Home forces 2,000	32,200
Other Army combat forces	Far East 7,500; Gulf 400; Mediterranean 4,100; other areas 100	12,100
Air Force general purpose combat forces	Air defence 300; U.K. headquarters and stations 3,200; overseas headquarters and stations 5,200; U.K. general support 4,400; overseas general support 2,300	15,400
Air mobility	Strategic transport 800; medium-range tactical transport 800; short-range transport 200; control and support 1,800	3,600
Reserve and auxiliary formations	Navy 300; Army 2,400; Air Force 400	3,100
Research and development	Military aircraft 7,200; guided-weapons 3,700; space 200; other electronics 3,500; ship and underwater warfare 3,400; ordnance and other Army 7,000; other research a and development 3,700	28,700
Training	Initial training 6,900; Service colleges 3,900; flying training 2,300; other training 11,400	24,500
Production, repair and associated facilities in the U.K.	Naval dockyards 48,500; factories 23,800; repair, maintenance and storage 54,300; inspection 13,300	139,900
Other support functions	Whitehall organisation 18,500; local administration 21,300; meteorological services 3,600; other 4,100; pensions 300; family services in the U.K. 11,200	59,000
		333,100

In the Royal Navy the total number of industrials employed is 58,800. Of these 31,900 are employed in the Dockyards at Portsmouth, Devonport, Chatham and Rosyth. Their main work is constructing, refitting and converting of naval vessels, and it provides the major industrial activity in the dockyard towns.

Other work for industrials is provided, for example, in the Supply and Transport Service and in the armament and victualling depots.

In the Army the total number of industrials is 63,100. Of these 15,200 are employed in the Royal Ordnance Factories at Birtley, Bishopton, Blackburn, Bridgwater, Chorley, Enfield, Glascoed, Leeds, Nottingham, Patricroft and Radway Green.[1]

The output from these in 1971–2 was expected to be £55·5m.[2] Most of the work in these complex industrial establishments, with their large numbers of employees, is for the services—e.g. tanks at Leeds, guns at Nottingham—but about 20 per cent is for overseas customers and about three per cent for 'civil purposes'.

Other work for industrials is provided in the Army Supply and Repair Organisation, e.g. the Royal Army Ordnance Corps Depots and the Royal Electrical and Mechanical Engineers Workshops. These vary in size but 38 Central Workshop at Chilwell is a significant engineering establishment.

In the Royal Air Force the total number of industrials employed is 19,500. Their use is spread over the various Commands which all depend on technical and supply backing to keep their aeroplanes in the air. The largest user is Maintenance Command which has a support function for all Commands.

Its work—repairing aircraft, receiving new aircraft for preservice check and modification, the storing and supplying of everything from spoons and furniture to highly-complex aircraft spares, is carried out in units whose organisation and outlook is very similar to that of outside industry. In fact the range of stores held in some maintenance units make those of the largest private firm look puny and their methods old-fashioned. The work at the engineering M.U. at St Athan, for example, is given only after tendering against outside industry.

[1] At the Leeds R.O.F. there are 1,900 civilian staff. See also Appendix D, p. 42, 'Government Industrial Establishments' (the Malabar Report), Cmnd 4713, July 1971.
[2] 'Statement on the Defence Estimates 1971', op. cit., p. 45. See also 'Supply Estimates Class XII', Defence, Feb. 1971, pp. 84-6.

There are other M.U.s at Kemble, Quedgley, Chilmark, Carlisle, Wroughton, Stafford, Aldergrove, Hartlebury, Shawbury, Sealand, Leconfield and Bicester. These all come under the control of the Commander-in-Chief of Maintenance Command who is, consequently, one of the largest employers in the country—and in my experience one who bothers about shop floor/manager relationships to a degree unknown in large-scale private industry.

Overall, the Ministry of Defence is a large employer in many fields—in particular it is a significant user of engineering skills.

Other Departments

The Department of the Environment and the Ministry of Defence employ some 90 per cent of all industrial civil servants. The remainder are employed by other departments in small groups providing services of a variety of kinds. The Home Office, for example, employs industrials in H.M. Prisons, Borstals and at the Police and Fire Service Training Centres.

There are two units which, by their nature, are worthy of note to put this sector of the civil service into perspective—the Royal Mint and the Stationery Office. The Treasury had responsibility for both until May 1972 when the latter was transferred to the ministerial control of the Civil Service Department.

The former employs 400 non-industrials and 1,400 industrials.[1] Production is moving from London to Llantrissant in South Wales where the work is to be concentrated; a move decided in the interests of regional planning. The industrial staff are employed mainly on melting, rolling, cutting, annealing and coining; also on die and seal work, weighing and telling, inspection and maintenance. The coins produced are for use at home and abroad.

The Stationery Office employs 3,350 non-industrials and 4,315 industrials. The industrial staff are employed mainly with printing presses and the servicing of office machinery—together with work in distribution, warehouses and bookshops. The non-industrial staff are predominantly executive, clerical and comparable staff with technical qualifications in the printing industry. There are two printing works in London itself, with others in

---

[1] Supplementary Estimates 1971–2, *op. cit.*, Class x, p. 10, and for full details of work see 'Royal Mint. Annual Report of the Deputy Master and Comptroller for the Year 1970'.

Harrow, Wembley, Oldham, Gateshead, Edinburgh and Bracknell.

Problems of Pay, Management and Accountability
The problems of pay, management and accountability are to be found in all parts of the Civil Service but they are of particular concern and are highlighted in the industrial/technical units which employ large numbers of industrials.

Non-industrials of course work in these units as managers, administrators, and scientists, while in practice, jobs classified as industrial in one sphere are non-industrial elsewhere[1]—consequently this discussion is based on the work unit as well as that of job classification.

The eventual fusing of the industrials and non-industrials recommended by the National Board for Prices and Incomes in 1970[2] will not only assist the task of management but will clarify discussion of its problems and those of pay and accountability.

The problem of pay, and not the least its low level, were not widely discussed until the publication of the first of the reports on the 'Pay of Industrial Civil Servants' in June 1966[3]—itself part of a much wider political discussion on prices and incomes.

Up to this time 'the rates of pay of industrials were fixed by reference to averages derived from basic time rates settled at industry level in a range of outside industry'.[4] This system was based on the Fair Wages Resolution of the House of Commons of 14 October 1946 which requires the government to pay its employees not less than the rates settled for comparable workers in outside industry.

In practice Report no. 18 of 1966 found that 'a high proportion of industrial civil servants found themselves at the lower end of

[1] 'Pay and Conditions of Industrial Civil Servants', Report no. 146, N.P.B.I., *Cmnd* 4351, pp. 23, 24, appendix C and Appendix 1 (footnote), April 1970.
[2] *Ibid.*, p. 28, para. 95.
[3] Report no. 18, N.B.P.I., *Cmnd* 3034, June 1966.
A relatively small number of industrial civil servants are paid 'trade rates'—that is the rates fixed by agreements governing the pay of their counterparts in industry and in the negotiation of which Government Departments take no part. Examples are printers employed by H.M. Stationery Office and a larger number of electricians and building trade workers. These were outside the terms of reference of the Report.
[4] Report no. 146, *op. cit.*, p. 3.

the range of industrial pay and that the differentials between the
pay of rank and rank were narrower than they were in industry
generally'.[1] There was consequently a difficulty in recruiting and
retaining labour of the right quality and numbers.

The report analysed the different industries to be found in the
Civil Service, it accepted the principle of comparability and the
need for the government to take into account the overall effect
of pay increases whether in the public or private sector—but
made clear the need for the particular problems and needs of
the industrial civil service to be considered. The government
should be positively responsible for its own industrial problems;
to follow by comparability was not enough.

As a result, new pay arrangements were brought into effect
from 1 July 1967. Not the least important was a new grouping
of the various 'industries' in the Civil Service which by July
1969 were reduced to four—engineering, dockyards, works services and stores, administrative and domestic. Most important of
all, there were real pay increases; the Industrial Civil Service did
not lose by a prices and incomes policy.

In April 1970 the N.B.P.I. reported on the 'Pay and Conditions
of Industrial Civil Servants'. Its recommendations were in the
field of pay negotiations—in particular that the four industrial
groups should be merged to provide a single structure of basic
pay—and also in the field of method study; work measurement
and job evaluation; and negotiating machinery.[2] Since that time
considerable progress has been made on these recommendations.
On 1 July 1970 there was a merger of the four industrial groups,
and by mid-1971 'over half of the Industrial Civil Service' was
covered by 'productivity agreements and other arrangements for
relating pay more closely to performance'.[3]

Much has been done in Defence in these respects as the
Defence Estimates for 1971 show. It was revealed that 'About
two-thirds of Royal Ordnance Factory Industrial employees are
covered by payment by results schemes, including peacework.
Of the remainder, about half are now included in productivity
agreements or incentive schemes.'[4] Indeed, there is much to
praise in the R.O.F.s in all aspects of their work from cost con-

[1] *Ibid.*, p. 3.
[2] Report no. 146, *op. cit.*, pp. 25-8.
[3] *H.C. Official Report*, vol. 819, no. 161, col. 145, 18 June 1971.
[4] Statement on the Defence Estimates 1971, *op. cit.*, p. 46.

sciousness to the calibre of management as the Malabar Report[1] made clear, and while the report could at the same time criticise an 'unhealthy situation' in terms of industrial efficiency in the dockyards, there is much to praise in Defence generally.

Defence leads, but there is a changed approach in the Civil Service as a whole, with productivity agreements in many fields— 'Board of Trade' airports, National Air Traffic Control and Tele- communications Engineering Establishments, the Royal Mint, and at the Department of the Environment in Works Main- tenance, Dredgers, Building Research Centre, Royal Parks, Supplies Division Stores, Transport Depots and M.T. Work- shops.[2]

There are problems peculiar to government that have to be faced in drawing up this type of agreement. For example, there are the scattered groups of industrials serving other departments, e.g. as caretakers, whose type of work does not lend itself to measurement. In the large establishment the work programmes are often out of the control of management because they are related to outside factors such as defence needs. For this and other reasons a reserve capacity has often to be retained. Govern- ment management and accountability has to take this aspect into account.

Report no. 18 of the National Board for Prices and Incomes showed an unsatisfactory state of affairs in management's attitude to manpower. It was summed up as a tendency to fix manpower at a level designed to meet peak levels. The general lack of flexibility led to local management always seeking authority for an over-large work force.[3]

Accordingly, the Report recommended that the government should consider allowing local managements greater discretion to decide numbers and grades of workers employed; a strengthen- ing of central management services, as a result of which new budgetary procedures and pilot schemes for promoting greater efficiency could be devised.[4]

Four years later Report no. 146 was able to claim a great

[1] 'The Malabar Report', *op. cit.* R.O.F.s—para 78, p. 18; Dockyards— para. 71, p. 80.
[2] Report no. 146, *op. cit.*, appendix H.
[3] Report no. 18, *op. cit.*, p. 14.
[4] *Ibid.*, p. 19.

deal of work being done with the object of raising efficiency.
In the Defence Estimates of 1971 it was reported that in the
R.O.F.s 'management processes are being improved and new
methods introduced; production engineering and method study
have led to new techniques in manufacture and assembly'.[1] In
the same establishments, management consultants had been
brought in and decentralised administration was beginning.

In the Army, significant changes were reported in R.A.O.C.
inventory management through the Central Inventory Control
Point at Bicester. Management accounting systems were
developing in the R.E.M.E. workshops. Similar changes have been
under way in the highly technical R.A.F. for some years, where
new management techniques constantly exercise the minds of
civilian and military managers.[2]

Further changes will follow from the Report of the Malabar
Committee first set up in 1968 by the then Prime Minister to
examine 'whether the existing organisation and systems of control and accountability of large-scale establishments in the
Ministry of Defence and Technology, engaged in production offer
impediments to the achievement of full efficiency, and to recommend how such impediments should be removed'.[3]

The question of accountability is exercising the mind of the
Civil Service, and not only in Defence; the Bellinger Committee referred to earlier has, for example, been advising in
this respect at the Stationery Office. These technical accounting processes matter, and without the information provided it is
impossible to run a modern concern efficiently.

In my view, ultimately, and given the objective criteria, government industrial establishments should be given financial objectives in much the same way as the nationalised industries.

The existing situation in this respect in the Stationery Office
and the Royal Mint is far too incomprehensible. Apparently they
are required to conform to the objectives laid down for government trading generally. This means, I was informed by the Civil
Service Department in June 1971,

[1] Statement on the Defence Estimates 1971, *op. cit.*, p. 46.
[2] Defence Estimates 1971, *op. cit.*, pp. 46-7.
[3] 'The Malabar Report' made two reports which were published in
Cmnd 4713, July 1971: 'Government Industrial Establishments'. The
Interim Report on the R.O.F.s is being considered by the new Defence
Procurement Executive; the broad principles of the Report on the
Dockyards have been accepted by the government.

In the case of the Royal Mint, broadly, that the Department is expected to achieve commercially favourable results in respect of the work (supply of coins, medals, etc.) undertaken for foreign governments and the private sector, including notional interest on fixed and working capital at rates specified by the Treasury. So far as the Mint's main task—the supply of U.K. coins for circulation—is concerned, the Mint at present receive from the banks the face value of the coins supplied, which very considerably exceeds their cost calculated on a commercial basis, and similarly the Mint repay the banks for withdrawn coin at face value. The difference between face value and cost of production is discounted in examination of the Mint's results, and the Mint are expected to work in such a way that those results should similarly meet the criteria applicable to commercial transactions. Certain changes in the Mint's accounting system are currently under consideration.

Greater clarity of objective than this is surely possible; the last sentence is therefore hopeful.[1]

A profit and loss account is not a sufficient yardstick of efficiency in private industry, and in management terms large firms have for some time used sophisticated financial objectives beyond the comprehension of the smaller firms. What matters in the Civil Service is to provide similar clarity of objective. This is ultimately the task for the politician.

Problems remain, but the last five years have brought great change to the Industrial Civil Service in general and the industrial units in particular. It is using new managerial techniques and evolving its own management criteria; in matters of wage determination it is moving away from simply tagging along behind the private sector. All this was needed because in the management of industrial-type units the Civil Service was behind the times.

It is in this part of government activities that hiving-off to a public agency would be particularly appropriate. Whatever the political merits or demerits of 'denationalisation' of the so-called state pubs in Carlisle and parts of Scotland, the existing adminis-

[1] In August 1972 it was announced that the Mint was to be made 'a unit of accountable management financed through a trading fund', thus making 'it easier to concentrate attention on the performance of the undertaking as a whole and not only on the cash flows reflected in annual Votes'. See *H.C. Official Report*, vol. 842, no. 173, cols. 314-5, 7 Aug. 1972.

trative arrangements in the Home Office did not lead to clear
objectives and administration, or political responsibility. A public
agency would have been one solution. The State Management
Districts' results, nevertheless, compared favourably with those
of the private brewing trade; they could have been much better.

There are other fields of government activity where hiving-
off would also be appropriate. Such a policy would be a form of
devolution that would avoid the management diseconomies of
scale to be found in all government departments—and not the
least in the new super departments. Some of the work in the
Department of the Environment formerly in the M.P.B.W. is an
obvious candidate.[1] As long as there is a logical reporting system
from the agency to the department, then the 'requirements of
parliamentary accountability can be met'.[2] It may be that such
agencies would be appropriate also in local or regional government. There are large firms in the private sector who could pro-
fitably investigate some hiving-off in their own activities which
would apply to management accountability and ownership.

Hived-off or not, the type of organisation within a government department matters. In the Ministry of Defence the decision
in 1971 to have a Minister of State for Defence Procurement
will enable the structure of this department in respect of its
industrial units to be reconsidered.[3] The previous decision in
1970 after the General Election to abolish the structure based on
a Minister of Defence for Equipment was over-hasty. New
governments should wait six months before changing a structure
they have not seen in practice.

It seemed to some that, given all their difficulties of efficiency
and accountability, the hiving-off of the R.O.F.s and the Royal

[1] The setting up of a Property Services Agency within the Department
of the Environment is a step towards hiving off, see page 57, footnote
(1).

[2] See 'Getting Things Done', article by Michael Shanks, The Times,
10 Sept. 1970—and for a fuller discussion of developments in the U.S.A.
and the U.K. see Bruce L. R. Smith and D. C. Hague (eds.) The Dilemma
of Accountability in Modern Government, Macmillan, 1971.

[3] See 'Government Organisation for Defence Procurement and Civil
Aerospace', Cmnd 4641, April 1971. N.B. also the decision announced
in December 1971 to develop the Employment Service as a departmental agency within the department of Employment and that
announced in April 1972 to set up a Central Computer Agency within
the Civil Service Department. See p. 20 for information concerning
the Industrial Development Executive within the D.T.I.

Dockyards to a government agency might prove to be a solution to these problems. However, the Malabar Committee did look most carefully at this idea but came to the conclusion that the advantages of hiving-off could equally well be obtained through the setting up of a 'Trading Fund' within the Ministry of Defence Vote.[1] Undoubtedly greater clarity of financing objectives will be obtained in this way and this is an important first step—the question of hiving-off can, therefore, be left for later consideration.

The whole question of the existing structure and its reorganisation matters in both the Industrial and the Non-Industrial Civil Service. Without it many of the objectives of the National Board for Prices and Incomes will not be achieved.

The total staff employed of 903,105 is an important part of the total labour force, but a numerical comparison alone is not the full story. The range of occupations involved, the control and effect the activities have on the community, render it even more significant. The Civil Service is extremely powerful.

Whatever political mythologists might believe, the Civil Service is not going to disappear overnight or even over the course of years. It has grown in size because of the developing needs of society with industrialisation—not because of a political whim. Those who talk of cutting its size in opposition are surprised that it goes on growing in government; forgetting that it is constantly being given new tasks.

The Civil Service is only one aspect of the growth of the central government activities; there is also the work of organisations which operate with funds from the government.

GRANT-AIDED ORGANISATIONS

There are many grant-aided bodies; the Central Statistical Office list includes only those which receive substantial grants.[2]

A number of these organisations, e.g. British Institute of Management; British Travel Association; British Standards Institution; Horserace Levy Betting Board; Horserace Totalisator Board; National Computing Centre, are treated as part of the company sector—bodies serving industry. Others—British Film Institute; College of Aeronautics; Commonwealth Institute;

[1] Malabar Report, *op. cit.*, para. 12, p. 3; para. 109, p. 88.
[2] 'National Accounts Statistics, Sources and Methods', *op. cit.*, annex 2, pp. 298-9.

Industrial Advisers to the Blind; General Practice Finance Corporation; Universities—are treated as part of the personal sector.

The organisations concerned here are those classified by the Central Statistical Office as part of central government. Overall they employ some 900,000 people; more than the Civil Service itself. The largest employer are two or three organisations, e.g. Regional Hospital Boards; only these and others of the more significant and interesting organisations are dealt with here.

Individual Organisations

Regional Hospital Boards and Boards of Governors of Teaching Hospitals[1] (Department of Health and Social Security, Scottish Office, Welsh Office)

The services provided by the National Health Service fall into three main groups—the general practitioner services; the local authority health and welfare services; and the hospital services. The general practitioners, whether doctors, dentists, opticians or chemists, are in the personal sector; the local authority services come obviously in their own sector; it is the hospital services which are classified in the central government sector—as are the local health executive administrators.

The hospital services are administered through 20 regional hospital boards and some 450 hospital management committees, and in the case of the teaching hospitals in England and Wales, by boards of governors.

The committees and boards are made up of appointed members representing local interests, e.g. local authority members, employers, trade unionists, etc. They employ large numbers of medical, administrative, clerical and industrial staff in the headquarters and in the general, maternity, infectious diseases, psychiatric hospitals—as also in convalescent homes, etc.

The total number employed in this way by the Regional Hospital Boards in the United Kingdom and Northern Ireland in September 1971 was some 655,000.

[1] 'Department of Health and Social Security Annual Report 1970', *Cmnd* 4714, 1971. N.B. This Report refers only to England. In August 1972 ('National Health Service Reorganisation: England', *Cmnd* 5055, 1972; see also 'National Health Service Reorganisation in Wales', *Cmnd* 5057, 1972) proposals for integrating the threefold structure of the N.H.S. were made. Changes are also to be made in Scotland. See p. 117 below.

In England, for example, there were in 1970 22,059 medical and dental staff; 33,168 professional and technical staff; 237,350 nursing and midwifery staff; 48,583 administrative and clerical staff; 146,863 full-time; and 70,602 part-time workers, maintenance and domestic staff.[1]

A comparison with the statistics for previous years indicate a growing labour force; the expenditure on complex medical equipment and on new buildings is also growing. This illustrates a major political problem—as it does in the U.S.A. in a different context—of how to raise the necessary money.[2] Modern society demands better health services; as an electorate it is not so keen on paying for them.

The Research Councils[3] (Department of Education and Science)
The bodies concerned are: the Agricultural Research Council; the Medical Research Council; National Environment Research Council; Science Research Council; and the Social Science Research Council.

The Councils are autonomous bodies set up to foster research and training by the provision of grants to support work undertaken in university departments and in other higher educational establishments; and of maintenance awards and fees to support students for further studies or training in research after their first degree. They also establish research units in the universities and provide expensive experiment facilities used by university research workers, e.g. Rutherford and Daresbury high energy physics laboratories of the Science Research Council.

The Agricultural Research Council was established in 1931 and consists of not less than 15 and not more than 18 members. The membership includes distinguished scientists and practical farmers. It is responsible for 14 independent state-aided agri-

---

[1] *Ibid.*, table 58, pp. 250-1.
[2] R. H. S. Crossman, 'Paying for the Social Services', Fabian Tract 399, 1969.
[3] 'Report of the Agricultural Research Council, 1969–70', H.C. 71, 1970; Medical Research Council Annual Report, April 1970–March 1971', H.C. 422, 1971; 'Natural Environment Research Council Report, 1 April 1970–31 March 1971', H.C. 531, 1971; 'Science Research Council, Report of the Council 1970–1', H.C. 517, 1971; 'Report of the Social Science Research Council, April 1970–March 1971', H.C. 529, 1971. See also 'A Framework for Government Research and Development', *Cmnd* 4814, 1971.

cultural research institutes and advises eight similar institutes in Scotland.

The Medical Research Council established in 1920 consists of from 12 to 16 members. The scientific members are appointed after consultation with the President of the Royal Society. Its chief function is to promote research into all aspects of health and disease. The National Institute for Medical Research at Mill Hill and Hampstead is the main research establishment; a new Clinical Research Centre is being built in Harrow. The Council has over 70 research units at universities and hospitals.

The National Environment Research Council, with between 10 and 16 members, was set up in 1965 to encourage plans and conduct research in those sciences, both physical and biological, that relate to man's natural environment. The Council is responsible for the Nature Conservancy, the British Antarctic Survey, the Institute of Geological Sciences and other scientific bodies.

The Social Science Research Council, which consists of 14 members, was set up in 1965 to encourage and carry out research in the social sciences—economics, political science, psychology, social anthropology, statistics, etc.

The Science Research Council, with up to 16 members, was established in 1965 to cover all branches of fundamental science other than those for which the other research councils are responsible. Its own establishments include the Royal Greenwich Observatory, the Radio and Space Research Station.

The total staff employed by the Councils on April 1971 was 5,840, as follows:

	Medical Research Council	Natural Environment Research Council	Science Research Council	Social Science Research Council	Natural History Museum
1 Scientific and Professional staff	1,053	544	570	31	99
2 Experimental Class and Scientific Assistants	—	543	520	1	226
3 Technical and other staff	1,703	550	625	—	218
4 Administrative staff	791	479	531	79	52
5 Industrial staff	481	116	656	—	—
TOTALS:	4,028	2,232	2,902	111	595

The whole future of the Research Council system has been under question since the publication of the Green Paper, 'A Framework for Government Research and Development', in November 1971. The recommendation of Sir Frederick Dainton's Working Group was for the setting up of a 'Board for the Research Councils' which would have the overall responsibility of ensuring that 'the requirements of executive departments for scientific support from the Research Councils were being met, on a service or contract basis where appropriate, and by the provision of independent and authoritative information and advice in other cases'.[1]

The recommendations of Lord Rothschild, Head of the Central Policy Review Staff, urged that government departments should have a bigger say in the work of the Research Councils and emphasised the customer/contractor relationship. It has been argued, however, that such an approach would seriously inhibit scientific freedom.

In July 1972 the government reached conclusions on a number of the main issues involved, in 'Framework for Government Research and Development'.[2] First it was decided to reconstitute the Council for Scientific Policy; second, to give Departments direct representation on the Research Councils; and third, to transfer some of the funds provided from the science budget of the D.E.S. to customer departments and brought within the scope of the customer/contractor principle.

United Kingdom Atomic Energy Authority[3] (Department of Trade and Industry)
This authority with 10 members was created in 1954 and is responsible for research and development in nuclear energy; and, since the Science and Technology Act of 1965, for research outside nuclear energy, e.g. desalinisation, ceramics, carbon fibres, etc.

The Authority had researched in and developed experimental and prototype nuclear reactors; it has played a significant world part in this field. On 1 April 1971 the assets and liabilities of

[1] *Cmnd* 4814, *op. cit.*, para. 51, p. 16, on 'The Future of the Research Council System'.
[2] *Cmnd* 5046, 1972, 'v The Research Councils'.
[3] 'United Kingdom Atomic Energy Authority 17th Annual Report and Accounts 1970–1', H.C. 552. See W. Marshall, 'Harwell's Work with Industry', *National Westminster Bank Quarterly Review*, May 1971.

the Authority's trading fund were transferred to two new companies, British Nuclear Fuels Ltd and the Radio Chemical Centre
Ltd. It is the intention to seek private participation in the capital
of the two companies.

The former company is responsible for the establishments at
Capenhurst, Chapelcross, Springfields and the Windscale and
Calder Works; the latter for the Radio Chemical Centre at Amer-
sham and the facilities at Harwell.[1]

The net assets at 31 March 1971 were £229·6m; those for
research and development activities were £171·7m. The
Authority had investments in Societé Anglo-Belge Vulcain S.A.,
50 per cent; British Nuclear Design and Construction Ltd, 20
per cent; Nuclear Power Group Ltd, 20 per cent; Amersham/
Searle Corporation U.S.A., 50 per cent; Combustibili Nucleari
S.P.A. Italy, 50 per cent; Nukleardienst G.m.b.H. Germany, 50
per cent.

The total staff was 29,427—13,150 industrials; 16,277 non-
industrials; 2,560 qualified scientists and engineers were engaged
on civil research and development with, for example, nearly
1,500 of these concerned with the further development of nuclear
energy for the generation of electricity.

Arts Council of Great Britain[2] (Department of Education and
Science, Scottish Office, Welsh Office)
The Arts Council, with 20 members, is an independent body
first set up in 1946 to promote drama, music, painting, literature
and sculpture.

There are Arts Councils in Scotland and Wales appointed by
the main council; together in 1971–2 they received a grant of
£11·2m.

The total staff was 225.

The British Council[3] (Foreign and Commonwealth Office)
This organisation, with 30 members, is responsible for promot-

[1] See *ibid.*, appendix V, 'List and Functions of Authority Establishments
as at 31 March 1971'.
[2] 'The Arts Council of Great Britain, 25th Annual Report and Accounts
Year Ended 31 March 1971'; N.B. there is a separate Arts Council for
Northern Ireland.
[3] 'The British Council Annual Report 1970–1'; N.B. under the Council's
Royal Charter a number of government departments have the right to
nominate a member—Chancellor of the Exchequer, etc.

ing a wider knowledge of Britain and the English language abroad, and for developing closer cultural relations with other countries.

The activities of the Council are to be found in nearly 80 countries, where it advises and assists in English teaching and other subjects including science, and fosters contact with foreigners engaged in educational and professional activities. It also maintains libraries and presents the arts abroad.

In the U.K. the Council looks after the interests of overseas students and visitors.

The total staff was 4,250 of whom 2,477 were overseas.

British Tourist Authority[1] (Department of Trade and Industry) This organisation, with nine members and set up in 1970, is responsible for the overseas promotion of tourism in Britain; working with the Tourist Boards for England, Scotland and Wales.

The total employed by the four boards is 607.

Commonwealth War Graves Commission[2] (Ministry of Defence) This Commission, with 24 members, was set up in 1917, it now has the responsibility of maintaining structurally and horticulturally the cemeteries and memorials of the two world wars in 'more than 140 countries and territories from northern Norway in the Arctic Circle, to the Falkland Islands in the South Atlantic'.

The total staff was 1,683, which included 1,094 engaged overseas.

Criminal Injuries Compensation Board[3] (Home Office, Scottish Office) This Board, with nine legally qualified members, adjudicates on applications for ex-gratia payments of compensation to victims of crimes of violence.

Total Employed was 70.

Forestry Commission[4] (Ministry of Agriculture, Fisheries and Food, Scottish Office, Welsh Office)

---

[1] 'British Tourist Authority Annual Report for Year Ended March 1971'; N.B. there is an independent board for Northern Ireland.
[2] 'Commonwealth War Graves Commission 52nd Annual Report, April 1970–March 1971'.
[3] 'Criminal Injuries Compensation Board 7th Report, Accounts for Year Ended 31 March 1971', *Cmnd* 4812, 1971.
[4] 'Forestry Commission 51st Annual Report and Accounts 1970–1', H.C. 70, 1971.

The Commission, with a chairman and five other part-time members, was set up in 1919. Through the forestry enterprise, it is concerned with the production of timber, recreational facilities, wold-life management, and countryside amenities. As the forestry authority it is responsible for administering the grant scheme to private woodland owners; for research, plant health and for tree-felling licensing.

The Commission has an investment in Cowal Ari Saw-milling Company in Strachur, Argyllshire.

The total estate of the Commission is about 3,000,000 acres and includes 380 forests. The total labour force was 2,510 non-industrials and 7,005 industrials.

Herring Industry Board[1] (Ministry of Agriculture, Fisheries and Food, Home Office, Scottish Office, Welsh Office)
This body, with four members, was set up in 1935 to promote the sales of herring and the application of new methods of catching, processing and distribution.

The Board administers the government grant and loan scheme for assistance towards the improvements and purchase of fishing vessels.

The total staff was 62.

Highlands and Islands Development Board[2] (Scottish Office)
This Board, with seven members, was set up in 1965 to stimulate economic and social development in the counties of Argyll, Caithness, Inverness, Orkney, Ross and Cromarty, Sutherland and Shetland. It concerns itself with, for example, industry, agriculture, fisheries, tourism, transport and housing; and operates through grants and loans. Indeed, it also may set up and operate business itself.

In 1970 joint Board/private investment totalled £14·5m; ordinary shares were held in Shetland Hotels Ltd, 10,000 £1 shares; Scottish Sea Farm Ltd, 20,000 £1 shares; Lennon & Kean Ltd, Glasgow, 15,000 £1 shares; Caithness Glass Ltd, Wick, 10,000 £1 shares; preference shares in Highland Colliery Ltd, Brora, 20,000 25p shares; debentures in Cairngorm Sports Development Ltd, Inverness, £38,400 7½ per cent debentures (1981–6).

[1] 'Herring Industry Board 36th Annual Report for the Year Ended 31 December 1970', *Cmnd* 4565, 1971.
[2] 'Highlands and Islands Development Board 5th Report, 1970'.

Industrial Estates Corporation[1] (Department of Trade and Industry)
There are three bodies—the English, Scottish and Welsh Industrial Estates Corporations—which were set up in their present form in 1966 to build factories and manage estates in development areas. Estates are to be found in all parts of the country, e.g. Aycliffe in England, Hillington in Scotland, Treforest in Wales, and they provide work for some 250,000 people.

Meat and Livestock Commission[2] (Ministry of Agriculture, Fisheries and Food, Scottish Office)
This body, with nine members, was set up in 1967. Its function is to promote greater efficiency in the livestock industry and the livestock products industry in Great Britain; the collection and publication of market intelligence; the introduction of carcase classification; the improvement of retail presentation and price marking; and the promotion and coordination of research. It has responsibilities also for the furthering of efficiency of the handling and marketing of stock through auction markets and at slaughterhouses.

The Commission is financed from a levy on the industry; except where it acts for the government by certifying animals for fatstock subsidy.

The total employed was 1,314; 769 primarily in fatstock certification work.

Race Relations Board[3] (Home Office)
This organisation, with 12 members, was set up in 1965 with the statutory duty to receive and investigate complaints of racial discrimination. It seeks conciliation through regional conciliation committees; only then is redress sought in the courts.

The total staff was 58.

The White Fish Authority[4] (Ministry of Agriculture, Fisheries and Food, Home Office, Scottish Office, Welsh Office)

[1] 'English Industrial Estates 1971'; 'Opportunity 1971', Scottish Industrial Estates Corporation; 'Adventure', Welsh Industrial Estates 1967.
[2] 'Meat and Livestock Commission 4th Annual Report in Respect of the Year Ended 30 September 1971'.
[3] 'Report of the Race Relations Board for 1970–1', H.C. 448, 1971.
[4] 'White Fish Authority Annual Report and Accounts for Year Ended 31 March 1971', H.C. 435; N.B. there is also a Scottish and Northern Ireland Committee with six members.

This organisation, with seven members, was set up in 1951 to reorganise, develop and regulate the white fish industry.

The authority administers government grant and loan schemes for the purchase of new fishing vessels and engines and the improvement of existing vessels. It operates a levy on the original sale of white fish and receives a government grant for research and development.

The total staff was 252.

Reasons for Development

The story of the development of government departments is one of response to developing needs; this is the story also of the grant-aided bodies.

Where it was thought necessary to meet a need by an 'independent' body, then the grant-aid approach was thought more appropriate than the expansion of departmental functions.

The Forestry Commission was a response to timber deficiency in the first world war; the Race Relations Board was to meet the need to give a lead on racial discrimination; the Research Councils concept was based on independence for scientists; and the Atomic Energy Authority was set up in a field inappropriate for private enterprise both on lack of investment profitability and security needs.

The grant-aided organisation approach is one form of hiving-off—the Countryside Commission civil service type is another—but where not all the problems of accountability have been solved.

Accountability

The classification of the grant-aided bodies into a central government group and then company and personal groups, corresponds approximately to the distinction between those accounts audited by the Comptroller and Auditor General—the first group—and the others which are not.[1]

From the aspect of parliamentary accountability the Public Accounts Committee can examine any account presented to parliament whether or not the c. and A.G. have audited or had previous access to it. This Committee has looked, for example, at aspects

[1] In practice the c. and A.G. audits accounts of the National Library of Wales and the National Museum of Wales; he also has access to the accounts of the universities.

of the work of the U.K.A.E.A.,[1] and issued a most valuable report on the Forestry Commission—when it expressed doubts as to the form of its accounts and their inability to measure efficiency and commercial success.[2] Nevertheless, only a small proportion of the accounts are examined by the P.A.C., faced as it is with its many responsibilities and a shortage of staff and time.

The Expenditure Committee has the same problem as it looks at the estimates and the allied topical issues. While it would be possible with more staff for this or the P.A.C. to look at grant-aided bodies, these committees by their origin and philosophy are not entirely suitable for this new task.

The Select Committee on the Nationalised Industries by its terms of reference looks at this type of industry and a number of other public corporations—Independent Television Authority, Cable and Wireless, and the Bank of England. It has also been given power to look at the Horserace Totalisator Board over which the Home Secretary has no control on policy and activities.[3] Given this curious extension of interest there would be no reason why the grant-aided bodies should not be brought in. This Select Committee, however, also already has an exacting task and, given its origin, is again not appropriate.

The Select Committee on Science and Technology has looked for example, at aspects of the work of the U.K.A.E.A. when it considered the 'United Kingdom Reactor Programme' and the 'Nuclear Power Industry'; it has also examined the National Environment Research Council.[4] It performs a valuable task and some of the grant-aided bodies fall within its purview. Nevertheless neither this type of specialist committee, nor others that might be set up which may have a relevance to others of these

[1] 'Third Report from the Committee of Public Accounts Session 1968', H.C. 362, pp. xlix-lix; N.B. the P.A.C. will have no power to look at the two new subsidiaries, British Nuclear Fuels Ltd and Radio Chemical Centre Ltd, once they take private capital. In the interim period the P.A.C. could look at the relationship of the companies to the U.K.A.E.A.
[2] Alan E. Thompson, 'The Forestry Commission. A Reappraisal of its Functions', *The Three Banks Review*, no. 91, Sept. 1971, p. 30.
[3] 'Special Report from the Select Committee on Nationalised Industries', H.C. 298, 1968, p. 49.
[4] 'Third Report from the Select Committee on Science and Technology', H.C. 381, 1967; 'Fourth Report from the Select Committee on Science and Technology', H.C. 410, 1968; 'Fifth Report from the Select Committee on Science and Technology', H.C. 400, 1969.

grant-aided organisations, e.g. a Select Committee on the Health Service, is appropriate for the task, given their broad remit.

What is urgently required is a new parliamentary committee geared to the needs of the growing number of grant-aided bodies, and particularly their administration and structure. While the government itself should bear the main responsibility—and with regard to the Forestry Commission, the 1972 'Interdepartmental Cost/Benefit Study' and White Paper 'Forestry Policy' show what can be done in this respect[1]—such a committee should also question their continuing reason-to-be.

This extension of the parliamentary committee system need not and must not derogate from the main function of the House of Commons itself—questioning the executive. At the moment, without more information, it cannot carry out this task with enough depth of information.

The grant-aided organisations are a significant part of the central government sector and with the possibility of more 'hiving off' from the government departments but still within this sector, there is every likelihood in the post-Fulton period of their further growth.

All the activities of the central government including those of the civil service itself are likely to go on growing—the only exception being the armed services, where the reduction in manpower has been proceeding with the curtailment of commitments in different parts of the world. What matters politically is to consider the consequences of this growth: to question old methods and old organisation; to ask if the old task is really required today and if a new task does not require a new approach.

The central government, through its direct and grant-aided activities, as well as through its control of the private sector, is a significant part of the public sector.

The central government does not carry out all its activities itself. It allocates its money to other organisations; one of the most important groups of these is the local authorities.

[1] 'Forestry in Great Britain', Treasury, 1972; 'Forestry Policy', June 1972.

Further Reading

Richard A. Chapman, *The Higher Civil Service in Britain*, Constable, 1970.

D. N. Chester and F. M. G. Willson, *The Organisation of British Central Government*, Allen & Unwin, 1968.

Sir John Craig, *A History of Red Tape. An Account of the Origin and Development of the Civil Service*, Macdonald & Evans, 1955.

Sir James Crombie, *Her Majesty's Customs & Excise*, Allen & Unwin, 1962.

Geoffrey Kingdom Fry, *Statesman in Disguise. The Changing Role of the Administrative Class of the British Home Civil Service 1853–1966*, Macmillan, 1969.

David Howell M.P., *Conservative Party: Whose Government Works?*, C.P.C., 1968.

B. V. Humphreys, *Clerical Unions in the Civil Service*, Basil Blackwell, 1958.

Sir Godfrey Ince, *The Ministry of Labour and National Service*, Allen & Unwin, 1960.

Sir Charles Jeffries, *The Colonial Office*, Allen & Unwin, 1956.

Sir Gilmour Jenkins, *The Ministry of Transport & Civil Aviation*, Allen & Unwin, 1959.

Sir Alexander Johnston, *The Inland Revenue*, Allen & Unwin, 1965.

Sir Geoffrey King, *The Ministry of Pensions and National Insurance*, Allen & Unwin, 1958.

T. D. Kingdom, 'The Confidential Advisors of Ministers', *Public Administration*, autumn 1966.

Roy M. MacLeod and E. Kay Andrews, 'The Origins of the D.S.I.R.; Reflections on Ideas and Men, 1915–16', *Public Administration*, spring 1970.

Sir Harry Melville, *The Department of Scientific and Industrial Research*, Allen & Unwin, 1962.

Sir David Milne, *The Scottish Office*, Allen & Unwin, 1957.

R. K. Mosley, *The Story of the Cabinet Office*, Routledge, 1969.

Sir Frank Newsom, *The Home Office*, Allen & Unwin, 1954.

Marjorie Ogilvy-Webb, *The Government Explains, a Study of the Information Services*, a Report of the Royal Institute of Public Administration, Allen & Unwin, 1965.

J. B. Poole and Kay Andrews (eds.), *The Government of Science in Britain*, Weidenfeld, 1972.

Lord Strang, *The Foreign Office*, Allen & Unwin, 1954.

Sir John Winnfrith, *The Ministry of Agriculture, Fisheries and Food*, Allen & Unwin, 1962.

'Second Report from the Select Committee on Science and Technology, Session 1968–9'; Defence Research.

'Defence Research and Development: the Government's Observations on the Second Report from the Select Committee on Science and Technology, *Cmnd* 4236, 1969.

'The Tenth Reports and Statements of Accounts of the Horserace

Betting Levy Board and the Horserace Totalisator Board for Year
    1 April 1970–31 March 1971'.
Britain 1972. An Official Handbook, H.M.S.O., 1972.
'Fulton. The Reshaping of the Civil Service: Developments during
    1970', Report by the Joint Committee of the National Whitley Council,
    March 1971 (annex: Merger of the Administrative, Executive and
    Clerical Classes Agreement, 1 January 1971).
The Administrators, the Reform of the Civil Service, Fabian Tract
    355.

Annual Reports: Associated Organisations
Report of the Charity Commissioners for England and Wales for the
    Year 1970, H.C. 409, 1971.
Commission on Industrial Relations, Second General Report, *Cmnd*
    4803, 1971.
Crown Estate Office, Report of the Commissioners for the Year ended
    31 March 1971.
Decimal Currency Board, Final Report 1971, H.C. 4, 1971.
Reports of the Chief Registrar of Friendly Societies for the Year 1970.
Report to the Lord Chancellor on H.M. Land Registry for the Year
    1970–1.
The Second Report of the Metrication Board 1971, Going Metric—
    Progress in 1970.
National Savings Committee for England and Wales, Annual Report
    1970–1.
First Report of the Parliamentary Commissioner for Administration,
    Annual Report for 1970, H.C. 261, 1971.
The Twelfth Annual Report of the Keeper of Public Records on the
    Work of the Advisory Council on Public Records, 1970, H.C. 364,
    1971.
Ninety-Sixth Annual Report of the Public Works Loan Board 1970–71,
    Restrictive Trading Agreements, Report of the Registrar, 1 July 1966
    to 30 June 1969, *Cmnd* 4303, 1970.
Eighth Annual Report of the Water Resources Board for the Year end-
    ing 30 September 1971, H.C. 73, 1972.

3 Local Authorities

3 Local Authorities

One of the main ways by which the state has become directly involved in the provision of facilities, both social and environmental, which have become vital to the successful running of a complicated modern industrial economy, is through the activities of a variety of local authorities.

Total Expenditure and Total Employed

These bodies raise revenues themselves, but a large proportion of the expenditure of the central government is spent through them. Their expenditure for 1971–2 was estimated by the government to be £5,486m—£3,577m on current and £1,909m on capital account[1]—already they incur nearly one-third of all public expenditure.

In mid-1971 these authorities employed nearly 2,500,000 people—some 10 per cent of the total employed labour force.[2] They are an important part of the public sector.

Definition

There are many governmental authorities operating locally under the ultimate control of the central government, and it is necessary therefore to be clear as to the definition of local authority to be used. The Central Statistical Office defines 'local authorities as public authorities of limited scope, having power to raise funds by certain forms of local taxation',[3] and who are obliged to make annual returns of income and expenditure under Local Government Acts. It is these authorities which are the concern here.

[1] 'Public Expenditure 1969–70 to 1974–5', Cmnd 4578, Jan. 1971, table 1.6, p. 15.
[2] See p. 99, below.
[3] Rita Maurice (ed.), National Accounts Statistics. Sources and Methods, Central Statistical Office, H.M.S.O., 1968, p. 356.

#STRUCTURE AND FINANCE

Local Government

As a consequence of this definition the local government sector consists basically of those local authorities with general administrative powers—the first-tier County Councils and County Boroughs; the second-tier Municipal Boroughs, Urban District Councils and Rural District Councils; and the third-tier Parish Councils and Parish Meetings which work to these R.D.C.S.

There is the Greater London Council with the Inner London Education Authority, the 32 London Boroughs, and the City of London.

These authorities vary in size: Lancashire is the largest County Council and Radnorshire the smallest. Birmingham is the largest County Borough and Canterbury the smallest. There are similar variations in the other types of authority.

Special Authorities

The sector includes various joint boards, e.g. Joint Burial Boards, Joint Sewage Boards formed by groups of authorities. Examples of Joint Fire Authorities are the Berkshire and Reading, and the Suffolk and Ipswich.

There are also local boards with special functions—local harbour boards, district fishery boards, drainage boards, river authorities, water boards, and a variety of small bodies 'such as the conservators of certain commons and the trustees of certain London squares'.[1] Amongst the most important of these local boards are the Port of London Authority, the Metropolitan Water Board, and the Mersey Docks and Harbour Board.[2] There are also, for example, the Mersey Tunnel Joint Committee, the St Austell Market, the St Saviour's Southwark Market. The new Passenger Transport Authorities set up under the 1968 Transport Act, e.g. Merseyside; South-East Lancashire North-East Cheshire; and West Midland have most of their members nominated by the local authorities in their area.[3]

[1] *Ibid.*, p. 306.
[2] Other Harbour Boards are, for example, Port of Tyne Authority, Dover Harbour Board, Tees and Hartlepool Port Authority.
[3] On P.T.A.s see pp. 98-9, below.

In this local authority sector are also classified, not only the provincial police who are plainly local government by their nature, but the Metropolitan Police which since its foundation has had a special and direct relationship with the Home Secretary.

Finance

Local authorities raise their revenue in a number of ways; the local authorities with general powers, from local rates, grants, and from miscellaneous charges. The rates are based on a property valuation and a subsequent declaration of a rate in the pound; the grants since 1 April 1967 have been principally a Rate Support Grant, which replaced the general, rate deficiency, and certain specific grants—designed to reduce the rate burden and to produce a fairer distribution of Exchequer assistance among local authorities; the miscellaneous charges include those received for services and facilities provided in old people's homes, etc., and from council house rents.

The following figures (in £m) show the great relative importance of government grants which have increased over the years; they show on the capital side the importance of loans.[1]

| Financial Year | Rateable value (c) | Revenue | | | | Capital | | | |
| | | Income | | | | Income | | | |
		Rates	Government grants	Miscellaneous	Total	Loans	Government grants	Miscellaneous	Total
1968–69	2,313.7	1,398.0	1,712.9	1,329.3	4,440.2	1,341.7	85.7	161.4	1,588.8

These loans are raised from stock on the money market; from the Public Works Loans Board—an independent statutory body appointed by the Crown and financed by the Treasury; from Mortgages, Bonds and, more recently, from borrowing overseas.[2]

The special-function type of local authority raises revenue from the rates often precepted on and collected by the general

---

[1] *Local Government Financial Statistics England and Wales, 1968–69*, published 1971, table x.
[2] P. W. Jackson, *Local Government*, Butterworth, 1970, pp. 215–9. See also H. R. Page, 'Local Authorities in the Capital Market', *Three Banks Review*, no. 71, Sept. 1966, p. 26. N.B. Such bodies as the London Transport Executive, Metropolitan Water Board, may borrow from the P.W.L.B.

type of authority, and also by charges on the user, e.g. by the Port of London Authority, which reports annually to the Department of the Environment under the Port of London Act of 1968 and, besides its temporary borrowing on the money market, receives loans from the government under the Harbours Act of 1964 and the Industrial Development Act of 1966.

The Metropolitan Water Board levies its own water rate; it raises capital from the Public Works Loans Board and from the market. The government has control by loan sanction over capital works and by the need for parliamentary approval for Orders which are required before significant changes in the water rate can be made. The M.W.B. is also subject to District Audit.

The Mersey Docks and Harbour Board operated as a public trust authority to control the port of Liverpool, but it ran into managerial and financial problems with which its form of organisation and philosophy was unable to cope. The Labour Government had general proposals for public ownership of all docks; its successor while not shutting its eyes to the possibility of municipalisation in this instance at least, turned the Trust into a Statutory Company in 1971. Technically this made the new company a part of the private sector, but no decision has yet been made on this by the Central Statistical Office. Government grants are still a possibility for this and any similar companies, but they are ad hoc and dependent on the philosophy of the government of the day. Under the Harbours Act of 1964 the Secretary of State for the Environment still has to approve all capital expenditures in excess of £500,000.

The new Passenger Transport Authorities have a planning responsibility for all forms of transport in their areas but organise directly the former municipal transport undertakings. Under the legislation which set them up the 'executives' which are responsible to the authorities are required to follow a more commercial attitude than that of the former municipal undertakings —e.g. the Executive concerned must be in credit in respect of the cumulative net balance of the consolidated revenue account, and charges to revenue account must include proper provision for depreciation or renewal of assets. Accounts also have to be presented as if each executive was formed under the relevant Companies Act.

Nevetheless their activities are scrutinised by the Department of the Environment, who require more information than that laid down by the Companies Acts. Loans are made available from the P.W.L.B. and also directly from the government, e.g. grants towards capital expenditure; new bus grants; etc.

FUNCTIONS

All Authorities

The social and environmental needs of the modern state require many services; the disposal services—refuse collection, and sewage; the physical protection of the community—police and fire services; the physical environment of the community—roads, planning, housing, slum clearance, parks and open spaces; the individual and community health services—health vistors and nurses, pre- and ante-natal services; the community welfare services—home and residential services for the aged, blind and deprived children; the education of the community—schools, further education and polytechnics; the cultural facilities—libraries, museums and art galleries.

There are others: aerodromes, animal diseases, approved schools, baths and wash-houses, coast protection, markets, street lighting, water supply, weights and measures.

These functions are shared between the different types of local authorities and delegated in some instances from the first- and second-tier authorities. They are carried out through a committee system which is a feature of local government and makes the role of the councillor or alderman so different from that of a Member of Parliament.

The all-purpose authorities are not the agents of the state; they are popularly elected and legally independent bodies with independent powers. They can only, however, do what Parliament tells them to do; they come under government control also by the fact of central control of grants and subsidies and by the need to obtain Treasury approval for borrowing.

The work of the special local authorities is self-evident from their titles—harbours, drainage boards, etc. They too are controlled by the decisions of Parliament and there are central government controls over their activities. The virtue of being popularly controlled which is claimed by the all-purpose authorities in any discussion of central/local government relationship is not so powerful in the case of these special authorities.

The whole range of services is wide and has broadened since the days when they were synonymous with sanitation. The age of Bentham and Chadwick was symbolised by the Poor Law Commission, the Parishes and the various Boards, e.g. Burial, Highways, etc. The Department of the Environment, and the Department of Education and Science are representative by their very titles of today—although a tang of the poor law still taints attitudes in both these departments and lingers on also in the corridors of power of local government as a whole.

Examples: G.L.C., Leeds, etc.

The largest local authority is the Greater London Council, first set up as a result of the London Government Act of 1963. Its budget in 1971–2—together with that of the Inner London Education Authority—totalled some £660m, of which £440m is revenue expenditure and £220m capital expenditure. It controls an area of 610 square miles, and provides services for about eight million people. The range and extent of these, although not typical of local government as a whole, puts the nature of this authority into perspective and may prove to be more representative in the future.

The G.L.C. is responsible for the construction, improvement, maintenance and lighting of some 560 miles of metropolitan roads; it owns and manages over 200,000 dwellings. Through the I.L.E.A. which covers the area of the 12 inner London Boroughs, it controls nearly 1,000 schools, including 32 boarding schools, 21 technical, commercial and art colleges, together with nine colleges of education. The I.L.E.A. spends nearly £8m a year on books, teaching material, equipment and furniture for schools and colleges.

The G.L.C. organises the largest Fire Brigade and Ambulance Service in the country. It manages the Royal Festival Hall complex and grant-aids the National Sports Centre at Crystal Palace. A Scientific Service with 12 laboratories provides advice relating to trade effluents, paints and decorative finishes, food and drugs, building materials, noise and ventilation. There is an Intelligence Unit which engages in statistical analysis, surveys and forecasting.

The G.L.C., like its predecessor the London County Council, in its scope of functions and budget is akin to some independent countries. Since 1 January 1970 the Council has become responsible for the broad policy and financial control of the central buses and underground train services provided by the London Transport Executive (L.T.E.) which has succeeded the London Transport Board; it also appoints the Chairman and members of the Executive which has the responsibility of managing the services provided.[1]

Before the G.L.C. took over its responsibility in this respect, the government wrote off London Transport's outstanding capital debt of £269·8m. With this clean sheet as a basis, the Executive has to meet the financial objectives set by the Council under the Transport (London) Act of 1969 and to conduct its affairs on commercial lines.

Apart from capital borrowings to meet the cost of new railway lines—e.g. Piccadilly Line extension to Heathrow Airport; the new Fleet Line from Baker Street to New Cross—the financial objectives mean that expenditure will be financed from revenue, together with grants from the G.L.C. and from the government. The L.T.E. employs over 60,000 staff, it carries over 2,200 million passengers a year. It has responsibilities for the design, construction and maintenance of 6,428 buses, 4,423 passenger rolling stock, and for signalling equipment. There are three main works at Acton, Chiswick and Aldenham, together with 21 railway depots, 246 stations and 68 garages. It generates and distributes electric power.

The Greater London Council has wide responsibilities; it performs them in a way that gives it a world-wide reputation.

Another example of the activities of a local authority is from my own City of Leeds which is governed by a Council of 30 aldermen and 90 councillors who represent the 30 wards of this city with a population in mid-1971 of some 500,000. The Council has an annual turnover of some £80m on revenue, and £20m on capital account; it operates a Central Purchasing Department to standardise goods in use and to purchase a wide variety of goods in bulk. In terms of land use the City Engineer's Department is engaged in proposals for planning, etc., estimated to

[1] For full details of the London Transport Executive see 'Annual Report and Accounts for the Year Ended 31 December 1970'. N.B. London Country Bus Services Ltd was set up to deal with such services outside the area of the G.L.C.

cost nearly £600m. The Works Department handles nearly £3m worth of work a year with direct and contract labour. In all, the city has 112 municipal housing estates with a total of over 60,000 dwellings. There are welfare services for the old and handicapped with 32 hostels—now part of a large and comprehensive Social Services Department. The Transport undertaking owns 696 vehicles; the Waterworks undertaking supplies over 600,000 people; there are nine swimming pools and five public laudries. The Education Committee is responsible for 255 schools, two Colleges of Education and eight further education establishments. There is a comprehensive library system.

The City has an excellent record in urban renewal; it has cooperated with the Department of the Environment in its approach to planning and transport. It shares control of an airport with Bradford and the West Riding County Council.

The Glasgow Corporation also operates a municipal airport; large housing schemes, buses and underground trains; its own Printing and Stationery Department; and Fire Insurance Scheme. Hull has its own telephone service; Birmingham a bank; there are municipally-owned docks in Bristol, Preston and Boston.

Sheffield Corporation is an outstanding local authority. Of unusual interest, because it is not typical of other authorities, is its Public Works Department which is one of the largest building and civil engineering organisations in the country. Since 1947 it has completed over £50m worth of work; its annual turnover is over £5m per annum. It maintains the Corporation's existing buildings—over 75,000 houses and flats, some 300 schools, clinics, etc., 94 public baths, wash-houses and conveniences, 21 libraries, art galleries and museums, health clinics and other property of the Health Committee, police buildings and fire stations, markets and abattoir, and transport properties— as well as the Town Hall with its annexes, and also 42 farms. Sheffield has the largest, most comprehensive Market and Abattoir undertaking in the country.

There are other significant authorities. There is the Lancashire County Council with, in 1971, nearly 2,500,000 people, and rateable value of £91·4m. There is the Birmingham County Borough with over a million people and rateable value of £54·5m. There is Slough, a Municipal Borough, with rateable value of £8m; Thurrock, an Urban District Council, with rateable value of £9m; and the Rural District of Eton with rateable value of

£5·2m. Of the London Boroughs, Harrow, of medium size, has a population of 206,000 and rateable value of £12·3m.[1] For 1972–3 its total budget was estimated to be £19·5m. Over 50 per cent of this was spent on education—the remainder on social services, health, housing, etc.

All these examples show local government to be big business.

Examples: Education, Housing, Police

Of all the functions carried out by local authorities the most significant both financially and socially is Education.

The work of the Inner London Education Authority already mentioned is an example of the range of activities carried out by an unusually large authority. The number of schools and colleges given earlier for Leeds is more typical of the activities of one of the countries largest cities. In all education authorities the Chairman of the Education Committee is a very important person who is responsible for large expenditures on buildings and staff and for the training of pupils and students. He carries out these responsibilities through the Chief Education Officer and his staff, and through the Education Committee itself with its various sub-committees.

The transformation of education in the United Kingdom since the 1944 Education Act; the remarkable changes in the philosophy of primary schools with a consequent change in school layout; the varied changes based on the Tawney concept of 'Secondary Education for all', from the replacement of the old Senior School by the Secondary Modern School and then the slow but relentless change to Comprehensive education; the completely new facilities in the field of further education from Colleges of Further Education to Polytechnics; and a responsibility for a large part of the expansion of teacher training facilities —have been carried out by local government.

Weaknesses there may be in methods of administration; there is need for more devolution to the schools themselves. Administrative response to changing educational ideas is sometimes too slow; the changeover to comprehensive education has not always been well thought out. Despite the Educational Priority Areas

[1] For details of rateable values, population, etc., see 'Rates and Rateable Values in England and Wales 1971–2', Department of the Environment and Welsh Office.

and the Urban Aid Programme in the 'down-town' areas, there
are still far too many schools, particularly in the primary sector,
that are Dickensian in their squalor, with ineffective heating and
hopelessly inadequate sanitary and safety arrangements. Nevertheless, overall and through the activities of local government,
there has been a remarkable story of change in education.

'Over the last fifty years there is little doubt that the housing
problem has been transformed'—so said the government in its
White Paper 'Fair Deal for Housing' in 1971.[1] It justified this
view thus: 'In 1914 there were some eight million dwellings in
England and Wales. Nine-tenths of them were rented from
private landlords. Today there are some 17 million dwellings.
Over half of these are owner-occupied. A fifth are rented from
private landlords; more than a quarter from local authorities. Of
these 17 million dwellings $6\frac{1}{2}$ million have been built since 1945
and another $1\frac{1}{2}$ million improved and modernised during the
same period.'[2]

The community responsibility for housing is shared between
the Housing Corporation, the Housing Development Corporations, the New Towns Commission and the local authorities. It
is the latter—the G.L.C. and the London Boroughs; the County
Boroughs, the Municipal Boroughs, the Urban and Rural Districts—which have borne the major part of this responsibility,
particularly since the last war, by not only building homes but
by the 'improvement' of older dwellings which in recent years
has become an important aspect of government policy.[3] The
figures on p. 92 below show the relative performance of different
housing agencies and the private sector for Great Britain since
1945.[4]

Local authorities have influenced the private sector by their
planning control over individual houses and the layout of the
surrounding area.

In Leeds in mid-1971 the City Corporation owned 63,658
Municipal Estate dwellings; in the five years up to the same

[1] *Cmnd* 4728, July 1971, p. 1.
[2] *Ibid.*, p. 1.
[3] See 'Report of the Ministry of Housing and Local Government 1969–
70', *Cmnd* 4753, p. 7; Older Houses, the Housing Act 1969, which gave
legislative effect to the changes proposed in the White Paper 'Old Houses
into New Homes', *Cmnd* 3602, 1968.
[4] *Housing Statistics Great Britain*, no. 21, May 1971, Department of the
Environment, Scottish Development Office, Welsh Office, H.M.S.O.

	L.A.'s	New Towns	Housing Associations	Govt Depts	Total Public Sector	Private Sector	Total
1945–60	2,296,104	89,271	45,975	78,640	2,509,990	1,180,162	3,690,152
1961–65	627,170	35,752	12,076	22,267	697,265	959,070	1,656,335
1966	161,435	8,510	4,558	5,634	180,137	205,372	385,509
1967	181,467	11,102	4,984	6,365	203,918	200,438	404,356
1968	170,214	9,846	6,291	5,371	191,722	221,993	413,715
1969	162,910	10,872	7,336	3,972	185,090	181,703	366,793
1970	157,067	12,208	8,493	2,361	180,129	170,304	350,433

date it built 10,110 such homes. It has a reputation, predating central government interest, in the improvement of older dwellings. It is to a large degree for this reason that the City of Leeds also owned 8,230 tenancies in 'miscellaneous properties'.

The housing transformation in this city since the prewar years is due to local government in partnership with central government. It is also due to the dedicated work of local officials and councillors, and Leeds will always owe a great deal to the Rev. Charles Jenkinson, a councillor in South Leeds where some of the worst housing conditions existed.[1] Any consideration of local government would be too mechanistic if it ignored the local participants.

Since the first parliamentary involvement in housing with Lord Shaftesbury's Labouring Classes Lodging Houses Act of 1851, there has grown up a specialised body of professional knowledge, particularly in housing, finance and administration.[2]

Following the Housing and Town Planning Act of 1919 and the Housing Act of 1923 there has been much development in the field of housing finance. Basically the situation by the late 1960s was that the central government controlled local authority borrowing for this purpose. It was normally over a 60-year period and housing had become the largest item in loan debt. The housing subsidies provided were intended to offset market forces which of themselves had not provided dwellings for the 'working classes'.

In July 1971 the Conservative government announced their new proposals in 'Fair Deal for Housing'.[3] There were to be

[1] H. J. Hammerton, *This Turbulent Priest*, Lutterworth, 1952.
[2] See J. B. Cullingworth, *Housing and Local Government in England and Wales*, Allen & Unwin, 1966.
[3] *Cmnd* 4728, July 1971.

'fair rents' with rebates in both the private and public sectors and a new basis for the house subsidies which was designed to ensure that the existing (1970–1) exchequer subsidies of about £157m and the rates subsidies of about £60–£65m were to be channelled to those in need, and their burden more fairly distributed.

There was to be a new basis for housing subsidies, the effect of which was to prevent a rise in both those from the exchequer and the rates. The new range of subsidies was designed to meet deficits on all housing activities, repairs, etc., and not just those in new housing, and also to concentrate their effect in areas of greatest need.

Changes in housing finance were undoubtedly required, for neither its principles nor its effects were logical, nevertheless the logic of these moves to greater selectivity contrasts strangely with the indiscriminate subsidy given to owner-occupiers through tax relief or the option mortgage scheme. It remains to be seen whether the new scheme will provide 'a decent home for every family at a price within their means'; there certainly will be greatly increased rents for council house tenants in general, who to some degree will subsidise others.

In administration there has grown up another field of specialised knowledge to deal with the needs of slum clearance, improvement, the aged, and the problems of multi-occupation. It operates through the housing departments of the local authorities, e.g. that of the G.L.C. where there are branches for management, development, construction and maintenance. The precise organisation in an area depends on population and social needs. In Leeds there is under a Director of Housing, a decentralised organisation dealing with applications, letting, rent collection, welfare and transfers, which fan out to the estate Housing Managers.[1] Housing administration is big business with an outlook and mores all of its own.

No one who recalls the interwar years can deny the housing transformation which has taken place over the last 25 years, but this does not mean that there are no problems left to solve.

There is the continued exodus to the suburbs by the middle and the growing lower-middle class with the resulting concentration of housing need in the inner city areas associated with

[1] See Cullingworth, *op. cit.*, ch. III, 'Local Authority Housing Administration'.

low incomes and employment in the service industries. There are the social problems of the slum clearance areas—poverty and petty crime—which often feed on the length of time taken to clear and rebuild an area.

As far as the existing council house tenants are concerned there is the need to give them a degree of participation in administration and a more legally based security of tenure. Given the steady drive to higher rents a growing demand for this will come from the tenants themselves.

These problems are for the local authorities not the private sector to solve, although interesting ideas on the private housing aspects of urban renewal have come from a working party of the Economic Development Committee for Building.[1] They are worthy of consideration, for even a marginal addition to local authority programmes would be valuable. It might do something also to stop the polarisation of cities into the tenanted inner areas and the owner-occupied suburbs. In this last respect the Trades Union Congress, have suggested a public building agency to help the lower-paid workers to buy their homes.

The Police are another example of the work of local government in association with the central government; in this instance the Home Office.

Under the Police Act 1964, the police authority for either a county or a county borough is a committee of the council—the police committee in the county, the watch committee in the county borough. In both cases, two-thirds of the committee are councillors or aldermen, one-third magistrates. When amalgamations take place similar proportions still apply.

The annual report of the H.M. Chief Inspector of Constabulary illustrates the range of police activities carried out and the cooperation that takes place between the provincial forces and the Home Office—with the Police Scientific Development Branch; the Police Research Services Branch; and the Home Office Scientific Advisory Council.[2]

The section on 'Communications' is a further example of technical/scientific work, as is the Report of the Commissioner

---

[1] New Homes in the Cities. The Role of the Private Developer in Urban Renewal in England and Wales, National Economic Development Office, H.M.S.O., 1971.
[2] 'Report of Her Majesty's Chief Inspector of Constabulary for Year 1970', June 1971.

of Police for the Metropolis with its information on the Police National Computer and the Management Services Department.[1] To illustrate further the full nature of police activities in the London area, there is, for example, the use of a large number of vehicles and the consequent need for a large vehicle fleet workshop; the same force owns 4,814 houses and flats and provides hostel accommodation for 2,931 men and 304 women.

The Metropolitan Police is under the direct control of the Home Secretary and its revenues are provided direct by the Treasury and by a precept on the local government bodies in its area. The provincial police forces are paid for by central government grant and aid from the rates.

Examples: Port of London Authority, Metropolitan Water Board, etc.

Of the local authorities with special functions the Port of London Authority (P.L.A.), like the Metropolitan Water Board, is significant because of the very scale of its activities.

Fifteen of the 16 members of the P.L.A. are appointed by the Secretary of State for the Environment after consultation with the G.L.C., Trinity House and the City of London Corporation. The Authority controls the Millwall, India, Royal and Tilbury Docks where in 1970 5,500,000 tons of goods passed through in 41,276 vessels; it deals with 19.1 per cent of U.K. foreign imports and 25.1 per cent of U.K. foreign exports; it administers 94 miles of river and estuary. The annual report of the P.L.A. shows it to be a substantial owner of goods-handling equipment and river craft, especially lighters.[2] It also has an 18.8 per cent interest in Thames Estuary Development Co. Ltd, which exists to carry out planning and feasibility studies for the Foulness Seaport and Airport Development Project.

The Metropolitan Water Board (M.W.B.) came into existence in 1903 to take over eight water companies which prior to that supplied water in the London area. It is composed of members appointed by the constituent authorities as follows: the G.L.C., six; the City of London, one; the relevant London Boroughs, 26; the County Councils of Essex, Hertfordshire, Kent and

---

[1] 'Report of the Commissioner of Police of the Metropolis for the Year 1970', *Cmnd* 4680, June 1971.
[2] P.L.A., 'Report', 31 Dec. 1970.

Surrey, one each; the Thames Conservancy and the Lee Conservancy Catchment Board, one each.

The Board's area of direct supply is 539 square miles from Ware in the north to Sevenoaks in the south; from Sunbury in the west to Southfleet in the east. Its supplies are obtained from the River Thames and the River Lee and from wells and springs in the Lee Valley and Kent. There are very large storage reservoirs, e.g. at Staines, Chingford, and Walton, with a capacity of 29,952 million gallons.

The Board makes no profit from the sale of water but is required by statute to charge such a rate as will, together with all other income on revenue account, produce an income 'as nearly as may be' equal to the estimated expenditure for the year in question.

The following statement was made by the Chief Executive Officer of the M.W.B. in a publication giving an account of the undertaking:[1]

> Over many decades the supply of unlimited, pure and cheap water has been accepted as a right, and the industry has been able to provide such a service without undue fuss and publicity. This is no longer true in 1970; it will be even less true in the next three decades. Given the men and the money there is no doubt that the industry as a whole—in all its many parts—can continue to serve both the Capital and the Country as well as it has done since the beginning of the century. But it will need both; and there will be some agonising decisions still to be made on land use, amenities and cost which the public must know of and appreciate. There are no more easy and cheap solutions left.

This sets out clearly the basic problems facing local government in the provision of water.

In fact, while the water-board-type authority is classified under the heading of 'local authority', as of course are the local authority water undertakings, e.g. Leeds Corporation, a substantial amount of private company ownership still exists. The activities of these companies, e.g. the Colne Valley Water Company on the borders of Hertfordshire and Middlesex, are circumscribed by Act of

---

[1] *Metropolitan Water Board. A Brief Description of the Undertaking,* 1970, see foreword.

Parliament in the same fashion as the Metropolitan Water Board.

Until 1963 each statutory water undertaking, whether public or private, was responsible not only for distribution of water but also for the planning of reservoirs, etc. Such planning has been described as 'piecemeal and unorganised' and responsibility was scattered among the then Ministry of Housing, the Ministry of Agriculture, the River Boards, the Drainage Boards, and the Public Health Authorities.[1] It was because of this and the growing demand for water in the community, with its consequent effect on drainage and flooding, effluents and pollution, navigation, fishing and amenity value, that the Water Resources Act 1963 was introduced and passed by Parliament.[2]

This Act set up 29 river authorities in England and Wales to manage and conserve water authorities—e.g. the Avon and Dorset; the Yorkshire Ouse and Hull River Authority—and in the London area, the functions of a river authority were placed upon the Thames Conservancy and Lee Conservancy Catchment Board. Water supply undertakings would in future need the consent of the appropriate river authority before making new abstractions.[3]

Organisationally the 1963 Act, together with the voluntary decline in the number of water companies, has transformed the structure to the point where it has been argued that 'nationalisation is either simple or unnecessary, depending on one's point of view'.[4] Nationalisation is, in any event, but one form of public ownership. The arguments for any future organisational change will depend on the solution to the problem of land use, amenities and cost referred to by the M.W.B. In Yorkshire, for example,

[1] C. I. Jackson and P. A. Bird, 'Water Supply—the Transformation of an Industry', *Three Banks Review*, March 1967, p. 27.

[2] *Ibid.*, p. 27, quoting from U.K. Central Advisory Water Committee Sub-Committee on the Growing Demand for Water, *Final Report*, H.M.S.O., 1962, para. 10.

[3] (i) See *Association of River Authorities Year Book and Directory 1971*.
(ii) The administrative arrangements for water supply in Scotland were reorganised by the Water (Scotland) Act of 1967, by which the functions of 200 local water authorities were transferred to 13 regional water boards. The Act also established the Central Scotland Water Development Board which supplies water in bulk to its seven constituent regional water boards. All the members of these boards are members of town or county councils.

[4] Jackson and Bird, *op. cit.*, p. 30.

and it is typical, sufficient resources are not being made available
to enable water undertakings to fulfil their statutory obligations.

New proposals were mooted by the Central Advisory Water
Committee in their report *The Future Management of Water
in England and Wales*,[1] when they suggested that the Water
Resources Board should become a national water authority and
that the River Authorities, together with the water supply and
sewage disposal undertakings, should be merged into between
six and 15 water authorities.

Later in that year the government accepted the basis of this
report by announcing the creation of ten regional water authorities
to which will be transferred the responsibilities of the British
Waterways Board for canals and certain rivers, and a National
Water Council to continue the work of the Water Resources
Board.[2]

These proposals must be judged on their organisational merits.
On the political plane of public versus private enterprise, and
given the public utility nature of private water companies, the
eventual solution should be to blend these changes into those
taking place in the structure of local government.

As far as the Mersey Docks and Harbour Board is concerned,
in its new form it is charged with 'carrying on' the Port of Liverpool, with the duties of conservancy of the port and with the
administration of pilotage services. Whether this form of organisation will work has yet to be seen—for profitability and wider
responsibilities conflict in this rapidly changing field of activity.

The Passenger Transport Authorities, as was noted earlier,
have a planning responsibility for all forms of transport but run
directly all the former municipal transport undertakings in their
areas. They are classified as 'local authority' undertakings in
respect of these direct responsibilities but not, of course, for the
activities of British Rail or the National Bus Company, some of
which they coordinate.

The P.T.A.s have responsibility for strategic transportation
policy, for associated social policy and for the ultimate control
of the Executives which are charged with the management of
operations.

[1] 'A Report by the Central Advisory Water Committee to the Secretary
of State for the Environment', H.M.S.O., 1971.
[2] *H.C. Official Report*, vol. 827, 2 Dec. 1971, cols. 677-90. See p. 140,
below.

The Annual Report of the P.T.A. and Executive of S.E.L.N.E.C. for 1970 stated the obvious need for a coordinated approach for public transport in that area. Problems in this respect had increased and answers were beyond the individual transport operators and the existing local authorities.[1] The report discussed the problems which had arisen out of the efforts to achieve such coordination in the field of organisation, finance, industrial relations and technical matters. It explained the basis of the new relationship being forged with British Rail, the National Bus Company and Lancashire United Transport. Losses as a result of new fare policies and changed routes would be made good by the central government and the P.T.A.[2]

These P.T.A.s are large industrial and commercial undertakings; a new and probably expanding part of the local authority sector whose overall functions cover a wide spectrum of social and economic activities.

EMPLOYMENT

Range of Occupations

In all these fields there are large numbers employed. In June 1970 the total employed by local authorities in the United Kingdom was 2,467,000 or 9.8 per cent of the total employed labour force.[3]

Although they refer to Great Britain only and are based on a different definition of local authority, the returns made to the Department of Employment in June 1970 serve to illustrate the range of occupations within this sector.[4]

[1] S.E.L.N.E.C., 'Joint Report of the Authority and the Executive 1970', para. 2.
[2] *Ibid.*, para. 5.
[3] *Economic Trends*, no. 212, June 1971, 'Employment in the public and private sectors of the U.K. economy in 1969 and 1970', p. xlvi, table: Employment by sector and by industry groups.
[4] *Employment and Productivity Gazette*, Nov. 1970, p. 1028.
N.B. (i) Despite the differences between these figures and those provided in *Economic Trends*, the latter are based on the D.E.P. figures. (ii) See pp. 1027-8 for definitional limits on these figures; staff employed by P.T.A.s are not included. (iii) The D.E.P. definition of Local Authority is not as wide as that used in the National Accounts referred to on p. 82, above.

Great Britain
Education department:

(a) Lecturers and teachers	608,449
(b) Other staffs (clerical staff school cleaners, school canteen staff, etc.)	596,396
Water supply	12,728
Construction	127,984
Transport services	51,096
Health services, day nurseries, children's, aged persons' and other homes	264,503
Restaurants and canteens (excluding school canteens); orchestras; entertainments; amusement parks; race courses; golf courses; etc.	18,210
All other local authority departments	603,801
Police forces (including Metropolitan Police)	103,166
Grand Total	2,386,333

The local authorities are by far the largest employer of teachers who work in a variety of institutions. It is significant to note that there appears to be an almost one to one relationship between those who teach and those who 'help', in the widest sense of the term, teachers. In the R.A.F. for every man who flies there are 24 civilians and servicemen on the ground. The R.A.F. uses its specially trained pilots more selectively than the local authorities use their teachers. Perhaps the teachers are more at fault in this respect than the L.E.A.s.

Water supply is self-explanatory but does not include river authorities or private water undertakings. Construction refers to staff employed in building houses by direct labour, on maintenance work on housing estates, and on road construction, etc. Transport services refer to road transport, docks, river and harbour services, and airports.

The 'all other local authority departments' covers a wide range of occupations which arise from the functions discussed earlier.

In the police forces of England and Wales, at the end of 1970 there were 90,719 employed, inclusive of 20,692 in the Metropolitan Police; there were also 3,595 women police. The total number of traffic wardens was 2,883 men and 2,160 women; there were 13,379 clerical workers, 5,630 technical, 4,312 domestics, and 3,494 male and 615 female cadets.[1] To give an

[1] 'Report of H.M. Chief Inspector of Constabulary', *op. cit.*, pp. 88-9.

example of an individual force—in the City of Leeds Police in mid-1971 there were 1,164 police officers, 39 cadets, 56 traffic wardens, 177 full-time and 19 part-time civilians.

Overall the local authorities employ a wide variety of employees from road sweepers, refuse collectors, stokers, sewage workers, gardeners, grave diggers, caretakers, cooks, traffic wardens, rent collectors, bus drivers and conductors; to solicitors, accountants, engineers, architects, planners, doctors, nurses, midwives, child-care officers, mental welfare staff, librarians, weights and measures inspectors.

Each local authority is an employer over this wide range though its actual position is limited by the functions performed, its size, and by its rateable value. The G.L.C. has nearly 60,000 full-time employees. In the City of Leeds there are 5,400 officers, 14,188 manual workers, 2,965 staff in the Transport Department, 3,578 full-time teachers and 474 part-time, 177 College of Education lecturers and 929 in further education establishments. At the Leeds/Bradford Airport there are 78 staff —including air traffic control staff and firemen.

To put the matter in perspective, there are four local authorities with one full-time employee each, and almost half the authorities in England and Wales employ less than 100 full-time staff each. Nevertheless, overall, local authorities, to varying degrees, employ a very large labour force, carrying out in many cases skills which are not used in the private sector.

Employer and Trade Union Organisation

The various local authorities are organised in associations which seek to represent their various interests—in the County Councils Associations, the Association of Municipal Corporations, the Urban District Council Associations, the Rural District Councils Association and the London Boroughs Association. These bodies have an open door to various government departments to press the views of their constituent membership.

Representatives of these associations, together with those of the G.L.C., are members of the Local Authorities' Conditions of Service Advisory Board which was established to coordinate the activities of the employers' side of local government wage-negotiating organisations. It provides a joint secretariat for some

22 such bodies, maintains liaison with other similar organisations and disseminates information on service conditions.

Industrial unionism is not typical of British industry. It is not typical of local government; though in the local government manual unions over the years there has been much talk of restructuring to meet this end.

The main unions are: for the professional and clerical staff—the National and Local Government Officers Association (N.A.L.G.O.); for the manual workers—General and Municipal Workers Union (G.M.W.U.), the National Union of Public Employees (N.U.P.E.), the Confederation of Health Service Employees (C.O.H.S.E.), the Transport and General Workers Union. (T.G.W.U.). Examples of the specialised unions and staff associations are the Fire Brigades Union, the Police Federation, Youth Service Association, the Association of Educational Psychologists, etc., which negotiate in their specialised fields.[1]

N.A.L.G.O., which is the largest white-collar union in the world and which in 1964 'plunged into the mainstream of the trade union movement' by joining the T.U.C.,[2] not only represents those who work in various types of local authorities including water supply, but also those in electricity, gas, health service, new towns, transport—illustrating earlier functions of local government—also those in industrial estates administration and non-teaching university staff. N.U.P.E. and C.O.H.S.E. have a similar local-government-orientated cross-section while the G.M.W.U. and T.G.W.U. represent also people in many types of industry—engineering, chemicals, etc.

These unions and associations represent their members on the relevant Whitley-type councils which have developed over the years, and particularly since the last war, nationally, provincially and locally.[3]

The Advisory Board referred to earlier, services the various negotiating bodies; there is a group for Administrative and Professional Staffs, one for Manual Workers, and another for Ser-

---

[1] See Appendix, Staff Associations, Trade Unions and Associations of Staffs and of Employees, page 120, below—this will put in perspective the negotiating system in local government in particular, and of trade unions in general.

[2] Alec Spoor, *White Collar Union. 60 Years of N.A.L.G.O.*, Heinemann, 1967, p. 561.

[3] *Ibid.*, ch. 17.

vices. Under the former, for example, there is an N.J.C. for Local Authorities' Administrative, Professional Technical and Clerical Services, a J.N.C. for Justices' Clerks, a J.N.C. for Approved Schools and Remand Homes, etc. Under the Manual Workers Group there is an N.J.C. for County Council Roadmen, another for Local Authorities Services with panels for Employees at Municipal Airports. For skilled workers under the same group there are J.N.C.s for Building Workers and Engineering Craftsmen.

Under the Services Group come the N.J.C. for Fire Brigades, another for Chief Officers in Fire Brigades and for the Probation Service. The Police Council is classified here; by virtue of the special law and order function involved this is historically organised on a different basis.[1]

The negotiating bodies in Education are associated with the Advisory Board. The main negotiating bodies are Burnham and its associated committees—Primary and Secondary, Further Education, etc.; there is a J.N.C. for Youth Leaders and Community Centre Wardens. The staff are represented by the various teaching unions and associations—National Union of Teachers, National Association of Schoolmasters, and the Joint Four—and, where appropriate, by N.A.L.G.O.

The Advisory Board is associated with Whitley Functional Councils for the Health Service.

This is an outline only of a negotiating machinery structure which has taken a long time to evolve in the face of strong social and economic pressures operating in the local authorities themselves, and in the historically allied fields of gas and the health service.[2] A consideration of this structure reveals another facet of the structure of local government itself. Its ramifications have to be taken into account in any general consideration of incomes policy. There are particular problems in this respect in local government.

Almost annually one is made aware of the unsatisfactory nature

[1] See Anthony Judge, *The First Fifty Years*, the Story of the Police Federation, Police Federation, 1968.
[2] For details of negotiating machinery for manual workers over a wide field of local government and its associated industries, see Report no. 29, N.B.P.I., 'The Pay and Conditions of Manual Workers in Local Authorities, the National Health Service, Gas and Water Supply', *Cmnd* 3230, March 1967, appendix 1.

of Burnham negotiations. In 1967 Report no. 45 of the National Board for Prices and Incomes revealed some of the pay problems of Chief and Senior Officers in the Local Government.[1] In the same year Report no. 29 of the N.B.P.I. did likewise for the local authorities, health service, gas and water supply.[2] This revealed many of the shortcomings of a system whose end product was a large concentration of workers with low average weekly earnings and with a much higher proportion of men 'at the lowest level of earnings than is the case in industry generally'.[3]

Some 680,000 of the people employed by local authorities were within the scope of this reference. It is significant that well over half of these were women, of whom more than 90 per cent were part-time workers.

The Board recommended a detailed examination of the complicated wages structure, using job evaluation techniques to end unnecessary demarcations and to reward genuinely higher skills. It accordingly made recommendations for an interim scheme of relating pay and productivity. Changes were also, and not surprisingly, recommended in the negotiating machinery then in existence, e.g. the amalgamation of some English and Scottish negotiating bodies and the ending of some local bodies then in being in the West and in Wales.

Changes have followed in the negotiating structure and genuine productivity agreements have been made. Progress has been achieved in the wider field of managerial efficiency of which productivity is a part. The Department of the Environment has worked with the N.J.C. for Local Authority Services (Manual Workers) and through the Local Authorities' Management Services and Computer Committee (L.A.M.S.A.C.) to emphasise to local authorities the importance of further developing the use of modern management techniques—especially work study. As a result, an increasing number of local authorities have established their own management services units 'and there has been a substantial increase in the rate at which work-study based incentive

[1] Report no. 45, 'Pay of Chief and Senior Officers in Local Government Service and in the G.L.C.', Cmnd 3473, Nov. 1967. See also Report no. 15 on the salaries of teachers in Scotland, nos. 16, 50, 63, 69, 78, 85, 95 and 196 on municipal busmen, and no. 81 on pay of staff employed by the Bristol Corporation Docks.
[2] Report no. 29, op. cit.
[3] Ibid., p. 18, para. 47.

bonus schemes have been introduced for manual workers'.[1]

As part of this trend there has been an increasing use of computers which spreads over the last decade, and there are now about 300 separate installations.[2] But the overall progress seems to have had little effect on wages, and after the strikes of dustmen and sewerage workers in 1970, the Scamp Report showed that wages had slipped back in relation to the national average.[3]

There was more to these strikes than just rates of pay, but the problem of low wages had not, nor has yet, been overcome. It is part of a wider problem facing the community as a whole— a solution to which would also solve many of the related problems of social security and welfare.[4]

The problem of low wages in local government, like the related problem of pay in the higher professional ranks, is part of a wider question of training and recruitment.

Training and Recruitment

Low wages have not always been the problem of local government service. In the interwar years it recruited from the growing output of secondary school students who at that time did not so automatically pass on to the variety of forms of higher education available today. Local government employment with its white-collar status was the promised land to a working-class parent.

[1] 'Report of the Ministry of Housing and Local Government 1969 and 1970', Cmnd 4573, Aug. 1971, p. 55. See also Nicholas Watts, 'Management Development', with examples from Manchester C.B. and Cheshire C.C., in Municipal and Public Services Journal, 9 July 1971.

[2] Cmnd 4573, op. cit., pp. 55, 56. The Department of the Environment supports L.A.M.S.A.C. which was set up to promote the development of all kinds of management services through 12 regional offices from which detailed advice and direct assistance can be given to local authorities.

L.A.M.S.A.C. have surveyed the history of computer development and recommended in 'Computer Development in Local Government', Sept. 1969, that local government should work towards a limited number of regional computer centres, locally owned and managed but with a measure of central coordination.

[3] 'Report of an Independent Committee of Inquiry under Sir Jack Scamp into the Trade Union Side's Claim of April 1970, made to the Joint Secretaries of the National Joint Council for Local Authorities' Services (Manual)'; N.B. see p. 2, para. 5, for the changed composition of the N.J.C., and p. 11, para. 31 for lower paid workers.

[4] Report no. 169, N.B.P.I., 'General Problems of Low Pay', Cmnd 4648, April 1971.

For manual workers in the period of mass unemployment, local government employ offered security with a pension. Wages were not high but they were better than nothing at all.

The post-war world is different. Local government has not been able to recruit on these terms. Accordingly, on the basis of the tradition of the qualified staff with their professional qualifications employed by local authorities, the N.J.C. for A.P.T. and C. services as early as 1946 laid down service conditions which encouraged the establishment of a qualified service and imposed a moral obligation on local authorities to give positive help to their staff to get professional qualifications with financial aid and release for study.

The N.J.C. set up a Local Government Examinations Board whose main task was to devise and administer for clerical and administrative staff a system of qualifications for promotion which would be comparable to the examinations already available to their professional and technical colleagues.[1] This did much to stimulate training in the educational sense of the term. In the 1960s there was a further step forward in this respect as a result of the wider concern for industrial training shown in the Industrial Training Act.

In local government itself there was also the work of the Maud Committee on 'The Management of Local Government',[2] and of the Mallaby Committee on 'The Staffing of Local Government',[3] which was concerned with non-manuals and emphasised the need for more management training, the need to emphasise the role of technicians, the case for an improved career structure, the need for improved status and training for administrative staff, and the need to take a new look at the training of clerical staff. It recommended a Local Government Training Board, and one was set up on a voluntary basis sponsored by the four local authority associations. Its responsibilities are much wider than just the range of staff discussed by the Mallaby Committee, for it has within its scope all employees of local authorities other than those already under statutory boards or with existing training schemes, e.g.

[1] Local Government Training Board, 'Report and Statement of Accounts, 31 March 1969', section 3.
[2] Committee on the Management of Local Government, Chairman Sir John Maud, vol. 1, 1967.
[3] Committee on the Staffing of Local Government, Chairman Sir George Mallaby, 1967.

teachers, firemen, etc. It also performs the work formerly carried out by the Examination Board.

In its early years the Board quickly determines its priorities by improving the arrangements for planning and training of staff at all levels. It concerned itself with management, the training of supervisors and of clerical staff. It saw the need to introduce basic training schemes for manual workers, e.g. school caretakers.[1] In its Annual Report for 1969–70 there is evidence of an extension of its interests into weights and measures and the social services.[2]

A great deal is being done for training and education in local government. There are not the cries of woe from individual local authorities about their levy that there are from individual firms who pay compulsorily to the Industrial Training Boards.

Local government takes many knocks; in this field it should be praised, particularly in comparison with the private sector. This is not to say that staffing is not still an important issue in this part of the public sector.

PROBLEMS

Staffing and Management

The main problem in this respect is recruitment. Given the job opportunities in industry and the professions, young people do not flock to local government. The career structure seems not to be exciting; the image of local government is poor.

The older men in local government who see the outside job opportunities available now are not the best advocates of local government recruitment. The hierarchical set-up in some local authorities, aided by the power of some chairmen of committees, does not help matters.

Some of the recommendations of the Mallaby Committee have been referred to—overall they are concerned with recruitment, career prospects, selection procedure, induction and professional training.[3] While in some quarters there has been criticism of the

[1] H. Victor Wiseman (ed.), *Local Government in England 1958–69*, Routledge, 1970, note on the Local Government Training Board by Dudley Lofts, p. 92.
[2] Local Government Training Board, 'Report and Statement of Accounts for the Year Ended 31 March 1970'.
[3] Mallaby, *op. cit.*, ch. XIV.

limited nature of this report and of the lack of perception on some
of the issues, it is evidence of the concern about the problem.
Mallaby was not the end; what matters are the developments
taking place since then.[1]

The problem of staffing is part of a wider aspect of management, and it was to deal with this that there was set up in 1964
the Maud Committee, referred to earlier, on 'The Management
of Local Government'—'to consider in the light of modern conditions how local government might best continue to attract and
retain people (both elected representatives and principal officers)
of the calibre necessary to ensure its maximum effectiveness'.

There were 79 recommendations on such matters as the internal
organisation of local authorities; the relations between central and
local government; and on the elected members.

There have been criticisms of this report also; mistakes of fact
in particular and inconsistency in general.[2] It is, however, the
'best report we have' and with all its warts it provides much
material to consider.

Certainly there is need to get clear the function of the chief
official in relation to his chairman and his committee. Overall
policy should be made clear by the elected representatives. There
were too many committees, there was need for 'cabinet'-type
overall policy making.

Whatever the role of the individual councillor in the organisation of the local authority itself, he is important as an 'Ombuds-
man' with knowledge of what is going on in his ward or division.
Bureaucratic decisions are often taken which act contrary to the
interests of local residents, and sometimes there is maladminis-
tration. The elected representative will be vital in this respect,
whatever becomes of the idea for local commissioners for
administration.[3] When the new large local authorities are set up

[1] Wiseman, op. cit., see ch. 4, 'The Mallaby Committee—the Staffing
of Local Government', by W. S. Steer, partic. p. 80.
[2] Wiseman, op. cit., see chapter 3, 'The Maud Committee Report', and
partic. p. 55.
[3] In the White Paper of Feb. 1970, 'Reform of Local Government in
England', Cmnd 4276, para. 82, it was announced that the then government considered that a number of local commissioners for administration should be appointed to investigate complaints of maladministra-
tion in the sphere of local government, which could work through local
councillors.

it will be good for overall planning efficiency; local councillors, however, will be thinner on the ground. This could cause a real problem for some of the down-town areas where social problems abound and local councillors are an important point of contact.

The work of locally elected councillors is an important matter; it is far more important than the status issue about the future of aldermen. Councillors can be helped by local authorities concerning themselves with informational publicity; this is a job also for local political ward parties. Above all, councillors need postal and telephone expenses and the use of a typing pool at the town or county hall.

The chairman of important committees should be full or nearly full-time. Payment for these jobs will have to come. Maud recommended additional payments in addition to those to be made to all members, for those on his proposed management boards. As these would be the committee chairman my point would be met.

The Maud report covers many aspects of management; we saw earlier the developments taking place in the field of work study and the use of computers. As a result of the then government's objectives on 'Public Purchasing and Industrial Efficiency' referred to on page 31, above, there was set up a Joint Review Body on Local Authority Purchasing. This reported in 1968 and in May 1970 the 'Local Authorities (Goods and Services) Act' came into force, empowering local authorities to cooperate with one another in the provision of goods and services to take advantage of the economies of bulk purchasing and to use specialist staff skilled in modern buying techniques and stock control.

In July 1970 the local authority associations and the G.L.C. set up a Joint Advisory Committee to advise local authorities on 'Local Authority Purchasing' to help achieve 'standardisation and variety reduction over the whole field of public sector purchasing'.

In September 1970 the then Ministry of Local Government asked local authorities to review their purchasing arrangements in the light of the powers in the new legislation.[1]

The new government was carrying on with the ideas of the old, but fuller use of all the new management ideas awaits changes in local government structure. This is also the case with financial

[1] See 'Report of the Ministry of Housing and Local Government 1969 and 1970', *op. cit.*, p. 56, Local Authority Purchasing.

reform—discussion of which is as old almost as local government itself.

Finance

It is generally accepted that the greater local autonomy which is always one of the main objectives of structural reform, will only be possible if local authorities have more control over their total expenditure.

As was seen earlier, the rates over the years provide a declining proportion of local revenues.[1] The question that immediately arises in the face of this is—what are the possible alternative revenues? It is at this point that the disagreements begin.

From 1969 onwards actual schemes of structural reform became a matter of practical politics, and in 1971 with action imminent in this respect, the government published a discussion Green Paper on local government finance. This examined one possibility after another—local income tax, site value rating, local value-added tax, local employment or payroll tax, motor fuel and motor vehicle duties.[2] They were all found wanting, as they have in discussion so many times before.

As a result, the Green Paper fell back on the rates, but with variants such as super-rating, i.e. higher rates on commerce and services, and on further developments of the rate rebate scheme started in 1966 which would ease the burden on the lower paid. It also suggested improvements in the government grant system designed to provide more scope for local judgment.

Rates and grants are the basis of the existing system and, although the Green Paper is for discussion, the conclusion seems to be that local authorities are just not going to be able to raise much more of their revenue locally. Local government expenditure is too crucial to the management of the economy for governments to slacken control too much. Whatever changes are made, it is argued, this fundamental financial control must remain. This is a basic premise which must affect decisions on structural and functional reform.

[1] See also Wiseman, *op. cit.*, ch. 6, 'Local Government Finance', table VIII, Revenue Income of Local Authorities, England and Wales.
[2] 'The Future Shape of Local Government Finance', *Cmnd* 4741, July 1971.

Structure

The present structure of local government areas is the result of centuries of development—from the medieval Justices of the Peace to the Boards of Guardians in 1834 and the reform of the chartered boroughs in 1835. Then through the Local Boards of Health, the Burial Boards and the Urban and Rural Sanitary Districts to the County Councils and the County Boroughs of 1888, and to the Urban and Rural District Councils of 1894.[1]

As far as London is concerned, the Metropolitan Board of Works of 1855 gave way to the London County Council in 1888, and the vestries to the Metropolitan Boroughs in 1899. In 1963 the Greater London Council took over the L.C.C. together with the Middlesex County Council and parts of Essex, Surrey and Kent.[2]

The structure of London has been settled, the rest is now being changed despite the conclusion of the White Paper of July 1956 that there was 'no convincing case for radically reshaping the existing form of local government in England and Wales'.[3]

The Local Government Commission for England which followed this White Paper did make a start in reviewing local government areas. Fundamental changes were made in the Black Country and in parts of the East Midlands; a new enlarged Teeside County came into existence on 1 April 1968. The new Secretary of State for Local Government, Mr Richard Crossman, early in his period of office, however, saw the weakness of the limited terms of reference of the Commission and the piecemeal nature of its recommendations. In December 1965 he rejected the proposals for Tyneside and the Commission voluntarily suspended its activities. In February 1966 the reviews were discontinued, after the announcement of a Royal Commission on Local Government in England under the Chairmanship of Lord Redcliffe-Maud and with the following terms of reference: 'To consider the structure of local government in England, outside Greater London, in relation to its existing functions, and to make recommendations for authorities and boundaries, and

[1] See K. B. Smellie, *A History of Local Government*, Allen & Unwin, 4th ed., 1968.
[2] *Ibid.*, ch. 8, 'London 1835–1967'.
[3] 'Areas and Status of Local Authorities in England and Wales', *Cmnd* 9831, July 1956, p. 6.

for functions and their division, having regard to the size and character of areas in which these can be most effectively exercised and the need to sustain a viable system of local democracy.'

The Commission reported in 1969;[1] it found that the existing areas did not fit the pattern of life and work in modern England; that the services provided were split haphazardly between the different authorities; and that many authorities were too small in size and revenue.

The proposed new structure for England should be

1. 61 new local government areas excluding London, consisting of:
    (i) 58 unitary authorities responsible for all services,
    (ii) 3 metropolitan areas in the West Midlands, Merseyside and Selnec where responsibility for services should be shared with a second tier of 20 metropolitan authorities.
2. The 61 areas together with the G.L.C. should be grouped into eight provinces with councils indirectly elected by the unitary and metropolitan areas.
3. Within the 58 unitary authorities and wherever they were wanted by the inhabitants of the three Metropolitan areas, local councils should be elected for the existing local authority areas as a link between the public and the new authorities.

The recommendations were accepted in principle by the government, which in February 1970 announced its own conclusions in a White Paper, 'Reform of Local Government in England'.[2]

The main changes were that two additional metropolitan areas were to be created in West Yorkshire and South Hampshire, thus leaving 51 unitary areas; and that the provincial council concept was to be deferred until after the Crowther Commission on the Constitution had reported.

In September of the same year for Scotland, the Wheatley Report recommended the replacement of the existing 430 local

[1] 'Royal Commission on Local Government in England 1966–69', vol. I, Report, *Cmnd* 4040, also vol. II, 'Memorandum of Dissent' by M. D. Senior, *Cmnd* 4040 I, and vol. III, Research Appendices, *Cmnd* 4040 II. N.B. Mr Senior's views were that there should be a two-level system of 35 directly elected regional authorities plus 148 directly elected authorities.
[2] *Cmnd* 4276, Feb. 1970.

LOCAL AUTHORITIES 113

authorities by 44 at two levels—seven major regional authorities and 37 second tier.[1]

The General Election of 1970 cut short the political line of development arising from these White Papers—indeed their very legislative needs required a new parliament. In March 1970 the government did give their views on Wales, which had been the subject of a White Paper published in 1967 without the benefit of the English and Scottish proposals.[2] It was decided to have a further review of Glamorgan and Monmouth to see if a satisfactory pattern could be worked out to avoid the continued division between County Boroughs and County Councils.

The final decisions for the three counties were thus bequeathed to the new Conservative government which in February 1971 revealed its thoughts on England.[3]

There were to be two groups of operational authorities. Metropolitan counties would remain, but in Merseyside, Selnec, West Midlands, West Yorkshire, South Yorkshire, and Tyne and Wear; and within them Metropolitan districts. Elsewhere there would be Counties and County Districts.

To allow the focussing of local opinion on matters affecting the neighbourhood there could be parish councils where appropriate; and elsewhere their equivalent, which could be one of the old statutory bodies or even a non-statutory organisation.[4]

The division of functions was proposed as follows:[5]

As far as Scotland was concerned the government decided in February 1971 to follow the Wheatley two-tier concept in general, and that in particular there should be one more region—the Borders; both Orkneys and Shetland should be given separate status; and the number of districts should be increased by 14 to 49.[6]

[1] 'Royal Commission on Local Government in Scotland 1966–69', *Cmnd* 4150, Sept. 1969.
[2] (i) 'Local Government—Wales', *Cmnd* 3340, July 1967; (ii) 'Local Government Reorganisation in Glamorgan and Monmouthshire', *Cmnd* 4310, March 1970.
[3] 'Local Government in England. Government Proposals for Reorganisation', *Cmnd* 4584, Feb. 1971. See also Circular 8/71, 16 Feb. 1971, from the Department of the Environment.
[4] *op. cit.*, p. 11, para. 38-40.
[5] *op. cit.*, appendix.
[6] Reform of Local Government in Scotland, *Cmnd* 4583, Feb. 1971, p. 9.

County Councils (outside metropolitan areas) and Metropolitan District Councils

Education
Personal social services
Libraries

All County Councils	*All District Councils*
Planning:	Planning:
Plan making	Most development control
Development control (strategic and reserved decisions)	Acquisition and disposal of land for planning purposes, development or redevelopment[1]
Acquisition and disposal of land for planning purposes, development or redevelopment[1]	
Highways, Traffic and Transport	
Housing:	Housing:
Certain reserve powers, e.g. for overspill	Including housebuilding
	Housing management
	Slum clearance
	House and area improvement
Building regulations	
Weights and measures	
Food and drugs	
Clean air	
Refuse disposal	
Environmental health[2]	Refuse collection
Museums and art galleries[1]	Environmental health[2]
Parks and open spaces[1]	Museums and art galleries[1]
Playing fields and swimming baths[1]	Parks and open spaces[1]
Coast protection[1]	Playing fields and swimming baths[1]
Police[3]	Coast protection[1]
Fire[3]	

Notes:

1 Concurrent powers exercisable by county councils and by district councils.
2 Future administration of water supply, sewerage and sewage disposal to be considered in the light of the report of the Central Advisory Water Committee. Detailed allocation of other environmental services to be discussed with the local authority associations.
3 Some counties will need to be amalgamated for police purposes and possibly for fire.

In Wales the government revealed its views on a consultative document 'The Reform of Local Government in Wales'.[1] The proposal briefly was that the whole of Wales should be reorganised as a two-tier structure of main authorities, with seven county councils and 36 district councils.

In the discussion that followed these proposals, and in preparation for the legislation, everyone agreed, as usual, on what was wrong with local government: too many authorities, the illogical division of functions, the artificial separation of town and country—but disagreed on the actual proposals.

The boundaries themselves provoked the main discussion— for example, Plymouth with its industrial needs did not want to be administered from Exeter. Cardiff wanted some recognition that it was the capital city of Wales. The fact that the surrounding areas were solidly Labour played its part in this too. The other part of the argument as far as England was concerned, centred on the change from the previous government's one-tier to the Conservative two-tier approach. This was at the basis of Labour's criticism.

Lord Redcliffe-Maud welcomed the White Paper in general but was worried that the old worm of warfare between town and country was still being maintained. On functions, housing and planning seemed to provoke most mention.

Sir Harry Page, the former Treasurer of Manchester City Council, was of the view that because the majority in local government found the proposals readily acceptable, then they were obviously not sufficiently radical.[2] The local authority associations are certainly not noted for their objectivity.

In preparation for the legislation for the session of 1971–2 discussions were carried on with the various interests on all the obvious points, and on a new management structure, through a steering committee of the local authority associations and the Department of the Environment.

The bill published by the government in 1971, in which details of the reform were eventually given, did not depart from the main ideas of the White Paper.

A new pattern of local government was at last almost on the statute book. It is doubtful, however, in the absence of funda-

[1] Feb. 1971.
[2] Sir Harry Page, 'Local Government in Decline', *Three Banks Review*, June 1971, no. 90, p. 13.

mental financial reforms, that it will bring truly local government.

In the longer run, when the whole reorganisation is over and this fact is realised, perhaps more consideration will be given to the relationship with the central government which, while accepting that most of the finances will come from the Exchequer, would concern itself with devolution of both policy and administration.

The intention of the government to remove many of their 1,000 controls or sanctions over local authorities is an important step in this direction.[1] This should be followed up by a determination to alter the relationship of the Department of the Environment and the Department of Education and Science, and similar departments such as the Home Office, with the local authorities. At the moment there is a duplication of function which is frustrating, bureaucratic and wasteful of the expertise of professionals who would be better employed locally at the sharp end of social and planning policy making.

These departments have a role in cross-fertilising the experiences of local authorities generally and of maintaining standards of building, etc., but this is different from the duplication involved by central government professionals—architects, planners, educationalists—checking the work of colleagues in the field.[2]

In general these departments need the sort of renovating administrative questioning and reform that took place in the Ministry of Defence after 1964. Of course the relationship with local authorities is vitally different from that between headquarters and the various service commands, but the central/local relationship is clouded with mythology, acquired antagonisms, as well as bureaucratic procedures. These do little to protect the freedom of local authorities—they do slow up decision taking. Only major decisions need to be taken at the top; this philosophy is followed in the administration of the Urban Aid Programme[3] which uses the local know-how of people in the localities.

[1] H.C. Official Report, vol. 817, no. 145, 19 May 1971, col. 1288, from speech by Secretary of State for the Environment. Also, for the story of the development of central control, 1832–1929, see Smellie, op. cit., ch. 5.
[2] Wiseman, op. cit., p. 87.
[3] The Urban Aid Programme is carried out under the Local Government Grants (Social Needs) Act of 1969.

Another issue that will need discussion when the structural changes are over is that of transference of functions to local government; in some cases, back to local government. The plain fact is that despite its tremendous record of success—it has been the vehicle of much of the social change in housing and education—despite the devoted services of thousands of elected representatives and of officials, local government has failed to adapt itself to the changed requirements of the modern state.

Over the years there has been a steady transfer of former municipal functions to the central government: trunk roads, hospitals, public assistance, rating valuation and assessment, regulation of passenger road services. Municipal public utilities have been transferred with others to central public corporations; electricity, gas, passenger road transport. Water supply is moving in the same direction.

The Conservative government are proceeding with proposals —basically similar to those of the previous administration—to bring under unified National Health Service administration the personal health services now administered by the local authorities through their health committees.[1] The Polytechnics as they find their academic feet seem to want a status they feel unobtainable within the local government system.

This is in the face of lip service to local democracy by all governments, who find themselves driven in the opposite direction by the Keynesian need to control public expenditure—*vide* the Conservative government's inability to allow individual education authorities to provide free school milk if they wish —and the need to ensure that services are well provided everywhere, e.g. the control over numbers of teachers, police, firemen, etc. The technical parameters of the supply of gas and electricity together with their economies of scale could not, and cannot be, confined by the existing concept of local government.

This whole question of reallocation of functions will be well worth a fresh appraisal when the local government structural changes have taken place, and particularly if provincial government, built on to the development already taking place in the Regional Economic Planning Boards and Councils, ever materialises.

In Transport the new Passenger Transport Authorities took

---

[1] 'National Health Service Reorganisation, England', *Cmnd* 5055, 1972.

functions away from local government. The White Paper on Local Government suggested that transport be allocated to the County Councils. A subsequent 'consultation paper' says that the functions and responsibilities of P.T.A.s will be assumed by the new metropolitan councils, including policy control of the Passenger Transport Executives, but as in the case of the G.L.C./ L.T.E., these metropolitan county councils could be given a power of general direction to strengthen this control. The objective is to ensure that public accountability lies properly with the political body while maintaining an appropriately independent management structure. The Passenger Transport Areas will become coterminous with the areas of the metropolitan county councils.

This G.L.C./L.T.E.-type approach is akin to that involved in the proposal to hive off central government functions to public agencies while still maintaining overall responsibility to the government and to parliament.

It may be that this approach would be a means of bringing local authorities back into the picture with so many of the activities in their areas over which they have no control. Water supply is a case in point as was mentioned earlier.

It will, however, take more than a technical/managerial argument to convince many of the staff of central organisations and other forms of local government that transfer to all-purpose local authorities would be beneficial. The resistance of the medical profession played a part in determining policy in 1948 when the hospitals were nationalised; it did likewise in the discussions on the personal health services from 1969 onwards.

Those who care for local government should ask themselves why this is so. Is the image of the interfering local worthy too strong? Is the old Poor Law tang still lingering? Is there a fear of too detailed a control through the committee system?

As a Minister between 1965 and 1970, I saw the relationship between central and local government in practice. In 1968 I transferred to the Home Office. My first meeting with a local authority delegation was illuminating. The attitude of one or two of the local politicians was unnecessarily antagonistic and neither the material nor the discussion provided by them or their officials stood up to much analysis.

Perhaps it can all be explained by the fact that the subject under discussion was the emotive one of 'immigrants and social policy'. Certainly it was different from my later experience with local authority representatives on the Central Fire Brigade Advisory Council. Here our problem was that the organisation and procedures were such that we all took an inordinate time to reach decisions. The implementation of the Holroyd Report, which the Fire Service awaited too long, will help here.[1]

It was also foreign to my experience in the City of Leeds, where I have always had the fullest cooperation from committee chairmen of different political persuasions, and of course always from the officials.

Nevertheless, there is an image of local government which is supported by my first experience in a Home Department. It is a widely-held view which does not help any discussion concerning transference of functions, as those of us who once argued the case for 'municipalisation of rented property' found at the hustings. It is a matter, however, that will have fresh significance when the structural reforms are complete. It may be that the Crowther Commission has it in mind—for devolution is one of the important problems of government as a whole.

With all the major decisions being taken in the early 1970s, we have reached a watershed in local government. This does not mean that its problems are over, or that new ones will not arise.

Regard and concern for local government must not mean an acceptance of a new status quo. What matters is that it should constantly adapt itself to change.

What is certain is that local government will continue to absorb an increasing share of national resources and of the total employed labour force.

[1] Sir Ronald Holroyd, 'Report of the Departmental Committee on the Fire Service', *Cmnd* 4371, May 1970.

APPENDIX

Staff Associations, Trade Unions and Associations of Staffs and of Employees

Administrative and Professional Staffs Group

Association of Agricultural Education Staffs of Local Authorities.
Association of Chief Education Officers.
Association of County Planning Officers.
Association of Educational Psychologists.
Association of Headmasters, Headmistresses and Matrons of Approved Schools.
Association of Hospital and Welfare Administrators.
Association of Local Government Engineers and Surveyors.
Association of Local Government Financial Officers.
Association of Municipal Transport Managers.
Association of Principals of Technical Institutions.
Association of Teachers in Technical Institutions.
British Association of Organisers and Lecturers in Physical Education.
British Dental Association.
British Medical Association.
Community Service Association.
Confederation of Health Service Employees.
County, City and Borough Architects' Joint Association.
Incorporated Association of Assistant Masters in Secondary Schools.
Incorporated Association of Assistant Mistresses.
Incorporated Association of Headmasters.
Incorporated Association of Headmistresses.
Institution of Water Engineers.
Institutional Management Association.
Justices' Clerks' Society.
National and Local Government Officers' Association.
National Association of Approved Schools Staffs.
National Association of Head Teachers.
National Association of Homes and Hostels.
National Association of Inspectors of Schools and Educational Organisers.
National Association of Justices' Clerks' Assistants.
National Association of Local Education Authority Youth Service Officers.
National Association of Remand Home Superintendents and Matrons.
National Association of Schoolmasters.
National Federation of Continuative Teachers.
National Society for Art Education.
National Union of General and Municipal Workers.
National Union of Public Employees.
National Union of Teachers.

New Towns Chief Officers' Association.
Society of Clerks of the Peace of Counties and of Clerks of County
    Councils.
Society of Rural District Council Clerks.
Society of Town Clerks.
Society of Clerks of Urban District Councils.
Staffs' Sides of Provincial Councils.
Transport and General Workers Union.
Youth Service Association.

Manual Workers Group

Confederation of Shipbuilding and Engineering Unions.
Heating and Domestic Engineers' Union
National Federation of Building Trade Operatives.
National League of the Blind.
National Union of Agricultural Workers.
National Union of General and Municipal Workers.
National Union of Public Employees.
Transport and General Workers' Union.

Services Group

Association of Chief Officers of Police.
Chief Constables' (Scotland) Association.
Chief Fire Officers' Association.
Fire Brigades Union.
National Association of Probation Officers.
National Association of Fire Officers.
National Union of General and Municipal Workers.
Police Federations for England and Wales and for Scotland.
Superintendents' Associations for England and Wales and for Scotland.

Further Reading

W. Barker, *Local Government Statistics*, Institute of Municipal Treasurers and Accountants, 1964.

G. Barron, *A Bibliographical Guide to the English Educational System*, Athlone Press, 1965.

A. S. Bishop, *The Rise of a Central Authority for English Education 1971*, Cambridge University Press.

A. Briggs, *Victorian Cities*, Penguin Books, 1968.

J. J. Clarke, *Outline of Local Government in the U.K.*, Pitman, 1969.

J. B. Cullingworth, *Housing and Local Government*, Allen & Unwin, 1966.

J. M. Drummond (revised by W. A. Kitching), *The Finance of Local Government*, Allen & Unwin, 1964.

J. A. G. Griffiths, *Central Departments and Local Authorities*, Allen & Unwin, 1966.

W. O. Lester Smith, *Government of Education*, Penguin Books, 1971.

J. P. Mackintosh, *Devolution of Power: Local Democracy, Regionalism and Nationalism*, Penguin Books, 1968.

J. G. Millwood, *Municipal Work Study*, British Institute of Management, 1968.

R. M. Punnett, *British Government and Politics*, Heinemann, 1970, see ch. 13, 'Local Government'.

A. M. Rees and T. Smith, *Town Councillors. A Study of Barking*, Acton Society Trust, 1964.

G. Rhodes and S. Ruck, *The Government of Greater London*, Allen & Unwin, 1970.

P. G. Richards, *The New Local Government System*, Allen & Unwin, 1968.

P. G. Richards, *Delegation in Local Government*, Allen & Unwin, 1956.

W. A. Robson, *Local Government in Crisis*, Allen & Unwin, 1966.

W. A. Thomas and E. R. Shaw, 'Role of Loans Bureaux in Local Authority Finance', *Moorgate and Wall Street*, Hill Samuel & Co., autumn 1971, p. 21.

Seventh Annual Report of the Water Resources Board for the Year ending 30 September 1970, H.M.S.O.

Management of Local Government, Chairman Sir John Maud, M.H.L.G., 1967; vol. 2, The Local Government Councillor, an enquiry carried out for the Committee by the Government Social Survey; vol. 3, The Local Government Elector, an enquiry carried out for the Committee by the Government Social Survey; vol. 4, Local Government Administration Abroad, by Dr A. H. Marshall; vol. 5, Local Government Administration in England and Wales: research enquiries carried out for the Committee.

4 Public Corporations

4 Public Corporations

The central government does not carry out all its activities itself. It allocates responsibilities to other organisations which are, by definition, not part of the government but ultimately responsible to it: these are known as public corporations.

They are managed in the 'public interest'—a phrase first used by the Crawford Committee in 1926 when considering the British Broadcasting Corporation[1]—and their activities are often basic to the economy. They tend to differ in economic experience and behaviour from both private sector companies and government trading bodies.

Total Expenditure: Total Employed

The total expenditure of these corporations in 1970 was £8,041m. The total revenue was the same, and of this figure only £134m was given as a subsidy.[2]

In terms of public expenditure, the estimated capital expenditure for 1971–2 was £1,701m.[3]

In terms of manpower, in June 1970 the total employed labour force of the corporations was 1,920,000 or 7.7 per cent of the whole.[4]

Definition

Public corporations have been defined as public trading companies which have a substantial degree of financial independence of the central government which created them.[5]

They have two main characteristics. First, the Sovereign, Parliament or a Minister appoints directly or indirectly the whole

[1] 'Report of the Broadcasting Committee', *Cmnd* 2599, 1926.
[2] *National Income and Expenditure, 1971*, Central Statistical Office, H.M.S.O., table 33.
[3] 'Public Expenditure 1969–70 to 1974–75', *Cmnd* 4578, 1971, table 1.6.
[4] *Economic Trends*, no. 212, June 1971, p. xlvi.
[5] R. Maurice (ed.), *National Accounts Statistics. Sources and Methods*, G.S.O., 1968, p. 237.

or the majority of the board of management; there are no pro-
prietors, no shareholders. Second, they are bodies corporate free
to manage their affairs without detailed control by Parliament
or other elected body, with the power to borrow within laid-down
limits and to maintain reserves. Their finances are not part of the
finances of government except where advances are made for
capital expenditure or where subsidies or temporary loans are
made. This freedom is in contrast to that of the other central
government trading bodies, i.e. the Royal Ordnance Factories,
or the local authority trading companies.

Within this public corporation group is another called the
'nationalised industries'. There is no clear or final definition of
this term, but they are taken generally to mean the public corporations with a statutory responsibility for the supply of energy
—other than petroleum products—and of steel; the provision of
postal and telecommunication services other than broadcasting;
and the provision of transport services.

This definition does not cover all the public corporations which
have been investigated by the Select Committee on Nationalised
Industries as it has evolved its programme over the years. It is,
however, the definition used by the Treasury when it refers to
the 'nationalised industries'. It is suitable for general analysis
and it is on this basis that the classification is used here.

List of Public Corporations[1]

In the following list those industries recognised as 'nationalised'
are given first and are marked with an asterisk.

*British Airports Authority
*British European Airways
*British Overseas Airways Corporation
*British Railways Board
*British Steel Corporation
*British Transport Docks Board
*British Waterways Board
*Electricity Council and Boards
*Gas Council and Boards
*National Bus Company

[1] *National Accounts Statistics, op. cit.*, annex., p. 249.
    N.B. Public Corporations include the activities of subsidiaries where
their accounts are consolidated with those of the parent corporation.

*National Coal Board
*National Freight Corporation
*North of Scotland Hydro-Electric Boards
*Post Office
*Scottish Transport Group
*South of Scotland Electricity Board
*Transport Holdings Company
Bank of England
British Broadcasting Corporation
Cable & Wireless Ltd
Commonwealth Development Corporation
Covent Garden Market Authority
Housing Corporation
Independent Television Authority
National Dock Labour Board
National Film Finance Corporation
National Ports Council
National Research Development Corporation
New Town Development Corporations and Commission for the New Towns
Scottish Special Housing Association
Sugar Board

Northern Ireland:

Electricity Board for Northern Ireland
Northern Ireland Housing Trust
Northern Ireland Transport Holding Company

Reasons for Public Ownership

The arguments for and against public ownership and in particular for 'nationalisation' have been one of the main issues dividing the political parties since the end of the first world war.

Indeed, the Labour Party has as one of its aims set down in its constitution 'to secure for the workers by hand or by brain the full fruits of their industry and the most equitable distribution thereof that may be possible, upon the basis of the common ownership of the means of production, distribution and exchange, and the best obtainable system of popular administration and control of each industry or service.'

This definition was the expression of a political philosophy dating back at least to the Spencean Socialists, and which had developed in a variety of political climates through the ideas of the Chartists; the continental Marxist Social Democrats; the early

Fabian municipal or 'gas and water' socialists; and the pre-1914 anti-parliamentary syndicalists and guild socialists.

These latter ideas received pragmatic support from the miners concerned with the practical problems of their industry—particularly in South Wales, where the peasant chapel background provided a fertile ground for philosophical concepts expressed not by academics but by union leaders such as Noah Ablett and A. J. Cook.[1]

The nationalisation of the coal industry was a major aim of the Labour Party of the 1920s, as was the allied desire for workers' participation and social responsibility in the running of industry. These aims washed off on to a wider political stage with the General Strike and the higher proportionate strength of mining representatives in the growing Parliamentary Labour Party.

Public ownership became an article of faith to many members of the Labour Party; it was reinforced by the intellectual-Christian-ethical ideas of Professor Tawney and his analysis of property and rights.[2]

There developed also an argument for public ownership as part of that for 'economic planning'. The earlier socialist arguments for this were reinforced by those of Lord Keynes—applied to some degree by Roosevelt in his New Deal and in the U.K. with the outbreak of the Second World War. The economic planning argument was more explicitly expressed in the 1930s by the Labour Party; by the Lloyd George Liberals; and by Tory Democrats such as Harold Macmillan.[3]

It was at this time that Herbert Morrison gave his authority to the Board-type 'autonomous' system of organisation.[4] This view was in contrast to that of the influential Haldane Committee on the Machinery of Government in 1919, which had argued in favour of direct ministerial control.

There is an anti-monopoly argument for public ownership, which makes the case for state ownership of the inevitable monopolies, e.g. railways.

[1] Michael Foot, *Aneurin Bevan*, vol. 1: *1897–1945*, MacGibbon & Kee, 1962, p. 28. and R. Page Arnot, *South Wales Miners. A History of the South Wales Miners' Federation 1898–1914*, p. 169.
[2] R. H. Tawney, 'Equality', Halley Stewart lectures, 1929.
[3] C. R. Attlee, *The Labour Party in Perspective*, Gollancz 1937, and D. Jay, *The Socialist Case*, Faber, 1937. Also see ch. 1, above.
[4] H. Morrison, *Socialism and Transport*, Constable, 1933.

There is the technical efficiency, modernisation, re-equipment, rationalisation case which has been relevant in so much of the post-1945-type public ownership. For example, the pre-nationalisation coal industry was not a paragon of textbook capitalist virtues, while the privately owned steel industry of the 1960s left a legacy of weak organisational structure allied with low investment. The argument for the public ownership of the electricity industry from pre-war years was almost entirely a technical one but tinged with a concern for the social needs of the countryside.

A 'defence of the realm' argument has also been present. The original setting up of Imperial Airways, a predecessor of B.O.A.C., was to some degree for defence reasons, i.e. control of routes to the Near East and to India. The 'public ownership' of Rolls-Royce in 1971—albeit by non-public corporative form of organisation—was also justified on defence grounds.

These basic arguments for public ownership are relevant but in varying degrees, to most of the public corporations. They apply with greater aggregate force to the nationalised industries; in the case of others, e.g. the I.T.A., the National Dock Labour Board and the National Ports Council—which but for the General Election of 1970 was to be replaced by a nationalised ports structure—the public corporation is a form of government control of part of the private sector.

The origins of public ownership lie long before 1945,[1] but it is since that time that the major development has taken place. Not all the arguments in favour of this type of organisation have come from socialists but, given the strength of anti-public ownership sentiment, particularly in the media, and the small amount of denationalisation undertaken by successive Conservative governments, the main reason for its maintenance would seem to be the economic logic of the argument.

Public ownership in its different forms has met a major need of the modern mixed economy. The real and significant discussion today is concerned with the problems of the existing forms of the public corporations and with ideas for new forms to meet emerging economic and social problems.

[1] See Edward Goodman, ch. III, 'The Public Corporation', *Forms of Public Ownership and Control*, Christophers, 1951; also W. Thornhill, *The Nationalised Industries—an Introduction*, Nelson, 1968.

ORGANISATION: STRUCTURE, FINANCE, ETC.

The functions of the corporations vary, and although by their very corporate status there are important similarities, there are differences in the various aspects of organisation.

The following information on the individual corporations is based on a division into structure; finance; occupations and labour relations; research and development; and consumer consultation. In each case, the year in which the corporation was first set up and the sponsoring department is given.

The purpose of the information is to illustrate the form taken by the public corporations. In some instances where it serves to aid such illustration the range of information given is wide and is made in some detail.

Full information on all the corporations is available in the Annual Reports from which the information is taken for 1970-1, unless otherwise stated.

British Airports Authority,[1] 1966 (Department of Trade and Industry)

Structure

The Authority, with six members (four part-time), is responsible for four major airports—Gatwick, Heathrow, Prestwick and Stansted. On 1 April 1971 Edinburgh-Turnhouse was taken over from the D.T.I.

In 1970-1 the four airports dealt with 455,000 aircraft movements; 20,710,000 passengers; 429,000 short tons of cargo; and 40,000 short tons of mail.

At the airports the Authority provides the runway, loading, and terminal facilities for British and foreign airline operators.

Finance

The net profit after interest, and before tax, was £5·71m; each of the four airports made a net profit. Average net assets were £72·78m and the return on these was 12.28 per cent compared with the objective of 14 per cent. Borrowing from the D.T.I. totalled £58·31m. Capital investment for the year was £8·66m.

[1] 'The British Airports Authority. Annual Report and Accounts for Year Ended 31 March 1971', H.C. 527.

Occupations and Labour Relations
The number of employees was 4,339.
Labour relations are conducted through a B.A.A. Central Joint
Council and a B.A.A. Joint Negotiating and Consultation Com-
mittee.

British European Airways Corporation[1] 1946 (Department of
Trade and Industry)

Structure
The Board of nine members (four part-time) controls an organisation which provides passenger and cargo flights within the
U.K., to Europe and to the fringes of Africa—with 102 aircraft,
8,665,824 passengers were carried over 3,274,514,168 miles;
110,605 tons of freight were carried over 45,882,735 ton miles.
On behalf of the Scottish Office an Air Ambulance Service carried
446 patients on 352 flights.
In 1971 the government set up a British Airways Board to
concern itself with the operational structure and to oversee the
financial and strategic policies of the public airways corporations.
This Corporation, with B.O.A.C., belongs to the coordinating Air
Corporations Committee.
The Corporation carries out its activities via a 'profit centre'
concept concerned also with the subsidiary and associated companies. These are—with percentage of shares held—

	%
The Airways Housing Trust Ltd	33
B.E.A. Airtours Ltd	100
B.E.A. Helicopters Ltd	100
British Air Services Ltd (which owns all share capital of Cambrian Airways Ltd and North East Air Lines Ltd	70
College of Air Training jointly owned with B.O.A.C.	
Cyprus Airways Ltd	23
Gibraltar Airways Ltd	49
International Aeradio Ltd	33
Malta Airways Ltd	34
Silver Wing Surface Arrangements Ltd	100
Société Internationale de Telecommunications Aeronautiques	4.29

[1] 'British European Airways Corporation, Annual Report and Accounts
for Year Ended 31 March 1971', H.C. 518.

Sovereign Group Hotels Ltd, formed in 1970	100
to hold the investments in hotel and associated companies, i.e.	
Airport Catering Services Ltd	40
European Hotel Corporation N.V. Holland	$16\frac{2}{3}$
European Hotel Corporation (U.K.) Ltd	$12\frac{1}{4}$
European Hotel Corporation (France) Ltd	4.9
Hotel Maatschappij Schiphol N.V.	11

Finance
Profit was £524,000 after charging interest of £7·96m on capital borrowings and after crediting £8m from the 'Special Account' set up in 1969.

Net assets were £175·67m, and the return on these of 5.1 per cent compared with the requirment of 8 per cent over the four-year period ending 31 March 1972.

Capital expenditure was £38·5m—£26·3m of which was for aircraft and spares.

Occupations and Labour Relations
The labour force in the U.K. totalled 22,603—with 2,455 overseas, of whom 2,325 were locally employed. There were 1,398 pilots and 1,496 air cabin staff.

Engineering training took place at the Air Corporation Training School at Cranebank (jointly owned with B.O.A.C.) and at London Airport. There is an Air Transport Staff College owned by B.E.A. but run for the benefit of B.E.A. and B.O.A.C.

Wage and salary negotiations are conducted through the medium of the National Joint Council for Civil Air Transport (see B.O.A.C.).

British Overseas Airways Corporation[1] 1940 (Department of Trade and Industry)

Structure
The Board of ten members (five part-time) controls an organisation which provides passenger and cargo flights to all parts of the world other than Europe—with 54 aircraft, 1,893,657 passengers were carried over 6,616,600,000 passenger miles; 258,800,000 load ton miles of cargo were carried.

[1] 'British Overseas Airways Corporation, Annual Accounts for the Year Ended 31 March 1971', H.C. 519.

The information given for B.E.A. earlier concerning the Airways Board and Air Corporation Committee is relevant here.

The Corporation carries out its activities through a functional Board of Management. There are also associated and subsidiary companies, e.g.

B.O.A.C. Associated Companies Ltd acts for B.O.A.C. in association with other companies and holds the shares of:

	%
Air Mauritius	24.5
Cathay Pacific Airways Ltd	15
Fiji Airways Ltd	22.6
Gulf Aviation Co. Ltd	21.53
Hunts of the Pacific Ltd	31.25
Malaysia-Singapore Airlines Ltd	4.08
Mideast Aircraft Service Company S.A.	100
New Hebrides Airways Ltd	30.96
Turkish Airlines (T.H.Y.)	1.96
B.I.H. Ltd	66.7
East Point Hotels Ltd	10
European Hotel Corporation N.V.	16.7
European Hotel Corporation U.K. Ltd	12.3
European Hotel Corporation (France) S.A.	4.9
Fiji Mocanbo Holdings Ltd	7.6
Fiji Resorts Ltd	9.2
Kenya Safari Lodges and Hotels Ltd	5
Mnarani Ltd	50
New Mauritius Hotels Ltd	21.5
Panafric Hotels Ltd	27
Pegasus Hotels of Ceylon Ltd	18.05
Pegasus Hotels of Guyana Ltd	64.3
Pegasus Hotels of Jamaica Ltd	35.5
B.O.A.C. Engine Overhaul Ltd	100
International Aeradio Ltd with holdings in Abu Dhabi, Libya, Caribbean, Far East, Pakistan, etc.	66
The Airways Housing Trust	67
B.O.A.C. Restaurants	100
Alta Travel Ltd	51

Finance

Profit was £3·44m after charging interest and taxation. Net assets were £264·6m and the return on these for the five years cumulatively was 13.6 per cent—3.2 per cent for the year compared with the financial objective of 12.5 per cent for the period 1966–72.

The net assets were financed by £65m of Public Dividend

Capital—the return on which was 7.5 per cent, and by borrowings of £80·30m on the open market.

Capital expenditure was £123·3m, of which £61·9m was for aircraft and spares.

Occupations and Labour Relations

The total labour force was 24,128—with 18,792 in the U.K.

Labour relations are conducted through the National Joint Council for Civil Air Transport. The employers' side consists of the public corporations together with International Aeradio Ltd; Airways Corporations Joint Medical Service; British Caledonian Airways Ltd; B.E.A. Helicopters Ltd; North East Air Lines Ltd; Cambrian Airways Ltd; B.E.A. Airtours Ltd; Dan Air Services Ltd.

The trade union side consists of the Association of Scientific, Technical and Managerial Staffs; National Union of Furniture Trade Operatives; Draughtsmen's and Allied Technicians' Association; Transport and General Workers Union; Electrical Electronic Telecommunications Union/Plumbing Trade Union; Merchant Navy and Airline Officers' Association; British Air Line Pilots' Association; Amalgamated Union of Engineering and Foundry Workers; Clerical and Administrative Workers Union; National Union of General and Municipal Workers; Association of Clerical, Technical and Supervisory Staffs; National Union of Vehicle Builders; National Union of Sheet Metal Workers and Coppersmiths; Amalgamated Society of Woodworkers; Amalgamated Society of Painters and Decorators.

British Railways Board[1] 1963 (Department of the Environment)

Structure

The Railways Board consists of 13 members (five part-time). There are five regional boards—London Midland, Scottish, Western and Eastern—with a Chairman and up to nine other members. The primary function of the Railway Management Group—the Regional General Managers and Executive Directors at Headquarters—is to develop strategies and priorities for action.

There are a number of subsidiaries whose name indicates their

[1] 'British Railways Board, Annual Report and Accounts 31 December 1970', H.C. May 1971.

task; British Transport Hotels Ltd, British Rail Engineering
Ltd, British Rail Hovercraft Ltd, Transportation Systems and
Market Research Ltd—together with British Rail Shipping and
International Services Division and British Rail Property Board.

British Rail Engineering with 15 rail workshops at Swindon,
Crewe, etc., is one of the largest engineering concerns in the
country. It also has a joint company B.R.E.-Metro Ltd—formed
with Metro Cammell Ltd to promote export sales of locomotives
and rolling stock.

The Railways Board has interests also in, for example, Freight-
liners Ltd, British Transport Advertising Ltd, Channel Tunnel
Co Ltd, the Fishguard and Rosslare Railways and Harbours Co,
Societé Anonyme de Navigation Angleterre-Lorraine-Alsace, and
Container Base (Leeds) Ltd (also Liverpool, Scotland and Man-
chester).

British Rail thus provide passenger and freight transport services; the type of goods carried varies from parcels—with its
Rail Express Parcels Service—to petroleum products. Traffic
totalled 199,000,000 tons. Train ferry traffic is important by B.R.
boats, through Sealink Travel Ltd and B.R. Hovercraft.

Finance
The consolidated profit was £51·7m but after the payment of
interest of £42·2m the balance was £9·5m.

Net assets were £878m but the financial target was not based
on these but was a target surplus of £17m over and above
interest on capital and historic depreciation. The effect of the
1968 Transport Act, which wrote down the value of fixed assets
by £713m, provided no margin for replacing written-down
assets as and when required at today's cost—in these circumstances a target return on capital was not meaningful.

The liability to the Department of the Environment was
£365m, which takes into account the capital transferred and
restructuring of recent years. Grants payable under Section 39(i)
of the Transport Act 1968 to enable uneconomic rail services to
be maintained, totalled £61·6m and a diminishing grant—in 1970
£12m—is being paid from 1969 to 1973, for maintaining, pending removal, track and signalling capacity in excess of the railways' long-term needs. The total payment in this respect is not
to exceed £50m.

Capital expenditure during the year was £85·5m.

Occupations and Labour Relations
The total employees at the end of the year were 273,063, the
largest number 213,236 being employed on the railways; of this
number 58,696 were salaried, the remainder were train crew,
signalmen, etc.

Labour relations machinery is amongst the most comprehensive
in Britain. Its purpose is (i) to consider and deal with matters
relating to wages, hours of duty, conditions of service, etc., and
(ii) to provide a channel through which the ideas and suggestions of the staff for the more efficient and economical working
of the railways can be canalised.

The various bodies set up in agreement with the National
Union of Railwaymen, Amalgamated Society of Locomotive
Engineers and Firemen, and the Transport Salaried Staffs Asso-
ciation, range from those at local level to the regions and through
to the Railway Staff National Council. There is also a Railway
Staff National Tribunal.

The Board spent some £2·7m to provide 110,000 employees
with training. There is a School of Transport at Derby, a Productivity Service Training Centre at Watford and a Staff College
at Woking.

Research and Development
Expenditure by the Research Department was £3·8m, and a staff
of about 1,000—including 440 qualified scientists and engineers
employed.

The main activities are centred at the Derby Railway Technical
Centre—the largest and most comprehensive of its kind in the
world, covering research, engineering design and development,
workshops and supplies. Work is proceeding on an advanced
passenger train, for which a new £200,000 laboratory for testing systems and structures was opened in 1970; prototype trains
should be running experimentally in 1974.

Other research is in the field of train control, track research,
wheel-rail adhesion and of new materials.[1]

The Scientific Services section of the department has outpost
laboratories which provide-on-the-spot analytical services at
Muswell Hill, Crewe, Derby, Doncaster, Swindon and Manchester.

[1] See *Advanced Transport Technology*, B.R.B.

Consultation

There have been changes in the machinery of consultation in the field of transport as a whole since 1947.[1]

The Transport Tribunal which considered charges was limited to London only in 1962; this responsibility was abolished in 1969.

The responsibilities of the Central Transport Consultative Committee and area Transport Users' Consultative Committees, which comprise independent chairmen and representative members, were 'to consider any matter, including charges, affecting the services and facilities provided'—but after 1962 they were debarred from considering questions of charges and reductions in services. They were given however a more specific role to play concerned with hardship, where there was a proposal to discontinue a service.

British Steel Corporation 1967[2] (Department of Trade and Industry)

Structure

The Corporation, with 11 members (three part-time), is responsible for the publicly-owned steel industry. Examples of the companies acquired on nationalisation are Richard Thomas & Baldwins Ltd (still in 1967 not denationalised and owned by the Iron & Steel Board Realisation Agency); Colvilles; English Steel Corporation; United Steel Company; British Steel and Tube Ltd.

There are six product divisions each with its own trading account. The General Steels Division produces crude steel and its principal products are plates, universal beams and sections, billets, rods and bars—with main units at Scunthorpe, Teeside and in Scotland.

The Strip Mills Division is responsible for strip, sheet, tinplate and other coated flat products; the major plants are in South Wales—Port Talbot, Llanwern and Ebbw Vale; North Wales—Shotton; and Scotland—Ravenscraig.

The Tubes Division produces steel tubes and pipes, spun iron

---

[1] 'Second Report from the Select Committee on Nationalised Industries 1970–1. Relations with the Public', H.C. 514, pp. x-xvi.
[2] 'British Steel Corporation, Annual Report and Account, 1970–1', H.C. 471.

pipes, concrete products and plastic pipes and fittings. It markets merchant pig iron, iron castings, etc. The various sub-groups are in Scotland, the North-east, the West Midlands and South Wales.

The Constructional Engineering Group—bridgework, civil engineering—is organised into nine operating branches—four in the Northern and Southern Works Groups and five in the Building and Contracting Group.

The Chemicals Division based on two wholly-owned subsidiaries of the Corporation—United Coke and Chemicals Co. Ltd and Dorman Long Chemicals Ltd—consisting of coal tar distillation units, benzole refineries and associated chemical plants and two coke oven plants producing metallurgical coke. The refined tar, etc., is used to produce chemicals, building materials, synthetic fibres, electrodes and refractories. This division is also responsible for technical and development aspects of coal carbonisation and for the Corporation's investments in a number of associated companies, e.g. Staveley Chemicals Ltd (45 per cent), Pthalic Anhydride Chemicals Ltd (45 per cent) and Bitmac Ltd (50 per cent).

The Corporation has investments in a large number of companies in the u.k. and some overseas, e.g. the British Steam Shipping Company, Corby (Northants), and District Water Company, Margam Co-operative Homes Ltd, Dorman Long (Ghana) Ltd.

There are further companies in which the Corporation has interests but which are not subsidiaries, e.g. the Bamburgh Shipping Co. Ltd, Benzole Producers Ltd, Corby Town Football Club, Pacific Steel Ltd (New Zealand), the Rhodesian Iron and Steel Co. Ltd, Victaulic Company of Canada Ltd.

Finance

The trading surplus in 1970–1 was £120m before interest and taxation; the deficit was £10m. Net assets were £1,244·5m, but in this financial year no agreement had yet been reached concerning financial objectives on these (see Table, pp. 180–1 below).

Under the Iron and Steel Act of 1969 a sum of £700m was designated Public Dividend Capital.[1] No dividend was paid on this.

---

[1] Reduced to £500m in 1971 as part of the capital reconstruction operation (see p. 184).

Capital expenditure was £143m.

Occupations and Labour Relations

The total number employed was 252,400, of which 185,000 were operatives and 67,400 were staff; 21 per cent of the latter were scientists, draughtsmen and technicians.

Labour relations are conducted at the various levels of the industry with the T.U.C. Steel Industry Consultative Committee consisting of the major unions involved.

The Corporation pays particular attention in its training activities to adult retraining, because of the continuing reduction in job opportunities.

Research and Development

Expenditure here was £9m—which included cost of day-to-day technical services to works, product development and of the Water and Clean Air Unit.

The main laboratories are located as follows:

Research Establishments	Location
Corporate Laboratories	
Battersea Laboratories	London
Hoyle Street Laboratories	Sheffield
Teesside Laboratories	Middlesbrough
General Steels Division	
Motherwell	Motherwell
Teesside (Dorman Long, Consett)	Middlesbrough, Consett
Special Steels Division	
Swiden House	Rotherham
Strip Mills Division	
Port Talbot	Port Talbot
Shotwick	Nr Shotton, Flints.
Tubes Division	
Corby	Corby, Northants
Chemicals Division	
Orgreave	Sheffield

Research is carried out in coal and coke, ore preparation, blast furnace operation and control, steelmaking and casting, fuel and furnaces, tube making, forging and extrusion, wire drawing, metallurgy, product developments, engineering, control engineering and instrumentation, chemicals, slags and slag utilisation, operational research, corrosion, welding and machines.

There are 43 research contracts at universities, e.g. Sheffield
—feasibility study of inflatable sheet steel structure; Oxford—
fluid motion during solidification.

There are other contracts placed with, for example, C.E.G.B.,
the Fire Research Station and the National Research Development Corporation.

British Transport Docks Board[1] 1963 (Department of the
Environment)

Structure

The Board of nine members (seven part-time) administers har-
bours at Ayr, Barrow, Barry, Cardiff, Fleetwood, Garston, Goole,
Grimsby and Immingham, Hull, Kings Lynn, Lowestoft, Lydney,
Newport, Penarth Harbour,[2] Plymouth (Millbay Docks), Port
Talbot, Silloth, Southampton, Swansea and Troon. Traffic
through these was 86,200,000 tons. There are Local Advisory
Boards for the Humber, Southampton and in South Wales.

The Board is the licensing authority under the Docks and
Harbours Act 1966 for all the ports except Garston, Kings Lynn
and Plymouth; and is the Pilotage Authority for the Humber
Pilotage District.

The Board wholly owns General Workers Stevedores Ltd at
Grimsby and Immingham, the Hull and Humber Handling Co.
which in the year acquired Jacobs, Larvin (Stevedores) Ltd of
Hull; and the Humber Pilots Steam Cutter Co. Ltd. There is
a 50-per-cent interest in the Southampton Cargo Handling Co.
Ltd, and in the International Cold Storage Co. Ltd.[3]

Finance

There was an operating surplus of £4·5m. The net deficit was
£1·8m after interest payments and depreciation allowances.

Average net assets were £127·2m. The agreed net return on
these was 5.5 per cent; the actual return was 3.5 per cent.

[1] 'British Transport Docks Board, Report and Accounts for Year Ended
31 December 1970', H.C. 406.
[2] The Penarth Dock itself was in process of being sold as was the
dock at Bo'ness.
[3] There were small investments in Containerbase (London West) Ltd,
Humber St Andrew's Engineering Co Ltd, and the Baltic Mercantile
and Shipping Exchange Ltd.

Capital expenditure was £10·3m—mainly in dock structure and roads.

Occupations and Labour Relations
The total labour force employed was 11,075.

Labour relations for manual grades are conducted through a system based on a National Joint Negotiating Council.

All training and education activities are directed from the staff college at Kings Lynn.

Research and Development[1]
The total expenditure on research was £110,000 and is centred at the Research Station at Southall. Collaborative work is carried out with the National Physical Laboratory and the Construction Industry Research and Information Association. There is a Research Advisory Group under the chairmanship of Dr J. Allen—'to provide access to knowledge not ordinarily open to the Board's Research Station'.

British Waterways Board[2] 1963 (Department of the Environment)

Structure
The Board, with eight members (five part-time), is responsible for 53 inland waterways and six harbours throughout the country, e.g. Aire and Calder Navigation, Grand Union Canal, Leeds and Liverpool Canal, Weaver Navigation, and Ardishaig Dock, Ellesmere Port Docks, Gloucester Docks, Regent's Canal Dock, Sharpness Docks and Weston Point Docks. Of the canals some, and part of some, are Commercial Waterways, others are Cruising Waterways. In this latter respect the Board has recreational activity responsibilities in conjunction with the Countryside Commission and the Sports Council. The Board owns hire cruisers and passenger craft. There is a waterways museum at Stoke Bruerne.

There are wharves at, for example, Rotherham, Nottingham and Enfield, and a new container terminal at Leeds. There are fleets of barges for general cargo, for coal and for petroleum products. In 1970 6,000,000 tons of cargo was carried.

[1] *Report on Research*, British Transport Docks Board, May 1971.
[2] 'British Waterways Board, Annual Report and Accounts for Year Ended 31 December 1970', H.C. 385.

The Board owns a number of reservoirs.

Occupations and Labour Relations
The total employed was 3,046—763 operating staff, 1,504 maintenance, 648 administrative and clerical, 131 miscellaneous.

Electricity Council and Boards[1] 1958 (Department of Trade and
Industry

Structure
This Industry consists of 14 statutory corporations—the Electricity Council, the Central Electricity Generating Board (C.E.G.B.)
and 12 Area Electricity Boards—London, South Eastern,
Southern Electricity, South Western, Eastern, East Midlands,
Midlands, South Wales, Merseyside and North Wales, Yorkshire, Northern Eastern, North Western.

The Council consists of six members (two part-time) appointed
by the Secretary of State. There are also three members from
the C.E.G.B., together with the 12 Chairmen of the Area Electricity Boards. It has a responsibility to advise the Secretary of
State on all matters affecting the industry and to promote and
assist the maintenance and development by the Generating Board
and the Area Boards of an efficient, coordinated and economical
system of electricity supply. The Council also has responsibilities
in finance, research and industrial relations.

The C.E.G.B. owns and operates the power stations and main
transmission lines and is responsible for the provision of bulk
supplies of electricity to the Area Boards. The Area Boards own
and operate the distribution networks and are responsible for the
retail sale of electricity to their customers; they also sell electrical appliances and undertake contracting work.

There were sales of some 170,000 million kwh to over
18,000,000 million customers from 187 power stations—coal-
and oil-fired, nuclear, diesel, gas turbine and hydro.

Finance
The operating profit was £205m but after paying interest of

[1] 'The Electricity Council, Annual Report and Accounts 1970–1', H.C.
560; C.E.G.B., 'Annual Report and Accounts 1970–1', H.C. 561; see also
Annual Report of each Area Board for 1970–1.

£261m there was a loss—for the first time since nationalisation
—of £56m. Net assets were £5,084m. The agreed net return on
average net assets employed is seven per cent, the actual return
was 4.1 per cent.

Government loans outstanding totalled £3,350m. British Electricity Stock outstanding totalled £96·6m. Capital expenditure for
the year was £390m.

Occupations and Labour Relations

The total number of employees was 188,235 (a reduction of
8,727 over the year) as follows:

Type of Employment	No.	%
Managerial and higher executive	1,724	0.9
Technical and scientific	25,735	13.7
Executive, clerical, accountancy, sales, etc.	47,007	25.0
Industrial	106,779	56.7
Technical trainees and apprentices	6,900	3.7

Labour relations are conducted through a system of works,
district and area committees and councils which vary with the
nature of the employment. In terms of consultation on safety,
health, welfare, etc., there are about 500 local advisory committees, 12 district joint advisory councils and a National Joint
Advisory Council.

In training there is, for example, a residential training centre
at Buxton, a training station for apprentices at Leeds, a training centre at Drakelow, and an 'overhead line' and welding training centre at Drakelow. Overall there has been a concentration
on work study and close liaison with the Electricity Supply
Industry Training Board.

Research and Development

The laboratories are located as follows:
Electricity Council:
　　Electricity Council Research Centre, Capenhurst, Chester.
Central Electricity Generating Board:
　　Central Electricity Research Laboratories, Leatherhead.
　　Berkeley Nuclear Laboratories, Gloucester.
　　Marchwood Engineering Laboratories, Southampton.
　　Marine Biology Laboratory, Fawley.
　　The C.E.G.B. is primarily concerned with technological research

on generation and mains transmission. Other technological research, together with economic and commercial research, is more the concern of the Council and the area boards. Research contracts are placed with universities and outside organisations.

Advise is received from the Electricity Supply Research Council under the chairmanship of Lord Kearton.

Total expenditure on research was £13·5m.

Consumer Consultation[1]

There are consultative councils for each of the area boards, which consist of a chairman and between 20 and 30 members of whom between 8-12 and 12-18 are chosen from those nominated by local authority associations; the rest by a variety of local interests. The chairman is *ex officio* a member of the area board. There are also area committees.

The councils consider any matter affecting the distribution of electricity—including tariffs, provision of new or improved services and facilities.

The area boards are required to inform the councils of their general plans and arrangements for performing their functions. The consultative councils are empowered to make representations on these to the relevant boards or to the Council itself.

These consultative councils are thus able to consider the wider interests of consumer and are not just a channel for complaints.

Gas Council and Boards[2] 1949 (Department of Trade and Industry)

Structure

The gas industry in the U.K. comprises a Gas Council and 12 area boards—Scottish, Northern, North Western, North Eastern, East Midlands, West Midlands, Wales, Eastern, North Thames, South Eastern, Southern, South Western.

The Gas Council has a general duty to advise the Minister on questions affecting the gas industry and to assist the area boards in carrying out their duties. It is accountable to the Minister,

[1] 'Second Report from the Select Committee on Nationalised Industries 1970–1', Relations with the Public, p. xviii to p. xxi; also Annual Report of each Consultative Council.
[2] 'The Gas Council Annual Report and Accounts 1970–1', H.C. 593. Also Annual Report for each Area Board 1970–1.

as are the autonomous boards which supply gas and other facilities to domestic consumers, e.g. gas appliances.

The Gas Council consists of 17 members—including the 12 area board chairmen—(three part-time). The area boards have an establishment of up to nine members, of whom the chairman is full-time—together with the chairman of the consumers' consultative council for the area.

In 1970–1 the industry sold 6,166,500,000 therms of coal, oil and natural gas to 13,371,800 consumers. There were 118 manufacturing stations and over 1,000 gas showrooms throughout the country.

The use of natural gas is affecting the structure of the industry. While previously the boards had been both manufacturer and retailer of gas, natural gas is purchased and distributed to area boards by the Gas Council. A new organisation, to come into being in 1973, will give to the Council more direct control over the development, finances and strategy of the industry.[1]

The Gas Council owned a number of subsidiary and associated companies, e.g. Gas Council (Exploration) Ltd and Hydrocarbons Great Britain Ltd. Most of the Boards have similar investments, e.g. North Eastern Gas Board are associated with Midland-Yorkshire Tar Distillers Ltd.

Finance

The gross surplus for the year was £109m but after payment of interest the net surplus was £2m. Net assets were £1,432m. The agreed net return on average net assets employed is 7.0 per cent; the actual return was 6.2 per cent. The return required from the area boards varies from 6.5 per cent in Scotland to 8.5 per cent in the West Midlands.

Capital expenditure was £197m.

Occupations and Labour Relations

The total number of employees was 115,845—54,722 manual and 61,123 staff.

Labour relations are conducted through an N.J.C. system, e.g.

---

[1] *H.C. Official Report*, vol. 822, no. 195, col. 1866, Statement by the Minister for Industry. In 1973, a British Gas Corporation combining the responsibilities of the Gas Council and the area boards, is to be set up. The internal management structure for the industry will be determined by the Corporation.

National Joint Industrial Council for the Gas Industry. Since 1965 there has been a Gas Advisory Council made up of representatives of the Gas Council and the Trade Unions—'to consider and advise the Gas Council about matters concerning the gas industry, in particular the plans and policies of the industry in relation to national objectives for economic growth'.

The industry spent over £2m in the provision of training resources. In 1971, for example, a new training centre was opened in Leeds for the North Eastern Gas Board. All area boards have central training facilities and employ over 400 training staff. Courses are available in management, and sales and clerical training.

Research and Development

Nearly £5m was spent on research in the fields of production, storage, transmission, distribution, etc.

The major research stations are located as follows:

Watson House (Fulham, London). Research is primarily concentrated on the domestic and commercial applications of gas.

Midland Research Station (Solihull). Primarily industrial applications of gas, but also deals with processes for gas manufacture.

London Research Station (Fulham, London). Basic research.

Engineering Research Station (Killingworth, Newcastle-upon-Tyne). Research is primarily concentrated on the engineering aspects of transmission, distribution and storage of gas.

In addition some of the area boards also maintain laboratories and research stations.

Collaboration with other gas industries continued through the Atlantic Gas Research Organisation and the European Gas Research Group.

Consumer Consultation[1]

There is a gas consultative council for each area board—consisting of a chairman and between 20 and 30 members. Not less than half and not more than three-quarters are drawn from local authorities in the area. The remaining members are appointed

[1] 'Second Report from the Select Committee on Nationalised Industries 1970–1', Relations with the Public, pp. xxiv-xxvii. Also Annual Report of each Consultative Council.

to represent commerce, industry, labour and the general interests of consumers.

Within the area of the boards themselves, local consultative committees are also set up.

The consultative councils are required to consider any matter affecting the supply of gas—tariffs, services, etc.—which is brought to their notice by consumers or by the boards themselves. They are in effect two-way communicating channels.

While there is no statutory consultative machinery above the level of the area boards, there are informal meetings twice a year between the Gas Council and the chairmen of the 12 area gas consultative councils.

In the year 1970–1 14,677 representations were considered by the consultative bodies—concerning sales, services, natural gas conversion and accounts.

National Bus Company[1] 1968 (Department of the Environment)

Structure
The N.B.C. with nine members (eight part-time) controls road passenger services on a regional basis in England and Wales as follows:

North Eastern: East Yorkshire; Gateshead & District; Hebble; Northern General Transport; Sunderland District; Tynemouth; Tyneside; United Automobile Services; Venture; West Riding; West Yorkshire; Yorkshire Traction; Yorkshire Woollen District.

North Western: Crosville; Cumberland; North Western; Ribble; Standerwick.

Eastern: Eastern Counties; Eastern National; East Midland; Lincolnshire; Mansfield District; Midland General; Tillings Travel (N.B.C.); Trent; United Counties (took over Luton Municipal).

Midlands: Midland Red; Potteries.

South Wales and West: Black & White; Cheltenham District; Devon General Greenslades; Red & White; South Wales Transport; Western National (took over Exeter Municipal); Western Welsh.

Southern: Aldershot & District; Brighton, Hove & District; City of Oxford; East Kent; Gosport & Fareham; Hants & Dorset; Maidstone & District; Shamrock & Rambler; Southdown; Southern Vectis; South Midland; Thames Valley; Timpson; Wilts & Dorset.

London Country Bus Services Ltd.

[1] 'National Bus Company, Annual Report and Accounts Year Ended 31 December 1970', H.C. 440.

2,568 passenger journeys were carried over 799,000,000 miles.

The N.B.C. also engages in bus manufacture jointly with British Leyland, through Bus Manufacturers (Holdings) Ltd, which consists of Bristol Commercial Vehicles Ltd, Eastern Coach Works Ltd, and the Leyland National integral bus project in Cumberland. There is also, for example, a 28.8-per-cent interest in Park Royal Vehicles.

Finance

The operating deficiency, before tax and interest, was £5·1m; revenue deficiency, after tax and interest, was £8·1m. Net assets were £92·9m but financial objective was not related to this. Capital expenditure was £13·9m.

Occupations and Labour Relations

Total employed was 84,015. Labour relations are conducted through the National Council for the Omnibus Industry and the National Joint Council for Non-Manual Staffs.

National Coal Board[1] 1947 (Department of Trade and Industry)

Structure

The N.C.B. consists of 12 members (four part-time) and is responsible for the running of the coal industry. The industry is divided into the following areas: Scottish North, Scottish South, Northumberland, North Durham, South Durham, North Yorkshire, Doncaster, Barnsley, South Yorkshire, North Western, North Derbyshire, North Nottinghamshire, South Nottinghamshire, South Midlands, Staffordshire, East Wales, West Wales, Kent.

The total output of coal was 142,200,000 tons in 292 collieries.

The Coal Products Division operates coking, manufactured fuel and by-product plants. There are coke ovens, for example, at Coedely, Monkton, Fishburn; a Phurnacite plant at Aberaman and 'Multiheat' plant at Cardiff. It conducts joint ventures with others in off-shore exploration for hydrocarbons, e.g. with Conoco

[1] 'National Coal Board, Report and Accounts 1970–1', vol. I, Report, H.C. 460; vol. II, Accounts and Statistical Tables, H.C. 543, and see 'The Finances of the Coal Industry', Cmnd 2805, Nov. 1965.

and Gulf Oil companies. It oversees the Board's interests in
associated chemical companies, e.g. Nypro U.K. Ltd, Pthalic
Anhydride Chemicals Ltd, Stavely Chemicals Ltd; the last-named
refines crude benzole from the Board's coking plants and produces chlorine, analine, etc. The same firm has a 50-per-cent
interest in Vinatex Ltd, with plants at Staveley and Havant,
Hants, to produce thermoplastics.

Individual brick-making companies are controlled by the
Board, who also have a share in Scottish Brick Co. Ltd. The
Board has, too, an interest in a number of concrete companies
and through these markets prefabricated brick panels.

The Board owns and manages substantial estates, comprising
houses, farms, industrial buildings. On nationalisation, for example, some 140,000 houses were vested in the Board, and 24,400
have been built since through the Coal Industry Housing Association. 142,769 acres of farm land are let to tenant farmers or
licencees; 111,500 acres of closed colliery and waste heap land
is also owned.

There is a minestone Executive whose job is to dispose of
minestone, red shale, etc., in construction work.

The N.C.B. has other activities through joint interest in private
firms engaged in the handling and distribution of solid fuel, e.g.
J. H. Sankey & Son, British Fuel Co., Lancashire Fuel Co. Other
joint enterprises are British Drilling Ltd, and International Reser-
vations Ltd in which the Board has a 50-per-cent interest. This
firm provides a service for booking hotel rooms—with about 750
hotels in Great Britain and Ireland on their list. J. H. Sankey has
itself many subsidiary companies, e.g. Walkers (Brighton),
Walkers (Fareham), Smyth Bros (Ipswich).

The N.C.B. wholly owns British Coal Utilisation Research
Association, and Colmec Transport Ltd.

Finance
The operating profit was £34·m. The surplus, after payment of
net interest charges, was £500,000m. Net assets were £666·7m
but no percentage returns on these has been set in this industry.

Outstanding loans from the D.T.I. totalled £675m. The Coal
Industry Act 1971 provided that part of the social costs of colliery
closures were to be met from the government itself—a diminishing total grant of £24m over the three years to 1974. The Act
also extended for three years the power of the government to

make redundancy payment schemes for workers in the industry. In this Act alone powers are given to the government to direct the Board to review and report on its ancillary companies and on the activities of companies in which it has interests. The Secretary of State at the D.T.I. has now also the power to direct the Board to discontinue or restrict its non-colliery activities.

The total value of capital investment projects in progress at the end of the financial year was £51m.

Occupations and Labour Relations

The total employees were 356,332. The total industrial workers were 320,452—286,034 in coal production.

Labour relations are conducted through separate machinery for colliery workers; workers in coke and by-product plants; and non-industrial staffs. For colliery workers machinery is at colliery, district, and national level.

There are also consultative committees at colliery, area and national level. These discuss safety, health and welfare; the organisation and conduct of the industry; and other matters of mutual interest to employees and the Board. The men's representatives are appointed by the appropriate trade union.

There is a comprehensive system of training and education with, for example, 7,488 apprentices in training under the Mining Apprenticeship scheme. There are schemes for Engineering Craft Apprentices and Student Apprentice Schemes. There are management training schemes at the N.C.B. Staff College at Chalfont St Giles and the associated training centres.

Research and Development

The Mining Research Development Establishment is located at Stanhope Bretby near Burton-on-Trent; the Coal Research Establishment is at Stoke Orchard near Cheltenham.

In 1970-1 emphasis was given to the development of ripping equipment and to the efficiency of coal-face and roadway excavation machinery. Progress was also made in power loading.

Research into all aspects of coal processing and combustion is concentrated at Stoke Orchard.

In marketing there have been developments in the field of district heating.

Consumer Consultation[1]

There are two coal Consumer Councils, the Industrial Coal Consumers' Council and the Domestic Coal Consumers' Council—the staff and expenses of which are paid by the Minister.

Both organisations consider matters concerning the supply of solid fuel brought to their notice by their respective consumers, and annual reports are made to the Minister.

National Freight Corporation[2] 1968. (Department of the Environment)

Structure

The Corporation, with eight members (six part-time), controls directly a number of companies—mainly road haulage—organised into four groups as follows:

Special Traffics: Pickfords Group, e.g. Pickfords Removal, Pickfords Heavy Haulage, Pickfords Tank Haulage, etc.; Harold Wood & Sons; Car Transport (B.R.S.) Ltd; companies in the Tayforth Group, e.g. Caledonian Bulk Liquids, etc.; Road-Air Cargo Express (International) Ltd; Air Link, 55 per cent (with B.E.A. and B.O.A.C.)

Parcels and Small Groups: Bristol Express Carriers Ltd; B.R.S. Parcels Parcels Ltd and subsidiaries—James Express Ltd, N. Francis & Co. Ltd, W. Cooper & Sons Ltd; National Carriers Ltd; B.E.C. Specialised Services Ltd—Bridges Transport Ltd, Hanson Haulage Ltd, H. S. Morgan Southampton Ltd, Scottish Parcel (Carriers) Ltd, Watson (Carriers) Ltd; Tartan Arrow Ltd and subsidiaries.

General Haulage and Container Traffics: British Road Services Ltd and subsidiaries—Castle Bros Haulage Ltd, Corringdon Ltd, F. Crowther & Son Wakefield Ltd, H. & G. S. Bell Ltd, Morton (B.R.S.) Ltd; B.R.S. Contracts Ltd; Freightliners Ltd, 51 per cent—49 per cent B.R.; Containerway & Roadferry Ltd and subsidiaries—Ferry Trailers Ltd, N.V. Containerway S.A.; Tayforth Group (a holding company, Scottish based, controlling many companies); Lawther & Harvey.

Shipping (later the government announced intention to sell): Associated Humber Lines; Atlantic Steam Navigation Co. Ltd.

---

[1] 'Second Report from the Select Committee on Nationalised Industries', *op. cit.*, pp. vi-x.
[2] 'National Freight Corporation, Annual Report and Accounts Year Ended 31 December 1970', H.C. 441.

The range of road transport is wide as is seen from the vehicle
statistics :

Traffic Vehicles and Containers Owned
Powered Units
    Number   27,800
    Aggregate tonnage capacity   252,000
Additional trailers
    Number   25,700
Container and Demountable bodies
    Number   9,200
    Vehicle mileage   564,000,000

The two shipping companies own 19 ships. Atlantic Steam
Navigation, for example, operate to Ireland, Associated Humber-
lines carry cargo and, in particular, passengers between Hull and
Rotterdam.

Overall the various parts of N.F.C. vary in size from B.R.S.
Parcels, N.C.L. and Freightliners to a small body-building company, Star Bodies Ltd at Hollinwood, Oldham.

There are also a number of associated companies owned by
the Transport Holding Company, for example Containerbase
Federation and individual firms, e.g. Containerbase (Leeds),
(Barking), etc.; Northern Ireland Carrier Ltd, 50 per cent; Auto
Freight (N.I.) Ltd, Shipping; Anglo-Irish Transport Ltd; Fisher
Line, etc.

Finance
Profit before long-term interest was £5·6m but after payment of
interest on capital liabilities, etc., the loss was £1·2m.

Net assets were £116·8m but no financial objective was set by
the government in this financial year.

N.B. (i) Under the 1968 Transport Act the Secretary of State
for the Environment makes grants towards losses on 'rail sundries
traffic' and other road collection and delivery—other than in the
freightliner and high capacity containers—formerly carried on by
B.R.S. In 1970 this grant was £13·4m.

(ii) In January 1971 the National Board for Prices and Incomes
reported on the pricing policy of the N.F.C. and its efficiency. The
conclusion was the increases in charges had been necessary and
that the various companies had been taking useful steps to
improve day-to-day operating and efficiency.

Occupations and Labour Relations
The total number of staff employed was 63,500. Given the nature
of the organisation, i.e. the number of companies concerned, the
approach to labour relations is different from other nationalised
industries.

During 1970, however, a Council representing the N.F.C. and
all the appropriate unions was set up to discuss the problems of
the industry and to provide information on which the trade
unions could assess the situation in the firms, and the impact on
their members.

North of Scotland Hydro-Electric Board[1] 1943 (Scottish Office)

Structure
This Board of nine members (eight part-time) was established to
undertake for public electricity supply the development of water
power in the Highlands and Islands and 'to collaborate in carrying
out any measures for the economic development and social
improvement of the North of Scotland.'

Under the Electricity Act of 1947 all public generation and
distribution of electricity in the North of Scotland was put under
the control of the Board.

Finance
Trading surplus was £14·9m; the net surplus after interest
charges, etc., was £92,804.

Net assets were £271·9m. The agreed return on average assets
—taking into account uneconomic rural distribution is six per
cent; the actual return was 5.5 per cent.

Capital expenditure was £11·3m.

Occupations and Labour Relations
The total number of employees was 3,863.

Consumer Consultation
This is the function of the Electricity Consultative Council for
the North of Scotland District.[2]

[1] 'North of Scotland Hydro-Electric Board, Report and Accounts to 31
March 1971', H.C. 411.
[2] See *ibid.*, appendix VIII.

Post Office Corporation[1] 1970 (Ministry of Posts and Telecommunications)

Structure
The Board with seven members (one part-time) controls an organisation which is responsible for Posts, Giro and Remittance Services, Telecommunications, and Data Processing.

The work of the third section is illustrated by that carried out at the computer centre in South Leeds, where for the Post Office there is assembled the information for public telephone directories, etc., with ten million entries, and maintained records and accounts of the Philatelic Bureau. For organisations outside the Post Office the records of the Save-as-you-earn Scheme of the Department of National Savings are kept together with the accounts of some Trustee Banks and the payroll of a number of firms.

Finance[2]
There was a profit of £20·5m—made up of a loss of £72·6m on Post, Giro, etc., a profit of £93·5m on Telecommunications and a loss of £400,000 on the Data Processing Service.

Net assets were £2,839·6m, which were financed mainly by loans from the Minister of £2,163m—with a Eurodollar loan of £7·5m. The financial objective of the Postal Services is to obtain two per cent surplus on total expenditure; in the event the shortfall was £81·5m.

In Telecommunications the aim is to obtain a return of 10 per cent on net assets; the actual return was 9.6 per cent.[3]

In Data Processing the objective is eight per cent; the actual return was 4.1 per cent.

Capital investment was £459·8m.

Occupations and Labour Relations
The staff in Posts, Giro, etc., was 177,248; in Telecommunications 232,377; in Data Processing 3,870—a total of 414,824 (excluding sub-postmasters).

[1] 'Post Office. Report and Accounts for Year Ended 31 March 1971', H.C. 608.
[2] The Giro accounts were shown separately in the 1971–2 accounts.
[3] The return of 10 per cent was, in fact, increased to this figure on 1 July 1970 from 8.5 per cent.

Labour relations are conducted through a system of individual negotiation by the relevant union for the grades concerned, e.g. Association of Post Office Executives, Post Office Engineering Union, Post Office Management Staffs Association, Union of Post Office Workers, etc.

Joint Consultation on efficiency, terms and conditions of employment, health and safety, etc., improvement of equipment, etc., is provided for at headquarters through a National Joint Council, with committees at Regional and Local levels.

In all parts of the Post Office are extensive training arrangements. There are training centres for postmen, etc., at Bletchley, Harrogate, Manchester, Wolverhampton, Bristol, Cardiff, Edinburgh and London. There are telecommunication training centres at, for example, London, Bexhill and Eastbourne. There is a Postal Management College at Rugby, a Post Office Technical Training College at Stone, Staffs, and computer training facilities at St Albans.

Research and Development
There is a great deal of R. & D. work carried out, particularly in telecommunications with work in digital techniques, data communications, waveguides.

The Research Department controls the following research stations (together with staff employed):

	Employed
Dollis Hill	1,131
Martlesham	331
Ipswich	100
Castleton (Cardiff)	31
Blackwell (Bath)	32
Carlton House (Wembley)	5
	1,630

Consumer Consultation[1]
There is a Post Office Users National Council whose membership of 33 represent a cross-section of Post Office users and representa-

[1] See 'Post Office Users National Council Report on the Exercise and Performance of its Functions for the Accounting Year Ended 31 March 1971', H.C. 532. Also, 'Report from the Select Committee on Nationalised Industries Session 1970–1, Relations with the Public', H.C. 514, pp. xxvii–xxxi.

tives of the individual councils for Scotland, Wales and Northern Ireland. Its duty is to consider any matter it wishes, together with those made by users and by the Post Office—which is required to consult before making major changes in its service.

In 1970, for example, the Council reacted sharply to proposals made for tariff changes in the postal service and telecommunication services. It made detailed investigations, in some instances with expert outside help, and followed with its own proposals—some of which were accepted.

There are also some 200 local and voluntary Post Office Advisory Committees set up by Chambers of Trade, etc., which have a link with the P.O.U.N.C.

Scottish Transport Group[1] 1968. (Scottish Office)

Structure
This Group with eight members (seven part-time) controls a variety of travel activities in Scotland—road passenger, insurance, travel and tourism, and shipping, as follows:

Road Passenger: Scottish Bus Group Ltd; W. Alexander & Sons (Fife) Ltd, W. Alexander & Sons (Midland) Ltd, W. Alexander & Sons (Northern) Ltd; Central S.M.T. Co. Ltd; Highland Omnibuses Ltd; Scottish Omnibuses Ltd; Western S.M.T. Co. Ltd.
Insurance: S.M.T. Insurance Co. Ltd.
Travel and Tourism: Travel Press & Publicity Co. Ltd.; Sanderson Travel Service Ltd; Duncan Duffy Ltd; the Garve Hotel Ltd.
Shipping: David MacBrayne Ltd; Caledonian Steam Packet Co. Ltd; Arran Piers Ltd; Bute Ferry Co. Ltd.

The Group operates 4,712 vehicles and owns 35 vessels with a predominance of car and vehicle ferries.

Finance
Loss after depreciation and before interest on long-term borrowings and taxation was £1·4m. Net assets were £25·9m.
Capital expenditure £3m.

Occupations and Labour Relations
Total staff employed was 18,410—mainly in the Road Passenger

[1] 'Scottish Transport Group, Annual Report and Accounts 1970', H.C. 309.

sector, where labour relations are conducted through the National
Council for the Omnibus Industry and training through the Road
Transport Industry Training Board.

South of Scotland Electricity Board[1] 1955. (Scottish Office)

Structure

The Board, with nine members (seven part-time), is responsible
for the generation, transmission and distribution of electricity in
the South of Scotland.

Finance

The balance before interest was £27·3m; after such payments
there was a deficit of £1·1m. Net assets were £455m. The agreed
return on these is seven per cent; the actual return was six per
cent.

Capital investment was £72·9m.

Occupations and Labour Relations

Total employed was 14,111. Labour relations are conducted
through a system common with those for the industry in England
and Wales. There is a separate National Joint Advisory Council
for the two Scottish Boards. There is a training scheme tapering
to the universities. At Cumbernauld there is a technical training
centre.

Consumer Consultation

The Report of the Electricity Council for the South of Scotland
District is appended to the Board's Report.

Transport Holdings Co.[2] 1962. (Department of the Environment)

Structure

The five directors are all part-time. At the end of the financial
year the Company had interests in the following Companies:

Subsidiaries: Thos. Cook & Son Ltd (100 per cent, except

---

[1] 'South of Scotland Electricity Board, Report and Accounts 1970–1',
H.C. 410.
[2] 'Transport Holdings Co., Annual Report and Accounts 1970', H.C.
404.

for 25 per cent minority interests in certain of its overseas subsidiaries); Pickfords Travel Service Ltd (100 per cent); Sir Henry
Lunn Ltd (Lunn-Poly) (95 per cent of ordinary shares).

Associated: Skyways Coach Air Ltd (50 per cent of ordinary
shares); Penarth Dock Engineering Co Ltd (37 per cent of
ordinary shares).

The Company took this reduced form in 1968 when the
National Freight Corporation, etc., was formed. Since the publication of the report, Pickfords Travel Service has been transferred
to the N.F.C.; all the other interests other than Thos. Cook have
been sold; the disposal of this firm will follow in 1972.[1]

Occupations
In the year 1970-1 the Companies in the T.H.C. employed some
3,900 people in the U.K., with some 2,500 overseas. The T.H.C.
itself employed no staff; management services were provided by
the N.F.C.

Bank of England[2] 1946. (Treasury)

Structure
The Court of Directors consists of 18 members, including the
Governor and Deputy Governor. The Bank Charter Act of 1844
which divided its work into that of the issue department and
banking department is still the basis of the structure of the Bank.

The main functions of the Bank are to act as banker to the
government and to implement monetary policy; it is the sole bank
of issue; it is the banker to the commercial banks and is still the
lender of the last resort. Since 1946 the Treasury may give
directions to the Bank.

Although a Central Bank, the Bank has branches in Birmingham, Bristol, Leeds, Liverpool, Manchester, Newcastle upon
Tyne, Southampton and the Law Courts (London). These receive
remittances on behalf of Customs and Excise and Inland
Revenue, handle accounts of official bodies such as Regional

[1] In May 1972 the company was sold to a consortium of Midland Bank
Ltd, Trust House Forte Ltd and the Automobile Association Ltd for
£22·5m.
[2] 'Bank of England, Report and Accounts for Year Ended 28 February
1971'.

Hospital Boards; receive applications for government and other issues undertaken by the Bank; maintain accounts of other banks; and provide facilities for cheque clearance and for exchange control. Branch officials maintain contact with local industry and commerce.[1]

The Bank held equity share capital totalling £185·6m. The principal holdings were:[2]

Agricultural Mortgage Corporation Ltd, shares of £1	24%
Commonwealth Development Finance Co Ltd, 'B' Ordinary Shares	93%
Finance Corporation for Industry Ltd, shares of £10	30%
Portals Holdings Ltd, ordinary stock	32%

The Bank does not seek to influence commercial and financial decisions.

Finance

When the Bank came into public ownership the capital represented by £14,553,000 Bank Stock was transferred to the Treasury. Instead of dividends on Bank Stock the Bank pays to the Treasury twice a year £873,180—the amount of the half-yearly dividend paid for many years to former stockholders and also the amount of the half-yearly interest on the compensation Treasury stock issued to those stockholders.

The profits of the issue department are paid into the National Loans Fund—£145,340,000 at 28 February 1971.

The operating profit of the banking department at the same date was £6·3m. Since 5 October 1971 the profits of this department are paid to the Treasury after agreed provision for reserves and working capital. This change came about as a consequence of the Report of the Select Committee on the Nationalised Industries.[3] Other changes made as a result of recommendations made by this body are that the Bank's accounts are published as part of the annual report; that changes are made for the full cost of the main services provided for government, e.g. exchange

[1] *Bank of England Quarterly Bulletin*, Dec. 1963, Branches of the Bank of England.
[2] The Bank has a shareholding of less than 10 per cent in I.C.F.C., see p. 28, above.
[3] 'Special Report from the Select Committee on the Nationalised Industries', the Committee's Order of Reference, 1968, H.C. 298.

control, management of Exchange Equalisation Account; and that information about the Bank's programme of capital expenditure is provided to the Treasury annually.

Occupations
In February 1971 full-time staff numbered 7,000, which included 1,300 non-clerical staff at the printing works; the banking staff totalled some 4,500.

British Broadcasting Corporation[1] 1926. (Ministry of Posts and Telecommunications)

Structure
The Board of Governors of the B.B.C. consists of 11 part-time members. The Chief Executive is the Director General.

The Corporation provides radio services—with emphasis on the various regions and through 20 local stations—and television services. It has special responsibility for external radio services. Unlike the I.T.A. it not only transmits programmes but is directly responsible for their content.

There are Broadcasting Councils for Scotland and Wales and a series of advisory councils for the expression of views on regional, local radio, agricultural, educational and musical interests.

Finance
The income for Home Services is the licence fees received via the Ministry of Posts and Telecommunications. The deficit was £6m. The income for the external services comes from a grant in aid from the government—in 1971, £13m. There was a small surplus of £63,550 on this account.

The net total assets of the Home Services were £54m; for external services £15·9m.

Occupations and Labour Relations
The total labour force was 23,671 (not including 1,090 part-time); of this total 12,790 were Programme, Technical and Executive.

[1] 'British Broadcasting Corporation, Annual Report and Accounts for Year 1970-1', *Cmnd* 4828, 1971.

Cable & Wireless Ltd[1] 1947. Ministry of Posts and Telecommunications

Structure
This limited liability company wholly owned by the Treasury is an unusual public corporation. The government of the day acquired £2·6m £1 shares in the company by virtue of the Imperial Telegraphs Act 1938 and the remainder of the equity —£27·4m shares—was bought by the government in accordance with the Cable & Wireless Act 1946. In 1950 the assets of the company in the U.K. were transferred to the Post Office. Although there is no statutory obligation on the company to do so, the report and accounts, made in accordance with Company Law, are always formally presented to the Chancellor of the Exchequer and to the Minister of Posts and Telecommunications.

Unlike a nationalised industry where the Minister's powers are closely defined by statute, in this instance as sole shareholders the government's powers are virtually unlimited in law. In practice it does not interfere in day-to-day matters.

The Board consists of ten members. The Chairman is appointed by the Minister, as with nationalised industries, but other appointments are formally made by a shareholders' resolution and are subject to renewal at each general meeting. In practice, three Post Office officials hold one share each as nominees of the Treasury, which holds the rest. This makes for a most curious annual meeting and means that the directors are themselves appointed by the government.

Cable & Wireless own the entire issue share capital of the following companies incorporated in Great Britain:

Cable and Wireless (West Indies) Ltd
Cable and Wireless (Mid-West) Ltd
The Eastern Telegraph Company Ltd
The Western Telegraph Company Ltd
The West Coast of America Telegraph Company Ltd
The Eastern Extension Australasia and China Telegraph Company Ltd
Mercury House Ltd

[1] 'Cable & Wireless Ltd Report and Accounts 31 March 1971'. Also *A Century of Service, a Brief History of Cable & Wireless Ltd 1868–1968*, Cable & Wireless, 1969.

There are other such subsidiaries in Belgium and in the U.S.A.—
with investments in Great Britain, Switzerland, Portugal, Brazil,
Chile, Argentine, Kenya, Nigeria, Sierra Leone, Philippines,
Puerto Rico, Trinidad and Tobago, Jamaica.

The telegraphic traffic carried by the company and its subsidiaries totalled 508,000,000 words; the international telephone
traffic totalled nearly 30,000,000 minutes; telex traffic totalled
over 7,000,000 minutes. The company operates internationally
through cable, radio and satellites.

Finance
The group profit was £3·4m; the net current assets were
£11·4m.

The company is self-financing although it submits annually
to the Treasury a five-year forecast of capital expenditure. Projects costing more than £100,000 must be approved by the
Treasury if they are not expected to yield a 10 per cent return.
The company's capital investment programme is subject to
Treasury scrutiny, on the same lines as the programmes of
nationalised industries, and the company is in general required
to follow, as far as it can, bearing in mind that it operates overseas
often on a concessionary basis, the principles laid down by the
government as regards the financial returns of nationalised
industries.

The company can borrow from the market and not from the
National Loans Fund.

The company comes within the purview of the Select Committee on Nationalised Industries.

Occupations and Labour Relations
The total staff employed by the group was 10,392; in the U.K.
1,281.

Commonwealth Development Corporation[1] 1948. (Foreign and
Commonwealth Office)

Structure
The Corporation consists of 12 part-time members. It replaced
the Colonial Development Corporation in 1963 and provides

[1] 'Commonwealth Development Corporation, Annual Report and Statement of Accounts for Year Ended 31 December 1970', H.C. 376.

finance and management for development projects in Commonwealth countries—and since 1969 in other countries, e.g.
Cameroons, Ethiopia and Indonesia.

The Corporation acts on a commercial basis and often in
partnership with private enterprise or territorial governments.
The Annual Report gives a list of companies in all parts of the
Commonwealth in which the Corporation is a shareholder—in
some cases a 100 per cent holding; in others as small as two
per cent. At 31 December 1970 there were 189 projects, e.g. in
the Caribbean—housing, farming, electricity projects; in Malaysia
—a Water Board, flour milling.

Finance
The surplus for the year was £453, 164. Capital liability to the
government was £123·7m.

Covent Garden Market Authority[1] 1961. (Ministry of Agriculture, Fisheries and Food)

Structure
The Authority of seven part-time members (one nominated by
the Minister of Transport Industries) has the main duties of
providing a market within the Covent Garden area and of re-
building it on the Nine Elms site.

Finance
Revenue consists of rents from trading premises and other
property owned by the Authority, of monies received by way
of tolls, and form car-parking charges.

On revenue account there was a surplus of £126,800, but the
deficit on the profit and loss account—after the interest charges
and payments on advances to the Minister—was £916,700.

The Authority's financial objective, as laid down in Section
37 of the 1961 Act, is to secure that income is sufficient to meet
revenue expenditure, taking one year with another. The Authority
have not been able to achieve this while the market remains at
Covent Garden, and the Government accept that the Authority
are unlikely to be able to do so until the market has settled down
in its new location and has successfully established itself there.

[1] 'Covent Garden Market Authority Report and Accounts for the
Accounting Period 30 September 1971'. See also the First Report 1961–2,
p. 4, for Duties and Powers of the Authority.

In the new market a very large part of the Authority's income will be needed to service the capital borrowed from the new market.

Occupations and Labour Relations
The staff employed was as follows: Administrative, 24; Industrial, 54.

The Housing Corporation[1] 1964. (Department of the Environment, Scottish and Welsh Office)

The Corporation of eight part-time members was set up to stimulate the formation of Housing Societies which provide dwellings either for co-ownership or for unsubsidised rent.[2]

The Corporation gives advice and assistance to the 1,275 registered societies on legal procedures, etc. Its regional staff visit estates and liaises with local authorities and the New Towns Corporation on the provision of land.

In the year ended 31 March 1971, 6,006 dwellings were completed; a total of 18,184. Activity is nationwide but concentrated in the south-east.[3]

Finance
Some building societies provide two-thirds of the cost of approved schemes, the Corporation provides the remaining third.

The total amounts outstanding to Housing Societies was £55·9m; the total government advances were £53·9m.

A small surplus of £68,249 was made because the average rate of interest on total amount borrowed was lower than the current rate chargeable.

Occupations
Total staff employed was 93 executive, administrative and clerical.

[1] 'Seventh Report of the Housing Corporation for the Year Ended 31 March 1971', H.C. 542. Also *H.C. Official Report*, 22 July 1971, vol. 821, col. 1595, Housing Corporation Advances.
[2] In July 1971 the Government announced a bigger role for the Corporation: principally that all associations providing houses for rent will be able to use financial resources provided; see 'Fair Deal for Housing', *Cmnd* 4728.
[3] See 'Annual Report', *op. cit.*, and *Living Ownership*, Housing Corporation.

Independent Television Authority[1] 1954. (Ministry of Posts and Telecommunications)

Structure

The Authority consists of 11 part-time members. The Chief Executive is the Director General.

The I.T.A. owns the transmitting stations and is responsible for content and quality of the programmes provided by the 15 programme companies.

There is a General Advisory Council and those for the expression of views on regional, religious, educational, medical and advertising matters.

Finance

The I.T.A. receives no licence revenue. Its revenue comes from the rent paid by the programme companies who also pay a levy to I.T.A. for onward transmission to the Exchequer.

The surplus after taxation was £1·98m. Net assets were £21·9m. The aim of the Authority since its inception has been to secure an income which is at least sufficient to meet its operating costs, to meet depreciation, to maintain a Reserve Fund, and to cover capital expenditure.

Occupations and Labour Relations

The total labour force was 981; with 538 at H.Q., 58 in the Regions and 385 at the stations. Some 50 per cent of these are classified as engineering and professional.

The programme companies are in the private sector and have their own negotiating arrangements.

National Dock Labour Board[2] 1947. (Department of Employment)

Structure

The Board consists of ten part-time members; in practice four members represent employers and four the trade unions.

---

[1] 'Independent Television Authority, Annual Report and Accounts, 1970–71', H.C. 3. N.B. As a result of the Sound Broadcasting Act (1972) which made possible independent local radio, the I.T.A. was renamed the Independent Broadcasting Authority on 12 July 1972.
[2] 'National Dock Labour Board, 24th Annual Report, together with Statement of Accounts at 2 January 1971'. See also *The Dock Workers Employment Scheme*, N.D.L.B., 1967.

The object of the Board is to implement the Dock Workers Employment Scheme of 1947 set up to regularise the casual system of employment and thus to secure and maintain an adequate number of efficient dock workers in regular employment. To this end there is maintained a register of work people and employers and facilities provided for medical care, welfare and training. There are representative local Dock Labour Boards in 20 groups of ports, e.g. Tyne and Wear, South Wales, etc., to implement the scheme locally.

The Board also administers the National Voluntary Severance Scheme at the request of the National Joint Council for the Port Transport Industry.

Finance
The funds for the Board's activities are raised by a levy on employers. Government loans are provided only for the National Voluntary Severance Scheme.

Occupations and Labour Relations
Total staff employed by the Board is 660—this includes 75 medical officers and nursing staff.

Collective bargaining in the industry is conducted through the National Joint Council for the Port Transport Industry.

There are training schools in Hull, London, Southampton, Bristol, Barry, Liverpool, Manchester and Grangemouth.

National Film Finance Corporation[1] 1949. (Department of Trade and Industry)

Structure
The Corporation, with five members (four part-time), has the function of providing a source of finance to the British Film Industry.

Among the films partially financed by the Corporation have been *The Third Man*, *Genevieve*, and *Saturday Night and Sunday Morning*.

[1] 'National Film Finance Corporation, Annual Report and Statement of Accounts for Year Ended 31 March 1971', *Cmnd* 4761. See also 'National Film Finance Consortium, Memorandum from the NFFC', Sept. 1971, and John Stapleton, 'Abandoned Cinema', *Socialist Commentary*, Nov. 1971.

Finance
The loss for the year was £305,786. Losses are more typical than profits in this speculative field.

Since 1949 the government has provided funds to the Corporation and in 1970 made available £5m to keep it in being for a further ten years. In June 1971 the government announced a change of policy—the Corporation would aim to achieve independence of government financial support and would act only through a joint consortium with private industry to which a maximum of £1,000,000 could be contributed. The policy of the consortium will have to be only commercially motivated.

Occupations and Labour Relations
The staff totals 13.

National Ports Council[1] 1964. (Department of the Environment)

Structure
The Council of 11 members (nine part-time) was set up following the Rochdale Committee and the Harbours Act of 1964. Its prime aim is to formulate and keep under review a national plan for the development of harbours in Great Britain. Based on this its duties are to promote the execution of plans after approval by the Department of Trade and Industry; to encourage harbour authorities to exercise and perform their functions as efficiently as possible; and to advise the government on action required to secure the improvement, maintenance and management of harbours and on the provision of adequate road and rail access to such harbours.

Finance
The Council is financed by a levy on harbour authorities—in particular the P.L.A. and B.T.D.B. A grant towards the cost of research is made by the government.

[1] 'National Ports Council, Annual Report and Statement of Accounts for Year Ended 31 December 1970', H.C. 408. See also 'Financial Policy for Ports', *Cmnd* 4794, 1971. N.B. In May 1971 it was announced that the Council was reconstituted so as to be completely disassociated from individual ports.

Occupations and Labour Relations

The total staff is 83, 41 of whom are professional, i.e. accountants, economists, engineers, master mariners, scientists and statisticians.

The primary aim of the Council's training policy are: the stimulation of training activities in all parts of the port industry; to conduct research into training needs; and to promote such training courses as are proved necessary where they are not provided elsewhere.

Research and Development

The Council have a responsibility in research and a small staff of scientists and engineers are employed who undertake minor reasearch projects but for bigger projects consultants are engaged. The four main areas for consideration have been—port approaches and docking facilities, dock operations and berth design, cargo distribution and assembly, research aids to planning and control.

Information on research results and statistical information generally is published for the use of the port owners.

National Research Development Corporation[1] 1949. (Department of Trade and Industry)

Structure

The Corporation, with 12 members (ten part-time), has the following functions:

(i) Securing, where the public interest so requires, the development or exploitation of inventions resulting from public research, and of any other invention as to which it appears to the Corporation that it is not being developed or exploited or sufficiently developed or exploited.

(ii) Acquiring, holding, disposing of and granting rights (whether gratuitously or for consideration) in connection with

[1] 'National Research Development Corporation, 22nd Annual Report and Accounts for Year Ended 31 March 1971', H.C. 553. See also N.R.D.C. leaflet no. 1, 'An Introduction'; no. 4, 'Help for the Inventor'; no. 5, 'Finance for Project and Development'; and 'National Research Development Corporation—a Service to Industry, Inventions for Industry', Sept. 1971, N.R.D.C. For a historical study see Peter Fairley, *Project X*, Mayflower Books, 1970.

inventions resulting from public research and, where the public interest so requires, in connection with inventions resulting from other sources.

(iii) Promoting and assisting, where the public interest so requires, research for satisfying specific practical requirements brought to the knowledge of the Corporation where they are of the opinion that the research is likely to lead to an invention.

(iv) Assisting, where the public interest so requires, the continuation of research where it appears to the Corporation that the research has resulted in any discovery such that the continuation of the research may lead to inventions of practical importance.

Internally the Corporation's activities are carried out by a Department of Applied Science—Biological and Agricultural Sciences Group, Industrial Chemistry Group, Scientific Equipment Group; a Department of Engineering—Mechanical and Civil Engineering Group, Computers and Automation Group, Electrical Engineering and Electronics Group, Production Machinery.

The subsidiary companies are:		Shares held
A.F. Hydraulics Ltd (hydraulic mechanisms)	Ordinary	50%
C.C.V. (Patent Holdings) Ltd (common cold vaccine)	"	100%
Dracone Developments Ltd (flexible barges)	"	51%
Energy Conversion Ltd (fuel cells)	"	100%
F.N.R.D. Ltd (automatic oil well drilling rig)	"	63%
Hovercraft Development Ltd (hovercraft)	"	100%
Tracked Hovercraft Ltd (tracked hovercraft)	"	100%

The associated companies, i.e. with equity share capital held of less than 50 per cent, were:

		Shares held
Advanced Materials Engg. Ltd	Ordinary	44%
Arcturus Electronics Ltd	"	33.3%
Auto Taxi Development Ltd	"	49%
British Hovercraft Corporation Ltd	"	10%
Cammell Laird (Sea Bed Engg.) Ltd	"	49%
Cotron Electronics Ltd	"	26%
Digimatics Ltd	"	20%
Floform Ltd	"	33.7%
G.N.R.D. (Patent Holdings) Ltd	"	25%
Klarcrete Ltd	"	44%
Oxford Aerosols Ltd	"	26%
Polaron Instruments Ltd	"	13%
Process Peripherals Ltd	"	26.1%
Revenue Systems Ltd	"	44.2%
Technograph Ltd	"	19.4%

Tekdata Ltd	„	30%
Whatman Biochemicals Ltd	„	24%
Wrexham Wire Co. Ltd	„	20%

During 1970-71, 96 new development projects were undertaken with total current projects of 404.

The type of support involved here ranged from the acceptance of all the administrative responsibility and finance to the sharing with a third party, e.g. a joint venture with industry—computer developments with International Computers, automation activities with Elliot Automation Ltd. Other projects have derived from publicly supported research carried out in Government research laboratories and from the Research Councils, Universities, and private sources.

The Corporation recoups its investments by levy arrangements and/or equity shareholdings (see companies above), or by royalties.

96 U.K. and overseas licence agreements were made, with a total of 560 in force, e.g. Cephalosporim—Medical Research Council/Oxford University; dental cement—Manchester University; carbon fibres—Royal Aircraft Establishment.

It will be noted that the 'company mechanism' for financial recovery purposes has been applied to only 25 situations out of 960.

Finance

The financial duty of the Corporation is to secure that 'the return to them from their activities shall be sufficient to meet their outgoings on revenue account, taking one year with another. In the event the profit interest was £68,960.'

For the first time income exceeded £6m. The consolidated licence income was £3·7m; levies from development projects were £2·4m. £5·8m was invested in development projects.

Occupations and Labour Relations

The total staff is some 260. Of these about 140 are secretaries, clerks, etc.; the remainder are scientifically, technically or otherwise professionally qualified.

The total staff of N.R.D.C. and its subsidiaries is 419. Tracked Hovercraft employ some 165 of these—which puts the size of the other companies in perspective.

Research and Development

The Corporation sets up research and development establishments where no facilities already exist, e.g. the production of acetylene from methane and the development of hovercraft in the past and tracked hovercraft now.

New Town Development Corporations[1] (various dates) (Department of the Environment, Welsh Office and Scottish Office)

Structure

The Corporations have been set up at varying dates since 1947, and new towns have been built in England and Wales at Aycliffe, Basildon, Bracknell, Corby, Cumbran, Harlow, Milton Keynes, Newtown, Northampton, Peterborough, Peterlee, Redditch, Runcorn, Skelmersdale, Stevenage, Telford, Warrington and Washington; in Scotland at Cumbernauld, East Kilbride, Glenrothes, Irvine and Livingstone.

The membership of each corporation is limited to nine part-time members. They are responsible for housing, planning, site development, public building and site—i.e. schools, churches, health centres, etc.—acquisition of land and industry. Their primary purpose is to relieve congestion in the great cities and to offer a healthier environment.

In each town there is a local coordinating committee for liaison on matters such as housing, arts, sport and recreation, main roads, etc.

The following information concerning the 18 towns in England and Wales illustrates the extent of their activities by 31 March 1971.

1 (a) Total dwellings constructed by development corporations   109,856
  (b) Total rented stock   106,650
2 Total population (estimated to 31 Dec. 1970)   1,025,000
3 Total factory space constructed by development corporations or on land made available to them   24,997,390 sq. ft.

[1] 'Reports of Development Corporations, 31 March 1971', H.C. 550. Also 'Reports of the Cumbernauld, East Kilbride, Glenrothes, Irvine and Livingstone Development Corporations for Year Ended 31 March 1971', H.C. 550. N.B. The Development Corporation for Central Lancashire New Town had not been effectively constituted by the end of the financial year; no report was submitted.

The following information illustrates the Scottish activities at the same date:

1 Total number of Corporation dwellings   40,129
2 Total population   198,166
3 Total factory space provided since designation   10,859,891 sq. ft.

Finance
Finance is provided by the government in the form of loans repayable over a period of 60 years with a fixed rate of interest. As at 31 March 1971, the total sum advanced by the Exchequer for the 18 towns was £561·7m; in Scotland £192·3m.

Total capital investment was £548m. Capital investment in the year was £87·7m.

Occupations and Labour Relations
Total number of employees in England and Wales on 30 June 1971 was 7,754, and in Scotland at 31 March 1971 it was 2,129.

Commission for the New Towns[1] 1962 (Department of the Environment)

Structure
The membership of the Commission is limited to nine part-time members. It is responsible for the management of houses, factories and shops in the four towns under its control—Crawley, Hatfield, Hemel Hempstead and Welwyn Garden City. These towns were formerly under development corporation control and it is anticipated that at a later stage the other corporations will hand over their properties to the Commission. In each town the Commission is advised by local committees' within the general policy of the Commission and the requirements of the Department'.

The following information illustrates the extent of the activities by 31 March 1971.

[1] 'Report of the Commission of the New Towns for the Period Ended 31 March 1971. Crawley, Hatfield, Hemel Hempstead, Welwyn Garden City', H.C. 551.

1 (a) Total dwellings constructed by the
      Commission   35,068
   (b) Dwellings built and let by the
      Commission   32,278
2 Total population   208,350
3 Total factory space constructed by the
   Commission or on land made available
   by them   10,969,511 sq. ft.

Finance
No advances were required, as the Commission was able to finance the whole of their capital programme from the proceeds of sale of land and buildings and the revenue surplus for the year.

Total capital invested was £113·3m. Capital investment in the year was £3·2m.

Occupations and Labour Relations
The total employees were 1,030.

The Scottish Special Housing Association[1] 1937 (Scottish Office)

Structure
This Association was established as a company limited by guarantee with no shares. Its Council of Management consists of seven part-time members.

The original purpose of the organisation was to erect houses for the working classes in 'special areas' of Scotland by supplementing the programme of the local authorities. In 1938 powers were given to build outside these but only by non-traditional methods for purposes of experiment and demonstration; in 1944 in any area where there was need; and in 1957, outside the area of an 'exporting authority', for overspill population.

In addition, houses have been built for miners transferred to developing districts, and since 1962 the association has been empowered to convert or improve. In Scotland it acts on behalf of the Housing Corporation, and of government departments, e.g. hospital boards needing houses for their staff. In the event

[1] 'Scottish Special Housing Association, Annual Report 31 March 1971'.

of unsatisfactory tenders, the association may build for local authorities.

The total houses owned is 74,574 and in 1970–1 4,202 houses were built; 2,676 by private contractors and 1,526 by the Direct Labour Department.

Finance
Income is received from rents and subsidies; deficit on housing revenue account was £1·3m. Capital expenditure was £14·9m; a total since 1937 of £168·3m.

Occupations and Labour Relations
The total staff employed was 714.

Research and Development
There is a Joint Housing Development Unit of the Association and the Scottish Development Department set up to carry out R. & D. into housing problems.

The association has paid special attention to computerised techniques in quantity surveying and, together with the Department of the Environment, is financing research by the Architectural Research Unit of Edinburgh University.

The Sugar Board[1] 1957 (Ministry of Agriculture, Fisheries and Food)

Structure
The Board of five members (four part-time) buys sugar under the Commonwealth Sugar Agreement and sells it commercially. The Sugar Corporation is a company in which the Board has £2·5m of shares, and contracts to buy the whole of the home-produced sugar beet crop from a specified acreage (at present 443,000 acres) at a scale of fixed charges determined as a result of the annual farm price review, and related to sugar content. The Corporation processes the beet into sugar and sells it on the open market. It also sells the by-products.

[1] 'Sugar Board, Thirteenth Report and Accounts for Year Ended 31 December 1970'.

Finance
The deficits of surpluses which result from the transactions of both the Corporation and the Board are shown in the accounts of the latter. When these shown a deficit a levy is charged on all sugar, imported or home-produced, entering the British market. When there is a surplus a distribution payment is made—so that taking one year with another the Board balances its accounts.

Occupations and Labour Relations
Total staff was 21.

Northern Ireland

The national accounts cover Northern Ireland; the following organisations which operate only in the province are included in the public corporations group.

Electricity Board for Northern Ireland[1] 1931 (Ministry of Commerce, N. Ireland)

The Board with six part-time members is responsible for the generation and distribution of electricity; it also sells electrical appliances, etc. With the Belfast Corporation and the Londonderry Development Commission the Board is controlled by the Northern Ireland Joint Electricity Authority.[2]

Northern Ireland Housing Trust[3] 1945 (Ministry of Development, N. Ireland)

This Trust, consisting of five part-time members, had the function of building houses to meet the housing shortage in the Province.

In October 1971 the Trust was ended and a new housing organisation, a Northern Ireland Housing Executive, was set up progressively to take over its function—together with those of the local authorities and the New Towns Commissions (see below).

[1] 'Electricity Board for Northern Ireland, 39th Annual Report and Accounts for year ended 31 March 1971'.
[2] From 1 April 1973 these organisations are to be subsigned into the N.1 Electrical Service.
[3] 'Final Report of the Northern Ireland Housing Trust 1971'.

Northern Ireland Transport Holding Company[1] 1968 (Ministry of Development, N. Ireland)

This company with eight part-time members took over the function of the Ulster Transport Authority in 1968. It is responsible for Northern Ireland Carriers Ltd, Ulsterbus Ltd, Northern Ireland Railways Company Ltd and, since September 1970, for Northern Ireland Airports Ltd.

New Town Development Commissions (various dates) (Ministry of Development)

These commissions are covered at present in the Central Statistical Office statistics under the heading New Towns Development Corporations (see p. 170).

The Northern Ireland Commissions are Craigavon (1965), Antrim and Ballymena (1967), Londonderry (1968).

General

Structure

The number of public corporations has increased since 1945 but within this increase new corporations have been born and others have died. For example, the Raw Cotton Commission, which commenced its activities on 1 January 1948, wound them up on 1 January 1968. The National Service Hostels Corporation Ltd existed from 1941 to 1956; the Festival Gardens Ltd from 1949 to 1953; and the Overseas Food Corporation from 1948 to April 1955.

In other instances existing corporations were succeeded by others, e.g. the Iron and Steel Corporation of Great Britain was in existence from 1951 to 1953, and was succeeded by the Iron and Steel Holding and Realisation Agency and its subsidiaries— the remaining one of which was vested in the British Steel Corporation when it was set up in July 1967. The Agency itself was dissolved in September 1967.

[1] 'Northern Ireland Transport Holding Company Report and Accounts, Year Ended 31 March 1971'.
[2] For full information see *National Accounts and Statistics, Sources and Methods*, *op. cit.*, annex pp. 249, 250. For details of recent changes see *National Income and Expenditure*, Central Statistical Office, 1971, p. 104.

In electricity there have been a succession of Corporations from the Central Electricity Board of 1926 to 1948; the British Electricity Authority and Area Boards of 1948 to 1955, when the Central Electricity Authority with Area Boards and South of Scotland Electricity Board was created. The Authority and Boards were reorganised into an Electricity Council, Central Electricity Generating Board and Area Electricity Boards in December 1957.

In transport the British Transport Commission was in existence from 1948 until 1952, when it was recreated as five separate corporations—the British Railways Board, the London Transport Board, the British Transport Docks Board, the British Waterways Board and the Transport Holdings Company. In 1968 there was a regrouping of businesses forming part of this T.H.C., when the National Freight Corporation and the National Bus Company were set up. The London Transport Board transferred to the local government sector on 1 January 1970—with its London County Services transferring to the National Bus Company.[1] The N.B.C. and the N.F.C. like the T.H.C. before them, was a new type of organisation in the public corporation field.

British South American Airways, created in 1946, was then absorbed by B.O.A.C. in 1949. All the activities of Cable and Wireless Ltd were incorporated in that public corporation from 1947 until 1950 when the U.K. assets were taken over by the Post Office. That part of the Great Northern Railway Board in Northern Ireland in existence from 1953 to 1958 was then absorbed in the Ulster Transport Authority, which itself was acquired by the Northern Ireland Transport Holding Company in April 1968.

In 1971 changes in the structure of the Gas Industry were announced to take effect in 1973; in the same year the first steps were taken to sell or transfer the remaining assets of the Transport Holding Company.

On 1 April 1972 the British Airways Board assumed its full responsibilities for B.O.A.C. and B.E.A.; its first report on organisation announced changes in the structure of the two individual Corporations which could lead to a merger.[2]

The basic common factor in the structure of the corporations

[1] See p. 88, above.
[2] British Airways Board, 'First Report on Organisation', H.C. 386, July 1972.

is a board whose members are selected to cover a wide range of experience in, for example, commerce or labour relations.

In this latter respect a former trade union official is often appointed but in no sense is such a person regarded as a representative of trade unions as a whole. In the case, however, of the 'non-nationalised' public corporations, there is a sense in which a part-time member could be regarded as a representative of interests involved. For example, Mr Jack Jones of the T.G.W.U. is a part-time member of the National Ports Council. Other non-union members of this body also have a representative function.

The chairman of the public corporation, and particularly of the nationalised industry, typifies one aspect of the modern industrial state—sometimes as a politician, *vide* Lord Robens of the N.C.B. or later Mr Richard Marsh of British Rail; sometimes a technocrat, *vide* Lord Beeching of British Rail or Sir Henry Jones of the Gas Council. Such men would find their way into any modern version of the *Forsyte Saga*. They are extremely powerful and often less amenable to governmental control than their private counterparts.[1]

The internal structure of the corporations varies from time to time to meet the new needs of the industry, including new and developing techniques of financial management. For example, in B.E.A. there has developed a 'profit centre' concept.

Finance

The annual profits, however defined, of the corporations are not meaningful without a knowledge of the pricing policy followed; the nature of the product or service provided—e.g. in 1970–1 all the world airlines were in 'profit' trouble; and the state of the industry before take-over, e.g. the under-investment of the 1960s in steel led to the inheritance of obsolescent and insufficiently maintained plant, one result of which is a low level of labour productivity. In some industries, e.g. coal and railways, profit is difficult to obtain because of the nature of the industry. In its time 'electricity' has made a profit and could still be adjudged inefficient.

The fact is that the term 'profit', in both the public or private sector, is not meaningful unless it is qualified with other relevant information. There have developed also more sophisticated

[1] C. A. R. Crosland, *The Future of Socialism*, Cape, 1956, p. 30.

accounting concepts in both sectors, and in the case of the public corporations the state has laid down certain criteria as financial objectives. These have changed over the years with changed political attitudes and with changes in the corporations themselves.

In the first instance the statutory duties of the public corporations were set out in the Acts of Parliament which set them up. Given the nature of the products and the services involved, it is in the nationalised group that discussion has taken place in this respect and the relevant changes introduced. In this group initially the duties broadly were to meet the demand for their product in the most efficient way, and to conduct their finances so that over time they at least broke even—after making a contribution to reserves.

No guidance was given on 'efficiency' and the standard of financial performance was defined in terms of surplus or deficit. This differs from the ordinary private sector concept of profit and loss, in that provision had to be made for all items properly chargeable to revenue under the statutes.

This standard of performance was made more specific in the White Paper of 1961 on the 'Financial and Economic Obligations of the Nationalised Industries', where the statutory provisions were interpreted as meaning that industries should aim to balance their accounts 'taking one year with another' over a period of five years—after providing for interest, and depreciation at historic cost. Provision was also to be made for future capital development programmes.[1]

Financial objectives or targets were to be determined for each undertaking in the light of its 'needs and capabilities'. In practice, as we have seen in the individual corporations, targets have been expressed as a rate of return on the undertaking's assets.

No such target has been made for coal; the one for steel only emerged in mid-1972.

In the White Paper of 1967 'Nationalised Industries. A Review of Economic and Financial Objectives', which returned to the same theme of financial performance, a broader and more sophisticated approach was revealed.[2] Investment projects were normally to show a satisfactory return in commercial terms unless they were justifiable on wider criteria involving an assessment of

[1] *Cmnd* 1337, April 1961.
[2] *Cmnd* 3437, Nov. 1967.

the social costs and benefits involved, or were provided to meet a statutory obligation.

On the matter of the commercial appraisal of investment the 'discounted cash flow technique' already in use to some degree was recommended. The test rate of discount was laid down at eight per cent.

On social cost—and this was a period of renewed discussion on this theme particularly in the field of transport—the concept of social cost benefit analysis was recommended.[1] As wider considerations were involved here than were the concern of the corporations themselves, then the analysis should be carried out with the relevant government department.

On prices—and this was the time of the Labour Party's agonies on prices and incomes—the policy was expressed thus: 'provided that industries, on balance, meet their targets over the period as a whole, they can, and should, carry out their pricing policies so as to fit in with the government's general overall policy for prices and incomes'. All major price increases had to be submitted to the National Board for Prices and Incomes.[2]

The summing up on financial performance in general was as follows:

> The setting of objectives for those industries which have not got them or the replacement of those which expire cannot be solely an arithmetical exercise, and in its discussions with the industries the Government will take into account the considerations—return on new investment, soundly based pricing policy, social obligations not covered by a subsidy, efficient operation, national prices and incomes policy—mentioned above. Unlike the common test rate of return on new investment, these objectives will in practice be different for each industry and for the various Area Boards because they will reflect different statutory and social obligations, conditions of demand, domestic costs and other factors peculiar to the individual undertaking. It will not be true therefore that a higher target necessarily indicates a more efficient industry.

Flexibility was maintained by the fact that the obligations

[1] See also 'Transport Policy', *Cmnd* 3057, July 1966.
[2] David Coombes, *State Enterprise. Business or Politics*, P.E.P., Allen & Unwin, 1971, ch. 7.

were to be fulfilled over a period of years and industries had not necessarily to meet their targets every year.

The current objectives are listed below.

THE NATIONALISED INDUSTRIES: FINANCIAL OBJECTIVES

Industry	Objective	Period Covered
National Coal Board	To earn revenue not less than sufficient for meeting all out-goings properly chargeable to revenue account	1970/71– 1971/72
Electricity Boards (England and Wales)	7% net*	1969/70– 1973/74
North of Scotland Hydro-Electric Board	6% net*	1970/71– 1973/74
South of Scotland Electricity Board	7% net*	1970/71– 1973/74
Gas Boards	7% net*	1969/70– 1973/74
British Steel Corporation**	Under discussion but to be set in the spring of 1972 to have effect for a period of 4 or 5 years	
Post Office Postal Services	To achieve a surplus equal to 2% of total expenditure as defined in Statement A on the 1966/67 Accounts	1968/69– 1972/73
Telecommunications	10% net*	July 1970 –1972/73
Data Processing Service	8% net*	1968/69– 1971/72
Giro	To make a positive contribution to Post Office finances within one year, and to cover its overheads including interest on assets and losses within 5 years, from the introduction of new tariffs on 1 July 1972	1972/77
British Overseas Airways Corporation	12½% net*	1966/67– 1971/72
British European Airways Corporation	8% net*	1968/69– 1971/72
British Airports Authority	14% net*	1969/70– 1971/72

Industry	Objective	Period Covered
British Railways Board	Target surplus of £17,000,000 over and above interest on capital and historic depreciation. To apply on an average of good and bad years	1971,
British Waterways Board	Each of these bodies has the statutory obligation to secure that the combined revenues of the authority and of its sub-	
Transport Holding Co.	sidiaries taken together are not less than sufficient to meet	
National Freight Corporation	their combined charges pro- perly chargeable to revenue	
Scottish Transport Group	account, taking one year with another	
British Transport Docks Board†	To earn a surplus after historic depreciation of £7,100,000 before interest.	1970
	To achieve by 1975 a return of not less than 9% on average net assets after provision for historic depreciation but before interest	1971–75
National Bus Co.‡	To earn an average surplus of £8,000,000 a year after pro- viding for depreciation on a historic cost basis but before interest and taxation and before providing for the dif- ference between depreciation charged on the historic cost basis and the current cost of replacing its assets	1971

Notes

* Income before interest but after depreciation at historic cost, expressed as a percentage of average net assets.

** The financial objective was announced by the Minister for Industry on 9 August 1972. At the same time he announced that for 1972–3 the British Steel Corporation would work within a loss limit of £70m and keep its increase in net borrowing within a limit of £300m. The corres- ponding limits set for 1971/72 were £100m and £300m.

† This objective set differs from that of most other industries. It was accepted that charges for the ports generally had been unrealistically low for some years and consequently the Department of the Environment agreed that the budgetted return for 1971 should be 5½ per cent on net assets with the longer-term target to be achieved by 1975.

The important element in the financial objectives set down
is return on capital. Capital is important in another respect; the
details given of the individual corporations show the large amount
of capital employed over a wide range of activities, with assets
in land, buildings and equipment of all kinds—road vehicles,
railway engines and aircraft. This is particularly true of the
nationalised industries to which on 30 June 1971 there was
outstanding £9,562m of advances.[1] In the Table following, the
size of their total net assets and of their fixed investment, reveals
their significance to the economy as a whole.

The annual capital expenditures, part of which is financed by,
and the whole of which is controllable by, the government—is
an important element in the Keynesian-type macro-control of
the economy.

By their very nature the public corporations have no shareholders and, as the above Table shows, in consequence large
sums of capital are borrowed from the government. The proportion these government loans form of total fixed investment varies,
but is high in the capital intensive industries.

At the time of public ownership, where appropriate, compensation stock was issued to the former owners. This became part of
the capital of the corporations and the interest on it was a charge
on the revenue.

Further capital needs were to be met from internal sources or
from the issue of further stock and, where an interest or capital
repayment guarantee was involved, Treasury approval was
required.

There was much discussion on this practice over the years in
the context of the need to maintain 'discipline' in the money
market, and eventually major capital requirements, other than
internal financing, came only from the government. Today the
source is the National Loans Fund which also makes similar

---

‡ No target was set by the government for 1972 because, in the words
of the Minister of Transport Industries, 'Having accepted that increases
in their charges in 1972 should be held to the 5 per cent limit
suggested by the C.B.I. both undertakings will inevitably make heavy
losses during the year.' It was evident that these losses would not be
recouped even over a reasonable period and the government decided
to make then the special grants under the Transport (Grants) Bill
introduced in early 1972.
[1] H.C. Official Report, vol. 827, no. 25, col. 256, 6 Dec. 1971.

NATIONALISED INDUSTRIES 1970–1[1]

	Average net Assets	Net income	Net income as a % of net assets	Fixed investment in U.K. Estimated Outturn (N.L.F. White Paper)	Government loans (Net Estimated Outturn (N.L.F. White Paper)	Government loans as a % of fixed Investment	Total Employees at March 1971
	£000	£000	%	£m	£m	%	000
1 National Coal Board	666,600	36,400	5.5	74.5	9.0	12.1	356
2 Electricity Council and Boards	4,958,000	204,700	4.1	380.0	187.0	49.2	188
3 N.S.H.-E.B.	269,400	14,900	5.5	12.6	14.3	113.5	4
4 S.S.E.B.	455,000	27,350	6.0	68.6	41.4	60.3	14
5 Gas Council and Boards	1,760,000	108,700	6.2	203.8	133.2	65.4	116
6 British Steel Corporation	1,234,669	40,955	3.3	130.0	43.0	33.1	252
7 Post Office	2,680,533	156,772	5.8	444.0	253.4	57.1	415
8 B.O.A.C.	251,246	10,569	4.2	79.2	−16.9	—	24
9 B.E.A.	166,165	8,480	5.1	35.4	41.1	116.1	25
10 British Airports Authority	72,782	8,934	12.3	10.5	− 0.3	—	4
11 British Railways Board	863,000	51,700	6.0	91.8	15.0	16.3	273
12 British Transport Docks Board	127,200	4,411	3.5	12.0	7.3	60.8	11
13 British Waterways Board	8,394	407	4.8	0.8	0.2	25.0	3
14 Transport Holding Company	7,484	−300	—	0.8	—	—	—
15 National Freight Company	108,300	5,600	5.2	26.0	15.0	57.7	63
16 National Bus Company	96,950	−4,700	—	13.9	2.0	14.4	84
17 Scottish Transport Group	24,819	−3,158	—	3.5	—	—	18
TOTALS 1-17	13,750,542	671,720	4.9	1,587.4	744.7	46.9	1,850

[1] For Government Financing see, 'Loans from the National Loans Fund 1971-2', Cmnd 4635, 1971. N.B. Surface transport figures refer to calendar year 1970.

loans to local authorities and parts of the private sector.[1]

The loans made to the nationalised industries in the year 1970–1 were estimated to be £704m. Further estimated loans of £151m were made to the New Towns and Development Corporations and Commission; Scottish Special Housing Association; Housing Corporation; Covent Garden Market Authority; Sugar Board; and at that time the Industrial Reorganisation Corporation.[2]

The Corporations may also borrow long-term from abroad and temporarily from the banks, etc.

Compensation, and thus the initial capital of the nationalised industries, was based on stock exchange valuations. This had little to do with real earnings and as a result some industries, e.g. coal and rail transport were over-capitalised. B.O.A.C. had the problem of aircraft obsolescence, which brought a similar result. On a number of occasions capital and revenue deficits have been written off by the government. Details since 1946 are as follows:[3]

Date	Nationalised Industry	Amount £m
31 Dec. 1962	British Transport Commission	487.4
31 March 1965	National Coal Board	415.0*
31 March 1965	British Overseas Airways Corporation ...	110.0†
31 March 1968	British European Airways	25.0
31 Dec. 1968	British Railways Board	1,262.1‡
31 Dec. 1968	British Waterways Board	15.5
1 January 1970	London Transport Board	269.8
		2,584.8

* Including £116m in respect of revenue losses.
† Including £30m reconstituted as a reserve, which has since been recapitalised.
‡ Including £705m debt suspended under the Transport Act 1962 and finally written off under the Transport Act 1968.

In December 1971 the government revealed that British Steel Corporation would be allowed to write off up to £350m of capital 'to cover existing and expected losses'.[4]

[1] In May 1972 the government announced that while the longer-term finance would continue to come from the N.L.F., 'greater flexibility' would be granted to the Corporations in arranging short-term finance.
[2] See 'Loans from the National Loans Fund 1971–72', op. cit., table 1.
[3] H.C. Official Report, vol. 827, no. 25, cols. 255, 256, 6 Dec. 1971.
[4] 'Memorandum on the Iron and Steel Bill, 1971', Cmnd 4839.

In recent years there has been another change in the nature of part of the capital debt of some of the nationalised public corporations with the emergence of an equity-type Public Dividend Capital.

The typical method of annual payment on capital to the government has been a fixed rate of interest. The Treasury, however, came to the view that 'for those nationalised industries which are fully viable but which are especially subject to fluctuating returns as a result of their trading conditions, the nature of their assets, etc.', an equity capital would be suitable.[1]

Public Dividend Capital is to be found, as we have seen in B.O.A.C. and the British Steel Corporation; the N.C.B. would like to convert half its capital debt into this type of Public Dividend Capital on which dividend rather than a fixed rate of interest would be payable. In poor years dividend payment would be deferred—in fact the N.C.B. has made an 'operating profit' each year except one. It may well be that this type of capital will increasingly be found in more public corporations as the nature of the existing industries change and new industries or firms come into the orbit of the state.[2]

Occupations and Labour Relations, etc.

The public corporations employ a significant proportion of the total labour force, with the nationalised industries predominating (see table, p. 183). Of the individual industries the National Coal Board, the Post Office and British Rail are significant employers. Overall, the span of employment by the public corporations is wide—from air pilots and train drivers; steelworkers and postmen; to scientists and economists.

These employees are not civil servants, neither have they the common staff arrangements found in local government service. Nevertheless, there are common factors in labour relations generally, arising from the statutes setting up the corporations which, for example, laid down a structure and procedures for

[1] Finance for Steel, B.S.C., 1969, p. 6.
[2] In May 1972 £200m of P.D.C. was given to the new British Airways Board—thus bringing its debt-equity ratio to about the level previously thought appropriate for B.O.A.C. alone. *H.C. Official Report*, vol. 842, 9 Aug. 1972, cols. 1775-1786.

collective bargaining, i.e. wages, hours, etc., and for joint consultation, i.e. safety, health and welfare.

Typical of the collective bargaining and joint consultation
procedures are those followed in rail and air transport, and in
the coal industry. In 'training' there is an overall similarity of
approach summed up by the use of training officers, training
centres and staff colleges.

In labour relations as a whole there is a similar approach to
that in the large private corporations, but the situation in the
public corporations compares favourably with the private sector
in general.

The great change that has taken place in recruitment and
training in rail transport is one measure of the remarkable technical changes there in recent years.

Research and Development
The amount of research and development varies in the different
corporations. Nevertheless, here also there is a common pattern.

The facilities in the present coal industry are quite remarkable
to anyone who knew the old; the railway industry needs and is
developing its arrangements to assist modernisation; the British
Steel Corporation with all its technical processes is rationalising
its research and development organisation; electricity and gas are
technological industries for whom research and development is
fundamental.

Across the board, and discounting individual problems that
arise in any form of industrial organisation, research and development facilities are good and their existence and structure is one
typical aspect of the organisation of public corporations.

Consumer Relations
The public corporations are not exposed to the full consequence
of commercial failure and possess at least to some degree a mono-
polistic position; as a result, there has been set up by statute
consumer consultative organisations.

The machinery set up is not uniform—'the date of the relevant
statute, and the climate of opinion seem to have been as
responsible for the variations as do the nature and structure of
the industries themselves'[1]—but there is once more a common

---

[1] 'Second Report from the Select Committee on Nationalised Industries
1970–71', H.C. 514, *Relations with the Public*, p. vi.

factor of similarity of purpose between the various consultative organisations. This similarity may be detected even in such diverse bodies as the Transport Tribunal and the various advisory bodies of the B.B.C. and I.T.A. Their overall purpose is to provide some element of public accountability in the field of price charged or service provided.

The Select Committee on the Nationalised Industries reported in 1970–1 on the machinery in various industries.[1]

Of the coal industry it said the machinery 'is as much to acquaint the Minister with the state of the Industry vis a vis its consumers as to protect them'.

The Transport Users' Consultative Committee 'see themselves as championing the interests of passengers but are, in the view of the sponsoring Department, now little more than a means for the ordinary user to secure the attention of British Rail on certain limited matters'.

In the gas and electricity industries 'the consultative committees are conceived to have a double role—communicating the views of the consumers to the industry and the position of the industry to the public'.

The Post Office Users' National Council 'regards its function as to represent the interest of the consumers'.

The structure of consumer consultation in the electricity industry typifies the pattern to be found in the public corporations. There is a real problem overall in providing a workable procedure—not made easier by the fact that these industries 'are subject to seemingly continuous criticism from the public which is far more captious than anything to which the private sector is liable'.[2]

Relations with Government and Parliament

Goverments in the United Kingdom are still responsible to Parliament; the relationship of government and parliament with the public corporations is conditioned by the nature of this

---

[1] *Ibid.* This report enquired 'into relations with the public of the electricity and gas industries, the National Coal Board, British Railways, the National Bus Company and the Post Office. The N.C.B. has no statutory consultative machinery', see para. 76, p. xxxii.

[2] *Ibid.*, p. vi.

responsibility. The basis of the relationship of the relevant departments, including the Treasury, to the corporations is laid down in the statutes.

The Minister has the power to appoint the members of the Boards; to approve the investment programmes; to control borrowings; and to approve programmes of research and development, and of training and education.[1]

The principal power given is that of giving general directions in the 'national interest'. In the 1967 White Paper 'Nationalised Industries—a Review of Economic and Financial Objectives'—it was stated 'the Government must accept a large measure of responsibility for the general lines of economic development which are followed in this vital sector of the economy'.[2] This is one aspect of the national interest.

At the other end of the scale is the view, expressed again in the 1967 White Paper, 'it is not the Government's intention to interfere in the day-to-day management of the industries'. It is between the two ends of this scale that parliament has to operate.

Discussion on the floor of the House of Commons of the public corporations and particularly the nationalised industries, is vitiated by a political fact of life—the Labour Party is 'for' and the Conservatives are 'against'. Add to this the nature of the broad-brushed Oxford Union type debates and the 'uproar' that accompanies the winding up—and there is a recipe for arid discussion. Solution to these problems leads into fields of parliamentary procedure but it does—except in the case of factual replies to questions and policy statements—mean that the pages of Hansard are not usually a very useful source of material on public ownership.

Within the range of activity possible in Parliament there are opportunities for Members at question time and in the late-night, short adjournment debates. Debates may take place on the private bills sponsored by the Corporations; on public bills; on the statutory instruments requiring parliamentary approval; and on the occasions when government seeks to increase the borrowing powers of individual corporations. There can be debates following the publication of their annual reports.

---

[1] 'First Report from the Select Committee on Nationalised Industries 1967–8', Ministerial Control of the Industries, vol. I, p. II.
[2] Op. cit., p. 14, para. 38.

The powerful Public Accounts Committee may examine the appropriation accounts of government departments; the Estimates Committee (now the Expenditure Committee) may examine any payments in the estimates of a government department. There are examples of such payments, or proposed payments, to public corporations, e.g. with the B.B.C. and their licence fee, and with the subsidies to the air corporations and rail transport, which made these candidates for enquiry. The weakness of this round-about approach to parliamentary accountability of the public corporations added force to the argument for and the development of a Select Committee on the Nationalised Industries. Given the political feelings about these industries and the real dilemmas which exist about public accountability, it is surprising that this committee has been so successful. There is little doubt that it has 'paved the way for other specialised committees' in recent years.[1]

There was much discussion before the committee was set up. Herbert Morrison wished to prevent the needs of the boards from developing a 'rather red tapeish, unadventurous and conventionally civil service frame of mind'. The T.U.C. was not in favour. Some on the conservative side in Parliament wanted the committee to provide some sort of 'efficiency audit'. As ever in the House of Commons it was the pragmatic middle ground that decided progress, together with the attitude of the various chairmen.

As a result of the activities of the Committee there has evolved a broader interpretation of the word 'nationalisation'. The argument for this was set out in a special report in 1968,[2] and by the session of 1970–1 the order of reference was that a Select Committee be appointed to examine the Reports and Accounts of the Nationalised Industries established by Statute whose controlling Boards are appointed by Ministers of the Crown and whose annual receipts are not wholly or mainly derived from moneys provided by Parliament or advanced from the Exchequer; and of the Independent Television Authority, Cable and Wireless Ltd, and the Horserace Totalisator Board, and to examine

[1] A. Morris (ed.), *The Growth of Parliamentary Scrutiny by Committee. A Symposium*, Pergamon Press, 1970, p. 71; see, in particular, 'The Select Committee on Nationalised Industries by Ian Mikardo.
[2] 'Special Report from the Select Committee on Nationalised Industries. The Committee's Order of Reference', H.C. 298, June 1968.

such activities of the Bank of England as are not—

(i) activities in the formulation and execution of monetary and financial policy, including responsibilities for the management of the gilt-edged, money and foreign exchange markets;

(ii) activities as agents of the Treasury, in managing the Exchange Equalisation Account and administering Exchange Control; or

(iii) activities as a banker to other banks and private customers.

Since 1956 the following boards have been investigated; North of Scotland Hydro-Electric Board; National Coal Board; British European Airways; British Overseas Airways Corporation; British Railways; the Gas Industry; the Electricity Industry; London Transport; the Post Office; and, since the change of reference in 1969, the Bank of England and the British Airports Authority.

The aspects investigated by the full Committee, and by sub-committee, have included research and development; education and training; staffing; and as we have seen the wider topics of financial objectivity, ministerial responsibility, and the committee's own terms of reference.[1]

These general reports had an effect, as we have seen, on government and parliamentary policy. Eventually the committee examined the Bank of England and important recommendations were accepted by the government.[2] There is little doubt also that the reports on individual corporations have had considerable influence on those responsible for their running.

The individual reports of the public corporations together with the collective discussion of their structure, finance, labour relations, etc., illustrate the characteristics and outlook of a developing method of government involvement in industry and commerce—and in the particular case of the nationalised industries a new form of industrial organisation.

It is not easy to measure success or failure and the passage of time makes comparison with former types of organisation less relevant. Nevertheless, the improvement in the annual percentage increase in traffic per man-hour on the railways; the annual increase in passenger miles per man-year of the airline corpora-

---

[1] See appendix, page 199, below, for details of enquiries completed by the Select Committee.

[2] See p. 158, above, and 'First Report from the Select Committee on Nationalised Industries 1969–70. Bank of England', H.C. 258.

tions; the annual increase in sale per man-hour in electricity; all compared with other countries, show that the public corporations in general put Britain high in the European league.[1]

In the coal industry, the changed organisation and techniques represent a silent revolution. There has been an increase in output per man-shift from 262 tons 25 years ago to 463 today.

In energy as a whole, as in rail transportation, there is a particular success story to tell that visits abroad do much by comparison to substantiate.

These industries have achieved their success in the face of the need to cut down their labour force. In 1947 there were 700,000 miners; today there are about half that number. In 1948 there were 650,000 railwaymen; today there are some 300,000. Such a decline severely affects internal morale and the external image of an industry.

There are, however, problems continuously arising in the public corporations that need analysis. Their existence is not a sign of failure and their recognition should not be regarded by the supporters of public ownership as defection to an enemy.

PROBLEMS

Individual Corporations

There are problems which are individual to each corporation. In the steel industry, for example, there is still that of making up for the low investment of the early 1960s.

This was made worse by the government of the early 1970s which controlled prices, thus leaving less surplus for internal financing, and was inhibited from providing sufficient investment capital by its belief that the public corporations should stand on their own feet.

Eventually the over capitalisation problem in the steel industry was, as we have seen, dealt with by capital write off. As a result of the long miners' strike in 1972, a similar policy will have to be followed in the coal industry. It should have been done earlier.[2]

[1] Michael Barrett Brown and Richard Pryke, *Stop Messing Them About*, Public Enterprise Group, pp. 14, 15.
[2] In the Coal Industry Bill at the end of 1972 there was a £275m write-down in capital assets and a write-off of £475m of debts owing to the N.L.F.

The new National Bus Company is operating in a declining industry and labour relations are complicated by the problems in the National Council for the Omnibus Industry. Forecasts on the timing of the N.B.P.I. proposals for an amalgamation of the N.C.O.I. and the National Joint Council for Municipal Bus Undertakings have proved optimistic.

The National Film Finance Corporation is operating in a field where it is difficult to get clear the right relationship between the state and a highly competitive, demand-dominated, industry.

The Post Office has difficulties in the labour-intensive mail section of its responsibilities. The British Waterways Board, with the weight of history on its shoulders, is not operating in an expanding market. The National Dock Labour Board and the National Ports Council are interventionist organisations operating in an area of the economy which most observers would regard as needing structural change.

The Select Committee on the Nationalised Industries found weaknesses in the organisation of the British Airports Authority —although overall it said, 'we would not wish these recommendations which we make in any way to detract from what the Authority has achieved and is engaged upon'. It described it as 'being operationally as efficient as any airport authority in the world'.[1]

These individual problems are the concern of the corporations —aided in some instances by the sponsoring department. The more general and overall problems need decisions by the government as a whole.

General

The concept of the financial objective given to nationalised concerns has been of great value; but with the Select Committee on Nationalised Industries it is still relevant to call in question the value of scientific reliability of using the single figure of a percentage target on capital employed as a measure of efficiency— and even more perhaps as a determinant of charges, especially in a monopoly or quasi-monopoly situation.

There is still the question of social needs to consider; it is of

[1] 'First Report from the Select Committee on Nationalised Industries, 1970–71, British Airports Authority', H.C. 275, p. xxxviii.

the essence of the question of public ownership. How far should it be taken into account? Is it a matter for the government and not the corporations?

On the control of prices, is it the role of the public corporations to lead and thus, in some cases, to provide a subsidy to the public sector?

There is lack of clarity in government policy on prices. In 1971, in collaboration with the Confederation of British Industries, there was announced a five-per-cent limit on price increases, to include the public corporations. Later that year the government announced grants of £27m to British Rail—in addition to 'infrastructure' grants and those to keep open uneconomic lines —and £7m to the National Bus Company, to enable these bodies to toe the C.B.I. line. This policy is obviously not temporary, for its implementation required special legislation; the 1968 Transport Act having removed all provision for deficit financing. It is a move away from the earlier 'lame duck' philosophy.

Is the staffing of the sponsoring department with responsibility for the public corporations sufficiently professional to deal with industrial matters? Is the civil service organisation suitable for speedy decisions?

As far as the Select Committee on the Nationalised Industries itself is concerned—has it enough staff to provide sufficient reports? Is it capable of the sort of analysis on prices that the N.B.P.I. once provided? Is there a need for a Ministry of Nationalised Industries to perform, besides sponsoring duties, some sort of efficiency audit? Perhaps such a Ministry would be the place to locate the old N.B.P.I. functions.[1] Now that there is an overall department—the Department of Trade and Industry —has experience shown that objective analysis of this sort can only come from an outside body, i.e. an efficiency audit commission?

In the field of labour relations there has grown up a special relationship between the trade unions and the corporations. The problems at Heathrow with the British Airports Authority show, however, that all is not well in this respect, as did the earlier delay in the introduction of liner trains on British Rail.

The miners' strike of early 1972 showed another aspect of the problems of labour relations but in this instance the dispute

[1] David Coombes, *State Enterprise. Business or Politics*, P.E.P., Allen & Unwin, ch. 7, 'The National Board for Prices and Incomes'.

was caught up in the meshes of the government's incomes policy. Nevertheless the 'special case' of the miners should have emerged without the aid of the Wilberforce enquiry.[1] An 'Incomes Board' for the Nationalised Industries to consider this type of fundamental structural question might be an approach to the matter.

On the basic question of worker participation, the prevailing attitude on the part of the trade unions is still that of the T.U.C. in 1944—participation is one thing, taking basic decisions is another.[2] The result of the experiment in the steel industry with 18 £1,000-a-year 'worker directors' on the advisory boards, is not encouraging. In one respect—'Workers won't trust us, we lose contact with them because we are appointed as individuals and not as their representatives.'[3] In general, however, the directors have been effective in determining social policy, redundancy and in aiding communication with the shop floor. As a result the B.S.C. is seeking to strengthen their role.

Nevertheless, there are many in a syndicalist tradition, however muted, who would wish to go even further.[4] In the world of Upper Clyde Shipbuilders there is a growing desire to be involved in ultimate decisions. Is it, as Richard Crossman has argued, that the managerial society needs worker participation?[5]

The weakest link in the organisation of the public corporations is undoubtedly the 'consumer consultative machinery'. It has only made a marginal impact on public awareness.[6] There is too much identification with the industries themselves; there is confusion between the function of advising the industry and that of watchdog for the consumer.

The Select Committee on the Nationalised Industries made interesting recommendations to improve the machinery in specific cases and on general principle in all industries—e.g. to demon-

---

[1] 'Report of a Court of Enquiry into a dispute between the National Coal Board and the National Union of Mineworkers under the Chairmanship of the Rt Hon Lord Wilberforce', Cmnd 4903, 1972.
[2] Report of T.U.C. Conference, 1944, pp. 408-12.
[3] Vincent Hanna, Sunday Times, 7 Nov. 1971', 'A Vote of No Confidence in Shop Floor Directors'.
[4] See (i) Industrial Democracy, Labour Party, 1967; (ii) Labour's Economic Strategy, Labour Party, 1971.
[5] R. H. S. Crossman, Socialism and the New Despotism, Fabian Tract 298, 1955.
[6] See Consumer Consultative Machinery in the Nationalised Industries, Consumer Council Study, H.M.S.O., 1968, p. 8.

strate independence, the cost of the consultative bodies should
not fall on the industry concerned; all consumers' bodies should
be enabled to comment on matters of general principle involving
their respective industries and on aspects which directly impinge
on the consumer.[1]

It may be that as part of a wider audit organisation one watchdog consultative body should be set up for all the industries. In
any event, the problem of the consumer is not one just for the
public sector—it is growing also in the private sector, arising
'from the relative isolation and ignorance of the consumer in the
modern world'.[2] The weaknesses in the position of the consumer
in the nationalised industries needs to be considered in a wider
context.

In this respect the abolition of the Consumer Council was a
step backward. The new ideas for local authority-operated consumer advice centres, modelled on similar centres in Austria,
Sweden and West Germany, is a move forward.[3] The Co-operative movement has much potential to offer the consumer in this
field.

Of the overall problems of the public corporations, probably
the most intrinsic and the most difficult to solve is that concerned with the control exercised by the central government
through the minister.

The Select Committee on Nationalised Industries, as we have
seen, devoted a report to this matter. There are many improvements to be made within the existing system, but a fundamental
change in the machinery itself was proposed by Mr Aubrey
Jones in his evidence concerning gas, electricity and coal. This
was for a holding company-type 'Energy Board' to take over all
appropriate assets in this field and to concentrate on commercial
matters away from political influence—away from the central
government.

The Select Committee rejected this idea on the grounds that
social and economic obligations must be considered together; they
preferred accordingly a Ministry of Nationalised Industries. While

[1] 'Second Report from the Select Committee on Nationalised Industries
1970-1, Relations with the Public', H.C. 514, 1971, p. xxxix. See also
W. Thornhill, *The Nationalised Industries, an Introduction*, p. 153.
[2] *Ibid.*, p. 529.
[3] J. Cartwright, 'Labour and the Consumer', *Socialist Commentary*,
Dec. 1971.

the holding company concept is not without wider significance
in this field, and whatever the precise form of governmental organisation—the main thing in the issue of ministerial control is to
clarify governmental objectives and make clear the lines of communication between the civil servants and the officials of the
public corporations.

There are many problems facing the public corporations. On
their solution depends their development as a relevant form of
public ownership.

In some respects, in structure, in methods of labour relations
and recruitment, the public corporations are similar to the large
firms of the private sector—e.g. I.C.I. and Unilever. Fundamentally, however, the corporations provide a new form of organisation with the main difference that there are no private shareholders. Overall they represent, and are part of, a new economic
environment—with interests in everything from coal; electricity;
steel; road, rail and air transport; to N.C.B. housing and the new
towns with 200,000 houses built to rent or for sale. The corporations are landowners; the B.S.C. has a 50 per cent interest in
Corby Town Football Club; British Rail and B.O.A.C. own luxury
hotels; the Post Office runs the Giro and the Data Processing
Service.

The public corporations bear the same relationship to this
new environment as the joint stock companies did to emergent
mid-Victorian capitalism. Just as the needs for large sums of
capital for new types of industry was one argument for limited
liability joint stock organisation, the impossibility of raising
sufficient sums of capital for public utility services and later for
modern technological industries such as steel, is one argument for
the public corporations.

The necessary legislation for public joint stock companies was
not passed by Parliament to the accompaniment of universal
praise. Indeed, the mid-nineteenth-century legislation to permit
joint stock limited liability companies brought the cry of 'the
rogues' charter'.[1] One age's radicalism becomes another's conventional wisdom.

The public corporation, despite the political arguments of the

[1] K. W. Wedderburn, *Company Law Reform*, Fabian Tract 363, 1965,
p. 2.

last quarter of a century, has been accepted in practice by successive Conservative governments, despite Mr Heath's 'we will ... put nationalisation into reverse', and Mr Powell's call for total denationalisation. I have argued earlier the force of economic logic here, but whatever the reason no real attempt has ever been made to reverse fundamentally the trend of this form of public ownership.

In more recent years there has been a conservative argument in favour of 'hiving off'. At its worst this has been a sop to political activists, at its best it raises legitimate questions concerning the frontiers of public ownership. To own some travel companies is one thing, but to own them 'by accident' and without a coherent philosophy is another.

However, to hive off B.S.C. special steels, N.C.B. computers, railway hotels and Thomas Cooks, ignores the diversification which has become typical of the large private sector 'conglomerate'. A glance at the diverse operations of the Imperial Tobacco Company gives an indication of the trend.

Within the Labour Party there has been a discussion on the whole philosophy of public ownership influenced by changes in the structure of industry and the experience of Morrisonian-type nationalisation—on which Richard Crossman expressed the view that 'socialism is not a state bureaucracy'.[1]

Hugh Gaitskell saw nationalisation as a means to an end in itself. Each further step in this direction should be justified by the facts of the situation; there were other forms of public ownership—municipalisation, state ownership of equity shares, state and mixed enterprises—operating through a holding company.[2]

The acceptance by the Labour Party itself of this new approach to public ownership came with the publication of *Industry and Society* in 1957.[3] In this policy document, based on the structural changes argument mentioned above—in particular the domination of the very large firm and the weakening power of the shareholder—the case for state participation in the ownership of private industry by the purchase of equity shares alongside new forms of public ownership was argued.

Since that time, and under the pragmatic influence of office,

[1] See, R. H. S. Crossman, *op. cit.*, Fabian Tract 298, 1956, p. 6.
[2] Hugh Gaitskell, *Socialism and Nationalism*, Fabian Tract 300, 1956.
[3] See also Declaration of the Socialist International at Frankfurt, July 1951.

the more flexible view on public ownership has developed. For example, it has been justified as a means of bringing techno-logical employment to the development areas, and to involve the state alongside the private sector in 'North Sea Gas' operations —where already the natural resources under the continental shelf below the North Sea are vested in the Crown; and the N.C.B., the Gas Council and British Petroleum are involved.[1]

At one time it seemed as if one development of this concept might be the purchase of equities by a National Superannuation Fund, but in office it seemed that fears of upsetting the equity market by large purchases of shares by a super insurance com-pany, prevented this line of approach.

Some of the public corporations, as we have seen, have them-selves moved into the private sector in this way through subsidiary and associated companies. The National Bus Company and the National Freight Corporation are practical examples of a holding company type of organisation which is clearly a new form of public ownership.

The public corporation, like industry itself, has over the years been changing its form. The philosophy of 1945 concerned itself with the major industries of that day but it did not lay down in tablets of stone, rules of organisation applicable to all conditions. What was basic was the disappearance of the shareholder; it is the significant aspect of this form of organisation when compared with the private sector.

[1] *North Sea Gas*, Labour Party, 1967.

Appendix

Enquiries Completed by Select Committees on Nationalised Industries

1956–57 North of Scotland Hydro-Eyectric Board
1957–58 National Coal Board
1958–59 The Air Corporations*
1959–60 British Railways
1960–61 The Gas Industry
1962–63 The Electricity Supply Industry*
1963–64 British Overseas Airways Corporation
1964–65 London Transport
1965–66 Post Office*
1966–67 British European Airways
1967–68 Exploitation of North Sea Gas
1967–68 Ministerial Control of the Nationalised Industries*
1968–69 National Coal Board
1969–70 Bank of England*
1970–71 British Airports Authority*
1970–71 Relations with the Public

The Committee made brief enquiries into Ministerial control of Nationalised Industries in 1956–57, and in 1961–62 they made a short enquiry into the action that had been taken on previous Reports. In December 1965 they held one-day hearings with the Chairmen of the Coal, Gas and Electricity industries, but published no findings.

* Enquiry started in the previous session.

Further Reading

C. F. Brand, *The British Labour Party*, Oxford University Press, 1965.

R. Boysun (ed.), *Goodbye to Nationalisation*, Churchill Press, 1971.

A. Briggs, *The History of Broadcasting in the United Kingdom*, vol. I,
The Birth of Broadcasting; vol. II, *The Golden Age of Wireless*; vol.
III, *The War of Words*; Oxford University Press, 1961–70.

A. Bullock, *The Life and Times of Ernest Bevin*, vol. I, *1881–1940*,
Heinemann, 1960; vol. II, *1940–45*, Heinemann, 1967.

P. D. Clayton, 'Accountability in Government Expenditure', *National
Westminster Bank Quarterly Review*, Nov. 1971, p. 43.

C. A. R. Crosland, *The Future of Socialism*, Cape, 1956.

A. H. Hanson (ed.), *Nationalisation. A Book of Readings*, Allen & Unwin,
1963.

R. Kelf Cohen, *Twenty Years of Nationalisation*, Macmillan, 1969.

R. Kelf Cohen, *Nationalisation in Britain. The End of a Dogma*, Macmillan, 1958.

C. D. Foster, *Politics, Finance and the Role of Economics*, Allen &
Unwin, 1971.

G. and P. Polanyi, 'The Efficiency of Nationalized Industries', *Moorgate and Wall Street Review*, Spring 1972, p. 50.

Enoch Powell, *Freedom and Reality*, Batsford, 1969.

Richard Pryke, *Public Enterprise in Practice*, Macgibbon & Kee, 1971.

W. A. Robson, *Nationalised Industry and Public Ownership*, Allen &
Unwin, 1962.

Michael Shanks (ed.), *Lessons of Public Enterprise*, a Fabian Study,
Cape, 1963.

Bruce L. R. Smith and D. C. Hague, *The Dilemma of Accountability in
Modern Government. Independence versus Control*, Macmillan,
1970.

John Strachey, *The Theory and Practice of Socialism*, Gollancz, 1936.

L. Tivey, *Nationalisation in British Industry*, Cape, 1966.

M. Thomas, 'The Consumer and the Corporations', *Public Enterprise*,
no. 1, 1971, p. 10.

Ralph Turvey, *Economic Analysis and Public Enterprises*, Allen &
Unwin, 1971.

Ralph Turvey (ed.), *Public Enterprise. Selected Readings*, Penguin,
1969.

National Board for Prices and Incomes, 'Proposals for Bus and Railway
Fare Increases in London', *Cmnd* 3561, 1968; 'Report on Gas Prices',
Cmnd 3567, 1968; 'Report on the Bulk Supply Tariff of the Central
Electricity Generating Board', *Cmnd* 3575, 1968; 'Public Boards',
Cmnd 4611, 1971.

Public Enterprise. Labour's Review of the Nationalised Industries,
Labour Party, 1957.

5 State Shareholdings

5 State Shareholdings

One major aspect of the mixed economy, as was seen in chapter 1, is the growing involvement of the government in private industry itself. Over the years the state has become so involved —not only by grants and 'launching aid' etc. but actually by the purchase of equity shares.

Place in National Accounts

Where such purchases have been made by public corporations and where their published accounts are consolidated, then the extended activities are regarded by the Central Statistical Office as part of the public sector. Where the central government has a shareholding in a limited liability company, this is not regarded as changing the status of the company which continues to be treated as within the private sector.

There are, no doubt, good statistical reasons for this approach, but in all logic the ownership of shares by the central government —either directly or through one of its agencies—surely makes the firms concerned fully or proportionately a part of a public sector.

Such a classification would have the additional merit of reflecting the growing mix between the public and private sectors— now hidden in the statistical shadows. Was not an early name for statistics political arithmetic?

Reasons for 'Public Ownership'

This type of public ownership has developed over the years but it was not preceded by, nor has it proceeded with, until more recently, philosophical discussion as to its merits or demerits.

It has been a pragmatic development—a reaction to events— justified by arguments for defence and security, as with British Petroleum and Rolls-Royce; for the maintenance of employment in shipbuilding and computers faced by foreign subsidised competition; and in the latter case to provide research and development money 'not available from the City'.[1] The involvement in agriculture has been in the main to assist the trading activities of the Land Settlement Association first set up in 1934 in conjunction with the National Council of Social Service, the Society of Friends, the Carnegie Trustees and other bodies to alleviate the unemployment and social distress of the Great Depression.

In the case of B.P. the State's involvement has not been unprofitable. Up to 31 December 1967 dividends paid amounted to £260·7m and 'capital appreciation on paper' amounted to some £500m.[2] The moral of this has not been lost on some who favour the 'B.P. approach'.

The range of shareholding activities is wide and is found in important parts of the economy. It is surprising therefore that with the exception of Rolls-Royce, which was acquired in a blaze of publicity after a short sharp argument in the Cabinet, that there is such little general knowledge of its extent.

EXTENT OF STATE SHAREHOLDINGS

Direct Holdings by Central Government

The extent of direct government shareholdings in private industry on 1 January 1972 is shown in the table on pp. 204–5.

Individual Firms

Beagle Aircraft Ltd.[3] This company was formed in 1960 to develop and manufacture light aircraft in Britain. In July 1966 it seemed that the company would cease operations and, in order to preserve a light aircraft industry in the U.K., finance was provided by the government, who kept close control on finances through a government-nominated financial director—pending the acquisition of the assets.

In July 1968, after legislation, the Minister of Technology did so acquire the assets and transferred them to a new company which was wholly government-owned and required to operate as a normal commercial company.

---

[1] *H.C. Official Report*, vol. 761, 21 March 1968, col. 610.
[2] Ibid., vol. 751, 24 Oct. 1967, col. 428.
[3] 'First, Second and Third Reports from the Committee of Public Accounts, Session 1970–1', H.C. 300-I, 375-I, 537, p. xxviii.

GOVERNMENT SHAREHOLDINGS AS AT 1 JANUARY 1972[1]

Name of Company	Number of shares held	Number of Government appointed Directors	Date of original acquisition	Reason for acquisition
Beagle Aircraft Ltd (in liquidation)	1,000,000 £1 Ordinary shares ...	—	1968	Maintenance of light aircraft industry
British Petroleum Co. Ltd ...	174,461,538 £1 Ordinary Stock 1,000 £1 8% Cumulative First Preference Stock	2	1914	Security of oil supplies
British Sugar Corporation ...	1,125,000 £1 Ordinary shares	3 (1 of whom must be Chairman)	1936	To safeguard sugar beet industry
Cammell Laird (Shipbuilding & Engineers) Ltd*	1,500,000 £1 Ordinary shares	—	1970	To support shipbuilding industry systems throughout the Commonwealth
International Computers (Holdings) Ltd	3,500,000 £1 'C' Ordinary shares† ...	1	1968	To support the creation of the company
Itabira Iron Ore Co Ltd (in liquidation)	61,220 £1 First Preference shares ... ... 380,000 £1 Second Preference shares 493,982 £1 Ordinary shares	—	1942	To secure supplies of iron ore

[1] *H.C. Official Report*, vol. 813, 10 March 1971, cols. 141-2. Changes between then and 1 January 1972 relate to Rolls-Royce—number of shares and directors; and to U.C.S. where the holdings of the Shipbuilding Industry Board had devolved to the Department of Trade and Industry. N.B. The Treasury put Cable & Wireless Ltd in this list of shareholdings even though it is a public corporation, 'Because it is a public corporation, in which the Government holds shares.' It has been omitted from this table because it is a public corporation.

Company	Shares held	Directors	Date	Reason
Power Jets (R. & D.) Ltd (in liquidation)	200,000 £1 Ordinary shares ...	Chairman and 2 Directors	1944	Defence
Rolls-Royce (1971) Ltd ...	30,000,000 £1 shares	Chairman and 7 Directors	1971	To ensure continuity of those activities of R.R. which are important to our national defence and to the air forces and civil airlines of many other countries
S.B. (Realisations) Ltd ...	42,050 5% Redeemable Cumulative £1 Preference shares 581,302 25p Ordinary shares 250,000 25p 'A' Ordinary shares	3	1943	Defence
Suez Finance Company ...	645,591 FFr10 Capital shares	2	1876	To secure Suez Canal route
Toplis & Harding (Middle East) Ltd	998 50p shares	—	1963	To support a company acting as agents for U.K. property in Egypt, following the Suez crisis
Upper Clyde Shipbuilders Ltd (in liquidation)	875,000 £1 Ordinary shares ... 7% Unsecured Loan Stock, 1975§ (£940,000) 12,000,000 25p shares (from Shipbuilding Industry Board)	—	1968 1966 1972	To support the shipbuilding industry
Welsh Highland Light Railway (in liquidation)	5% Debenture Stock (£35,774)	—	1922–4	Under Light Railways Act 1896, to alleviate unemployment

* The Public Trustee holds these shares on behalf of the Secretary of State for Trade and Industry.

† The Government have so far paid only 10p for each share. The balance of 90p per share is due on 28 Sept. 1972.

§ This Loan Stock is in Fairfields (Glasgow) Ltd, which is a wholly owned non-operative subsidiary of Upper Clyde Shipbuilders.

In September 1969 a revised programme for future activities was put forward by the company to provide a wider product range which would enable the company to continue in existence. The government was not prepared to provide the further £6m required and the concern went into liquidation.

British Petroleum.[1] This holding company, through its associated and subsidiary companies, is engaged in all phases of the oil industry, including searching for oil and natural gas and producing, transporting, refining and marketing petroleum and petroleum products, and in petro-chemicals.

The principal producing areas are in the Middle East and in Africa. Exploration for crude oil and natural gas is taking place in these areas and in Australasia, Canada, U.S.A. and Europe—including the North Sea.

There are subsidiary companies in chemicals, tankers, refineries, real estate and in other petrol and oil companies, e.g. Duckham Oil, National Benzole—with a variety of proportion of holdings in companies in the United Kingdom, Austria, Belgium, Denmark, Eire, Finland, France, Germany, Gibraltar, Greece, Holland, Italy, Luxembourg, Malta, Norway, Portugal, Spain, Sweden, Switzerland, Turkey; and in the Middle East, Africa, India and Pakistan, Far East, Australasia, Canada, Colombia, Trinidad, U.S.A.

In 1914 the British government acquired a controlling interest of 51 per cent in the then-named Anglo-Persian Oil Company because of the strategic importance of oil. Since 1966, when more shares were issued, the interest has been only 48.6 per cent of ordinary stock.

The Treasury view was that there was no need to maintain the previous percentage shareholding in order to keep an effective controlling interest.[2]

Since 1914 under the company's articles of association the government has the right to nominate two members of the board with power to veto any resolution. The government pledged itself not to interfere in the company's commercial affairs, and undertook not to exercise the right of veto except in regard to certain specific

[1] 'British Petroleum Annual Report and Accounts for 1970'.
[2] *H.C. Official Report*, vol. 740, 31 Jan. 1967, col. 44. See also *ibid.*, vol. 739, 24 Jan. 1967, cols. 221-3, for agreement with Distillers Co., when B.P. purchased by stock transfer, shares in the chemical and plastics interests of this company.

matters of general policy, e.g. 'the supervision of the activities
of the company as they may affect questions of foreign and
military policy, any proposed sale of the undertaking, or any
change of status of the company, and new exploitation and other
matters directly bearing on the fulfilment of current contracts for
the Admiralty'. This right of veto has never been used.

British Sugar Corporation.[1] This corporation is the sole pro-
cessor of home-grown sugar beet and is required to purchase
all grown on the authorised acreage at the guaranteed price determined by the government. When it cannot thus operate at a profit,
the Sugar Board pays it the difference between this guaranteed
price and a standard price determined by an incentive agreement
arranged by the government and the corporation.

Besides the 11.25 per cent share capital owned by the Treasury,
a further £2·5m of £1 ordinary shares—25 per cent—are owned
by the Sugar Board. The only other significant shareholder is
the Eagle Star Insurance Company with 22,000 shares. The corporation may have from seven to 14 directors. Its Articles of
Association empower the Minister of Agriculture, Fisheries and
veto any resolution of the board which may prevent the Corporation from discharging its duties under the Sugar Act, 1956.

Cammell Laird (Shipbuilding and Engineers) Ltd.[2] In 1970
Food jointly with the Secretary of State for Scotland, and with
Treasury approval, to appoint three directors including the Chairman. Appointments are normally for three years. There is also
provision whereby the Chairman may, after consulting Ministers,
the government purchased a 50 per cent shareholding in this
Birkenhead company which builds merchant vessels, warships
and marine engines—following losses which led to a liquidity
crisis in the group as a whole.

Loans were also made by the I.R.C. when it seemed that the
powers of the Shipbuilding Industry Board to assist the re-equip-

[1] 'Select Committee on Nationalised Industries, 1967–8', H.C. 298,
appendix I, 'Bodies of a Trading Nature in which the Government has
a Controlling Interest', p. 44; and 'Sugar Board, Thirteenth Annual
Report for Year Ended 31 December 1970', H.C. 336, appendix II,
'Accounts of British Sugar Corporation for Year Ended 30 September
1970'.
[2] H.C. *Official Report*, vol. 801, 7 May 1970, cols. 590–8; and 'Cammell
Laird & Co. (Shipbuilders and Engineers) Ltd, Report and Accounts
for the Year 1970'.

ment and reorganisation of the year were not appropriate to solve the wider problems of the group.

International Computers (Holdings) Ltd.[1] This company was formed as a result of a merger between I.C.T. (International Computers and Tabulators) and English Electric, with the participation of Plessey.

As a result, the new organisation became the largest company outside the U.S.A. specialising in commercial and scientific computers. Its main subsidiary is I.C.L., which in turn has its own subsidiaries, e.g. Baric Computing Service Ltd, Data Recording Instrument Co. and International Computers Ltd—India, New Zealand, Central Africa, etc. The holding company also has a number of associated companies and investments.

There is also a joint development company with Plessey to study and develop the convergence between computers and communications.

The government were to hold 10.5 per cent of the ordinary shares with 53.5 per cent by former I.C.T. shareholders, 18 per cent by English Electric and 18 per cent by Plessey. The then Minister of Technology, Mr Anthony Wedgwood Benn, announced that 'The Government will have a director on the board of the new company, but do not intend to intervene in the day-to-day management.'[2]

The initial commitment of the government was to participate in the finance of the new Company's operations to the extent of £17m over a period of five years. In August 1971 the government announced a number of measures to help I.C.L. and confirmed that their shareholding was to continue.[3] In June 1972 the new Minister for Industrial Development in the light of a report of the Select Committee on Science and Technology, announced a further support of £14·2m for the period up to September 1973—in order to maintain the momentum of its R. & D. programme.[4]

[1] *H.C. Official Report*, vol. 761, 21 March 1968, cols. 607-13. See also 'International Computers (Holdings) Ltd Annual Report and Accounts 1971'. N.B. I.C.L. is the only direct subsidiary of the holdings company.
[2] *H.C. Official Report, op. cit.*, col. 608.
[3] *Ibid.*, vol. 822, no. 191, 30 July 1971, cols. 196-7.
[4] *Official Report*, vol. 840, no. 147, cols. 34-9.

Itabira Iron Ore Company.[1] This company owned a deposit of iron ore in Brazil and 'with a view to ensuring the supply of iron ore to this country' its shares were compulsorily acquired in 1942.

An agreement was entered into between the U.S.A., the U.K. and the Brazilian Government under which the mine was transferred without charge to the Brazilian Government, who undertook to develop it to a specified output. The U.S. government agreed to arrange financial accommodation and material.

The company went into liquidation in 1944 and compensation terms are still under discussion with the Brazilian Government.

Power Jets Ltd.[2] From 1939 to 1944 the private company, Power Jets, which had developed the jet engine, was virtually a state-controlled establishment; in the latter year it was completely taken over by the then Ministry of Aircraft Production.

The company was, in practice, a research and development organisation, and following the institutional changes in the field of government, it went into voluntary liquidation in 1966. Difficulties have been experienced in the transfer of title to the Company's patents and it has consequently been kept in existence as a patent-holding company. The procedure is, however, expected to be completed 'fairly soon'.

Rolls-Royce.[3] This Company, long the premier aircraft engine company in the U.K., but with other interests, e.g. motor cars, marine and tank engines, etc., was allowed by the government to go into liquidation in 1971.

The prime reason for this liquidation was the prior decision by the government not to give further loans for the company to meet the RB211 contract.[4]

The Rolls-Royce (Purchase) Bill made provision for the acquisition 'for the benefit of the Crown of any part of the undertaking and assets of Rolls-Royce Ltd or its subsidiaries, and the carrying on of any undertaking so acquired'.[5]

After the passage of the Bill a new company was set up and two directors appointed—one the former Chief of the Defence

[1] *H.C. Official Report*, vol. 390, 10 June 1943, cols. 857-8.
[2] *House of Lords Official Report*, vol. 132, 14 June 1944, cols. 223-36.
[3] H. Nockolds, *The Magic of a Name*, Foulis, 1966.
[4] 'Rolls-Royce Ltd and the RB211 Aero Engine', *Cmnd* 4860, Jan. 1972.
[5] Rolls-Royce (Purchase) Bill, 1971.

Staff. Those assets, essential to British national defence, to collaborative programmes with other countries and civil airlines, were
purchased from the receiver—including the valuable Rolls-Royce
patents.

The new Rolls-Royce company at the end of November 1971
employed some 62,000 staff. Its subsidiaries included Rolls-
Royce Composite Materials Ltd and Hyfil Ltd (i.e. carbon fibre
production) and the shareholding in British Aircraft Corporation.

The remainder of the assets, e.g. Rolls-Royce Motors Ltd were
to be sold by the liquidator.

SB Realisations Ltd.[1] This wholly-owned holding company
holds 69.5 per cent of the issued share capital of Short Bros and
Harland Ltd of Belfast. The Minister of Technology is entitled
to nominate eight directors to the board of this aircraft firm,
which makes the Skyvan and, following the modern trend, parts
of other aircraft, e.g. the Lockheed Tristar, as well as guided
weapons; they are instructed to act in conformity with 'the best
commercial principles'.

The Minister's approval is required before incurring any substantial expenditure on capital account; issuing any further share
or loan capital or exercising any borrowing powers; investing
company funds in any subsidiary company; appointing a Chairman; or entering upon a course of action which might raise con-
troversial public issues.

The original takeover of the shares of Short Bros was in 1943;
there were obviously internal management problems that could
not be allowed to affect the war effort.[2]

Suez Finance Co.[3] The government acquired its holdings in
this company in 1958 in exchange for the government's former
interest in the Suez Canal Company which dates back to 1876.
Additional shares were acquired in 1969.

The Suez Finance Company is a wholly owned subsidiary of
Compagnie Financière de Suez et de l'Union Parisienne; it is

[1] Select Committee on Nationalised Industries 1967–8, *op. cit.*, p. 55;
see also 'Short Bros & Harland Ltd Directors' Report and Statement
of Accounts Year Ended 31 August 1971'.
[2] *H.C. Official Report*, vol. 388, 31 March 1943, cols. 157–8; 14 April
1943, cols. 1193–4.
[3] 'Compagnie de Suez et de l'Union Parisienne Report and Accounts
1970'.

this body whose shares are held by the government. Its interests, either by portfolio investment or by direct investment, extend from banks and investment companies to manufacturers and distributive undertakings, e.g. breweries, motor trade, civil engineering and oil—in France and other European countries.

Toplis & Harding (Middle East) Ltd.[1] The shares in this firm of loss adjustors and international surveyors, were acquired 'to support a company acting as agents for British nationals with claims against the U.A.R. in the post-Suez period'.[2]

Prior to the majority shareholding there was already a substantial financial interest in the firm by the government. It was at the point of a further deteriorating financial situation that the government acquired equity. A receiver/manager was appointed in 1963 to look after government interests.

Upper Clyde Shipbuilding Group. The Geddes Report in 1966 recommended the reorganisation of the shipbuilding industry. Consequently there took place in August 1967 a merger of five companies—John Brown (Clydebank yard), Fairfields (Govan yard), Connell (Scotstown yard), Stephens (Linthouse), and Yarrow which split off from the group in 1971.

The government already had a 50-per-cent holding in Fairfields when it became part of the group, and in February 1968 exchanged it for a 17.5 per cent share of the equity of U.C.S. The number of government-appointed directors was in proportion to the percentage of equity owned.

In June 1971 the group was refused further government money whether in the form of grant or equity and went into liquidation. There was an outcry, but following a government-commissioned Report on Shipbuilding on the Upper Clyde, the government decided not to support U.C.S. and establish only a successor company at Govan/Linthouse.[3]

U.C.S. was put in the hands of the liquidator and there followed the work-in with the aim of maintaining the fours yards in operation.[4]

In February 1972 the government decided that 'Govan Ship-

---

[1] *H.C. Official Report*, vol. 686, 16 Dec. 1963, cols. 155-6.
[2] *Ibid.*, vol. 758, 14 Feb. 1968, col. 387.
[3] 'Report of the Advisory Group on Shipbuilding on the Upper Clyde 1971', H.C. 544.
[4] See Alasdair Buchan, *The Right to Work. The Story of the Upper Clyde Confrontation*, Calder & Boyars, 1971.

builders', a paper company with two £1 shares owned by a
private interest, should be provided with £35m to meet early
losses in and capital investment for three yards at Govan, Linthouse and Scotstoun. The company began trading on 1 July
1972.

Welsh Highland Light Railway.[1] In 1972 a public enquiry
was held by the Welsh Railway Commissioner, as a result of
which the Welsh Highland (Railway) Light Railway Company to
link the North Wales Narrow Gauge with the Portmadoc Beddge-
lert and South Snowdon railway was incorporated in March 1922.
The government agreed to subscribe an amount to the debenture
stock of the company equal to half the cost of completing the
railway from Portmadoc to Dinas, provided the sum so advanced
did not exceed £37,500. The Ministry of Transport advanced
£35,774 to the company, and it was stipulated that the company should not raise more than £175,000 of share or loan capital
without the Minister's consent.

In November 1933 the local authorities with investments in
the railway asked the debenture holders to close the line, but
Portmadoc U.D.C. asked for the Portmadoc sections to be left
open. Following refusals to take over these sections by the L.M.S.
and the G.W.R., the Welsh Highland Railway was leased to the
Festiniog Railway in 1934. The railway closed to passengers in
1937; demolition was started in 1941 and continued to 1948. The
government made an Order for the winding up of the company
in 1944 but it is not yet completed.

A company called the Welsh Highland Light Railway (1964)
Ltd has been formed to reopen a section of the original line—
but the government has no shares.

Agricultural Enterprises
Another type of ownership over the years has been in agricultural
cooperatives—defined as mixed agricultural enterprises. Their
extent in January 1972 was as follows:[2]

[1] C. E. Lee, *The Welsh Highland Railway*, 1962.
[2] *H.C. Official Report*, vol. 829, 25 Jan. 1972, cols. 381-2, together
with other information from the Ministry of Agriculture, Fisheries
and Food. See also *ibid.*, vol. 830, 2 Feb. 1972, cols. 144-5.

Name of Company	No. of shares held	Total value (nominal) £	Date of acquisition
Avoncroft Cattle Breeders Ltd	1	1.00	1950
Blaenpenal and District Agricultural Co-operative Society	1	1.00	1947
Brandsby Agricultural Trading Association	1	1.00	1955
Carmarthen Farmers Co-operative Society Ltd	4	1.00	1941
Clynderwen and District Farmers Association Ltd	1	1.00	1942
Co-operative Wholesale Society Ltd	56	280.00	1959
Eastern Counties Farmers Ltd	80	20.00	1962
Eifionydd Farmers Association Ltd	5	5.00	1945*
Foel Agricultural Co-operative Society Ltd	1	0.50	1944*
Gloucestershire Marketing Society	250	250.00	1964
Haverfordwest Agricultural Co-operative Society Ltd	1	1.00	1942
Hitchen Bacon Factory Ltd (in liquidation)	200	200.00	1948
Isle of Scilly Growers Ltd	10	10.00	1967
Kent Wool Growers Limited	1	1.00	1940*
Kintyre Farmers Ltd	5	5.00	1965
Littleton and Badsey Growers Ltd	150½	150.50	1941, 1964
Lyonesse Growers Ltd	1	1.00	1968
Midland Shires Farmers Ltd	21	10.50	1942, 1965
National Seeds Development Organisation Ltd	8	8.00	1967
North Cardiganshire Farmers Co-operative Society	2	2.00	1946
North Devon Farmers Trading Society	2	8.00	1949
North Western Farmers Ltd	25	25.00	1965
Nursery Trades (Lee Valley) Ltd	317	317.00	1958, 1962, 1969
Preston and District Farmers Trading Society Ltd	10	5.00	1959
Pumpsaint and District Agricultural Co-operative Society Ltd	2	2.00	1942, 1946
South Western Farmers	10	10.00	1964
Southern Counties Agricultural Trading Society	30	30.00	1941, 1956
St Edmunds Bacon Factory Ltd	136	136.00	1948, 1954, 1957
Thames Valley Eggs Ltd	487	487.00	1947, 1949, 1955, 1957

Name of Company	No. of shares held	Total value (nominal) £	Date of acquisition
West Breconshire Farmers Association Ltd	1	1.00	1945
West Cumberland Farmers Trading Society Ltd	40	40.00	1944, 1947
West Midland Farmers Association Ltd	8	8.00	1957
Yorks and Northern Wool Growers Ltd	1	1.00	1950
Yorkshire Egg Producers Ltd	412	206.00	1947, 1964, 1967
Yorkshire Farmers Bacon Factory (1932) Ltd	378	94.50	1948, 1953, 1966, 1967*

* In process of redemption or redeemed

Most of these co-operative shareholdings are held by the Land Settlement Association in order to assist the trading activities of this organisation, which provides purchasing and marketing services for tenants on a number of smallholding estates which it manages as agent for the Minister of Agriculture, Fisheries and Food.[1] Most of the co-operatives are buying co-operatives which negotiate favourably purchasing terms for their members; and the only way to participate is to become a member.

The remainder of the co-operative shareholdings—with the exception of the National Seed Development Organisation—are held by the various experimental husbandry farms and experimental horticultural stations throughout the country; again to obtain the advantages of trading through a buying co-operative.

In agriculture there are three other concerns in which the state is involved.

The first is the Agricultural Mortgage Corporation Ltd, a public company whose shareholders are the London clearing banks and whose function is under the Agricultural Credits Act 1928 to make 'loans on mortgages of agricultural land on terms most favourable to borrowers'.

The Minister of Agriculture has the power to make advances to the Corporation's Guarantee Fund which is used to back issues

[1] 'Departmental Committee of Inquiry into Statutory Smallholdings, Final Report', ch. I-IV, *Cmnd* 3303, 1967.

of debentures and the right to approve alterations to the Corporation's Memorandum and Articles of Association. Of the eight directors one is nominated by the Treasury and two by the Minister of Agriculture; they are, according to the latter department, not answerable to the Government.

The second is the Scottish Agricultural Securities Corporation Ltd, whose share capital is held by three Scottish banks and was set up under the Agricultural Credits (Scotland) Act of 1929; it is described in the Treasury memorandum to the Select Committee on Nationalised Industries as the 'Scottish counterpart of the A.M.C.'.[1] Yet there it also states: 'The government have no powers to dictate the Corporation's policy, although a certain influence can be executed through the appointed Directors and by general consultation.'

The third company is the National Seed Development Organisation Ltd set up in March 1967 to market plant varieties bred with the aid of public funds in the United Kingdom.

The Company may use income from sales and royalties to defray expenses and in 1970–1 it earned a surplus of income over expenditure of £196,310 before tax. The Organisation is registered under the Companies Act 1948, is limited by guarantee and has a share capital of £100 with an issued share capital of £8. The eight share certificates are held by the governing body, who are appointed by the Minister of Agriculture, Secretary of State for Scotland and Secretary of State for the Home Office.

These three Ministers have wide formal powers of control through the 'service of directors'.[2] The organisation is, however, autonomous in its day-to-day management of commercial operations.

Other State Shareholdings

We saw in the chapter on the public corporations the extent of their involvement in private industry—and by British Steel Corporation, British Rail and the Air Corporations in particular.

The scope of such shareholding is wide; the reasons for it are

[1] Select Committee on Nationalised Industries, 1967–8, op. cit., p. 61.
[2] 'Special Report from the Select Committee on Nationalised Industries', op. cit., p. 45.

sometimes historical but increasingly economically motivated. For example, Mr Richard Marsh wrote as follows concerning British Rail:

> Bearing in mind that the main burden of our task is to provide enough income to replace the railway assets we have added to our statutory obligations the goal of generating sufficient cash flow to meet our investment requirements over a rolling ten year period. From our subsidiary activities such as shipping, hotels, etc., we look for a maximum contribution to the main task be it capital or income and to help us achieve this we have set target returns on capital employed broadly in line with private sector competition.

The Bank of England has integrated vertically into Portals Ltd to protect its supply of paper. In the case of the Agricultural Development Finance Corporation, the Commonwealth Development Finance Company, and the Finance Corporation for Industry, the Bank played a major part in their foundation because there was a gap in the market machinery and it wished to encourage by example other institutions to put up capital in the public interest and on less than commercially attractive prospects.

As a matter of policy the Bank does not seek to influence the commercial or financial decisions of these companies.

Some of the government agencies, e.g. the U.K. Atomic Energy Authority, have investments in outside firms. In Northern Ireland the provincial government is an equity shareholder in Harland & Wolff.[1]

The Industrial Reconstruction Corporation, which was set up by by the Labour Government to help promote rationalisation, mergers and restructuring of industry, became a substantial shareholder in the private sector. The Conservative government ended its activities but the following holdings were held on 1 November 1971 by the Secretary of State for Industry as a legatee—but awaiting disposal.[2]

---

[1] H.C. Official Report, vol. 820, 6 July 1971, cols. 340-1.
[2] H.C. Official Report, vol. 826, 15 Nov. 1971, cols 28-30; N.B. there were still outstanding loans made by the I.R.C. and repayable to the Secretary of State for Trade and Industry, e.g. £35m unsecured loan British Leyland Motor Corporation; £2·5m British Oxygen; £3m to Plessey Numerical Controls Ltd.

Equity and Preference Shares		Cost £
British Nuclear and Construction Ltd	260,000 Ordinary shares of £1	260,000
Brown Bayley Ltd	2,400,000 Ordinary shares of £1	*
Chrysler (U.K.) Ltd	7,561,140 7% Cumulative Preferred Ordinary Shares of 20p	1,512,228
George Kent Ltd	3,017,577 Ordinary Shares of 50p 1,244,180 Deferred Ordinary Shares of 50p	6,504,861
Herbert-Ingersoll Ltd	38,250 'A' Ordinary Shares of £1 36,750 'B' Ordinary Shares of £1	525,000
Kearney & Trecker Ltd	300,000 Redeemable Convertible Third Preference Shares of £1	300,000
Nuclear Enterprises Ltd	7,353 'B' Ordinary Shares of £1	300,000
The Laird Group Ltd	4,900,830 Ordinary Shares of 25p	1,225,208

* The following investments were held by Brown Bayley Ltd:

Brown Bayley Steels Ltd	2,404,000 shares of 50p	1,470,453
Ransome Hoffman	2,700,000 8% Convertible Unsecured loan stock 1984	2,700,000
	1,200,000 Deferred Ordinary Shares of 25p	588,911

The following loans 'convertible into equity' were still outstanding

Marwin (Holdings) Ltd	£750,000 8% Convertible Loan
Ransome Hoffman Pollard Ltd	£6,211,004 8% Convertible Unsecured Loan Stock 1984 (subscribed at par)
Rolls-Royce Ltd	£10,000,000 Unsecured Convertible Loan
Spirella Group Ltd	£400,000 10% Convertible Unsecured Loan Stock 1977 (subscribed at par)

By 1 January 1972 the shares in the Laird Group Ltd had been sold and early in the same year saw the disposal of shareholdings and loan interests in Chrysler (U.K.) Ltd and in Ransome Hoffman Pollard Ltd.

The I.R.C. is ended and thus eventually this method of state shareholding. There is no sign of a diminution of such involvement by the public corporations. On the parallel of private industry there is every reason to expect an increase; it was not surprising to learn that after the hiving off of Thomas Cooks from

the Transport Holding Company, B.E.A. and B.O.A.C. joined a
consortium to bid for its ownership.[1]

In the case of the direct holdings of the government itself
there are no indications that these are to be reduced. Indeed,
the experience of the Conservative government with Rolls-Royce
would indicate an increase in this type of involvement as do the
powers taken in the Industry Act of 1972 for state acquisition
of loan or share capital. Necessity is stronger than ideology.

RELATIONS WITH GOVERNMENT
AND PARLIAMENT

Government

There does seem to be some lack of clarity in government departments concerning the extent and nature of government ownership of shares in private industry, e.g. as to the nature of both
Cable and Wireless and the Transport Holding Company—both
in fact public corporations.

By the very ad-hoc development of this type of ownership over
the years, and unlike the public corporations and the directly
controlled organisations, e.g. R.O.F.s, there does seem to be no
systematic arrangements for the 'control' of the companies concerned which were not under the aegis of the Industrial Reconstruction Corporation.

The view of the government on these arrangements in the
particular case of the Beagle Aircraft Company was given in reply
to a Report of the Public Accounts Committee.[2]

The P.A.C. expressed concern at the 'inadequacy of continuing
information to the government and continuing appraisal of the
government's position' on Beagle.[3] The reply by the Treasury
and the D.T.I. was that

A Government shareholding in a company registered with
limited liability under the Companies Acts does not of itself
alter the legal rights and duties of shareholders, or of the
Board, its officers and the company itself, or of third parties
having dealings with the company. Moreover, when the

[1] In the event Thos Cooks was bought by a consortium of Midland
Bank Ltd, Trust House Forte Ltd, and the Automobile Association.
[2] 'Third Report from the Committee of Public Accounts, Session 1970–1',
H.C. 300 I. 375, pp. xxviii–xxxi and 299–330.
[3] H.C. Official Report, vol. 827, no. 23, 2 Dec. 1971, col. 694.

Government creates or acquires such a wholly Government-owned company to carry on a commercial undertaking, it expects the Board and officers of the company and those doing business with it to proceed on a normal commercial basis and with full regard for the legal rights and duties of the various parties. The Treasury and the Department of Trade and Industry agree that the arrangements between the government as a sole shareholder and a wholly-owned commercial company must be such as to enable government to be adequately informed of the company's policy and progress, but with due regard for the need to give the Board the proper degree of freedom to manage the affairs of the company commercially and without prejudice to the legal rights and responsibilities of the Board and its officers and of those doing business with the company[1]

This drew the following response in the House of Commons from Mr Harold Lever, Chairman of the P.A.C.[2]

That does not quite answer the problem. When the Government intervene as a shareholder, they are rarely wholly passive. They tend to appoint directors to the board, to exercise some degree of supervision and in some ways to become responsible for what the company does.

When the Government have a major financial stake in a company, the first question to be asked is: what are their obligations to creditors? The Government cannot ride off by saying 'We told the directors to act commercially and, therefore, any liability to creditors is a liability of the company and not of the Government.'

He went on,

Whether one is a Government or an honourable private citizen, if one is financing a company and actively participating in its affairs with knowledge one has no right to spawn companies which can take on credit without any reasonable expectation of paying the debts one is incurring.

[1] Treasury Minute on the Reports from the Committee on Public Accounts, Session 1970-1 and Abstract of Appropriation Accounts, paras. 49-58, p. 6.
[2] H.C. Official Report, op. cit., cols. 695-7.

Again, he stated

It is not good enough to appoint gentlemen of distinction to the board—an eminent accountant or general; talent of the kind that Governments are apt to find for these jobs—and then say, 'We were not to know that the losses would be so great. We would have been ready to pay up for a smaller loss, but not for this gigantic loss, and we now wish to withdraw.' In those circumstances, they cannot bow out without meeting the creditors. It follows that the appraisal and information must be continuous.

Something else follows, too. Before Governments undertake these ventures they must obtain an expert and dispassionate commercial judgment about the prospects and they should found their decision on that.

The Financial Secretary to the Treasury replied as follows:[1]

The Committee recommended that when the Government take a shareholding in a limited liability company and intend to accept no liability beyond that of any normal shareholder, this should be stated publicly so that creditors will not be misled. This recommendation raises immensely complex issues which are still under consideration.

The second question concerns information. Perhaps I can be of more help in this regard. We agree, as the Treasury Minute points out, that where the Government are the sole shareholder in a commercial company, there must be arrangements to ensure that they are adequately informed about the company's affairs in general, its trading position, developments in its activities and prospects. The Government accepts that principle entirely and the arrangements which exist—they must obviously vary from one individual case to another—are reviewed from time to time. It is not essential that the arrangements should be uniform in all cases. The main thing is to make sure that they work well in practice. The Government are reviewing the arrangements in individual cases to make sure of this.

On the arrangements for control the government had still to make up its mind on 'complex issues' and was still reviewing procedures. On general principle it was clear:

[1] *Ibid.*, cols. 767-8.

At the same time, this does not mean that Government Departments should seek to involve themselves in day-to-day affairs of wholly-owned companies. Again, as the Treasury Minute points out, the fact that such a company is wholly-owned by the Government does not in any way alter the fact that it has to operate under the Companies Acts, and clearly boards of directors must be given the proper degree of freedom to manage the affairs of the company commercially without prejudice to their rights and responsibilities under the law.

With regard to the government directors responsibilities Mr Harold Wilson when Prime Minister summed up these when referring to British Petroleum as follows: 'The Government directors have a general obligation to report on all matters which they consider should be referred to, or brought to the notice of H.M. Government.'[1]

A provocative remark by the Financial Secretary to the Treasury in the Beagle debate—when he made clear that the discussion concerning fully-owned companies applied also to companies only partially owned and to those receiving loan finance —broadened the area of discussion.[2] Such an approach broadens the possibility of future policy.

The whole matter of the relationship of government with the companies it owns or aids needs far more investigation and discussion. This has happened in the case of the public corporations; it is necessary in the case of the various grand-aided organisations as was argued earlier; it is vitally necessary in the case of shareholdings where government gets enmeshed in the private sector. The Industrial Reconstruction Corporation was so important in this respect, and for this reason alone its demise left a gap which needs to be filled.

Parliament

With regard to the relationship of Parliament to the companies owned by the government, accountability may be exercised in a number of procedural ways—general debates on major matters of government policy with regard to the firms and parliamentary questions not concerned with day-to-day administration.

[1] *Ibid.*, vol. 711, 4 May 1965. Also see cols. 1111-3.
[2] *Ibid.*, cols. 767-8.

There have, for example, been many debates on U.C.S. and Rolls-Royce; ever since the initial shareholding of the government in B.P., questions have been asked on the attitude of the government as a shareholder.

As far as the Public Accounts Committee is concerned there are no powers to examine the accounts or activities of a commercial company simply because of the government shareholding. Where grants are made, e.g. to Short Bros and Harland, it is open to the Committee to examine the Accounting Officer of the government department concerned on the relationships of government to that company and the extent to which government objectives were being met.

The P.A.C. report on Beagle Aircraft Ltd and the debate that followed, reveals another reason for investigation, i.e. a possible open-ended commitment to company creditors in the event of collapse.

There is parliamentary accountability, but whether it is relevant to a growing form of public ownership is another matter. This aspect of parliamentary procedure is ripe for the type of full discussion that arose in the 1950s and 60s when the full implications for parliament of nationalisation were realised in practice.

In the case of the public corporations with their shareholdings there is usually an internal organisational management link which follows the line of vertical integration, e.g. B.O.A.C. with its hotel investments.

Insofar as the corporations are themselves responsible to parliament, so are their subsidiary and associated companies. Nevertheless, because of their growing importance and probable development, the Select Committee on the Nationalised Industries should examine these from an accountability point of view —and issue a general report on the problems involved and the procedures that ought to be followed.

In this respect the following excerpt from the Annual Report of a public corporation is relevant—

Cable & Wireless Ltd owns 99.95 per cent and 95.60 per cent of the issued share capital of two further companies and of these total holdings 96.96 per cent and 46.60 per cent respectively are held by subsidiary companies. Details of these companies are not included above on the grounds that disclosure would be harmful to the interests of such companies, but their accounts for the year ended 31 March 1971 are included in the consolidated accounts.[1]

There are, no doubt, good commercial reasons for this mysterious approach; but it is not good enough for a body responsible to parliament.

The basic accountability problem, however, lies with the direct state shareholdings. In this respect there is another approach which would follow from a changed organisation relationship between them and the government and from a wider future use of this type of public ownership.

FUTURE POLICY

With regard both to an appropriate form of organisation to deal with the problems of the existing shareholdings, and to a consideration of an extension of this type of public ownership—the developments that have taken place in two other mixed economies, in Sweden and Italy, are very relevant.

Sweden and Italy[2]

In Sweden there is a long history of public ownership. Until recently it was of two main types—state undertakings, e.g. railways, post office, forest service, etc.; and companies in which the state had complete or majority share control, e.g. wines and spirits, iron ore deposits, air transport, engineering, shipbuilding, etc.

Since 1970 and following a Royal Commission there has been set up a holding company to own most of the companies. Other changes have put the state undertakings into a Public Enterprises Commission which coordinates their activities and their relations with the holding company; there has also been an unification of ministerial responsibility.

In Italy where there is also state enterprise of the conventional type—posts, railways—there are state holding companies, of which the two most important are Istituto per la Ricostruzione Industriale and Ente Nazionale Idrocarburi.

[1] 'Cable & Wireless Ltd, Report and Accounts, 31 March 1971', p. 18.
[2] David Coombes, *Business or Politics*, P.E.P., Allen & Unwin, 1971, ch. 10, Sweden; ch. 11, Italy.

The former, I.R.I., controls over 100 firms in banking, mining, shipbuilding, merchant shipping, chemicals, air transport, civil engineering (and in particular motorway construction), motor vehicles and radio/television, etc. The activities are comprehensive and diverse as I found when I visited many of them.[1]

The latter, E.N.I., is basically concerned with the production and distribution of oil, natural gas and nuclear energy.

The firms, which are controlled by the holding companies, compete with other firms and raise part of their capital on the open market. On the other hand, they receive interest-free loans from the government through a sponsoring Ministry of State Holdings which has statutory powers of control, e.g. on investment programmes.

Guided though the holding companies are by the profit motive, they engage in socially-motivated operations, particularly in the field of regional development. The giant steel works at Tarento is a prime example of this type of activity.

Although in neither Sweden nor Italy is the holding company organisation set-up free from criticism on a variety of grounds— e.g. in Italy, lack of enterprise and concern for the long-term needs of the country—and bearing in mind the differing backgrounds, this form of public ownership and control has a particular relevance to this country.

State Holding Company[2]

There are a variety of shareholdings held by the state in the U.K. The confused state of information and philosophy on their very existence would at the least be clarified with the setting up of a state holding company—whether it be the lack of information revealed over Beagle, the lack of principle in B.P., or the lack of both in the sage of U.C.S.

A state holding company would also enable the government to find a less politically embarrassing solution of the need to replace the I.R.C. The need to rationalise industry is still vital,

[1] See 'Annual Report' (English Abridged Version), I.R.I., 1971.
[2] See *H.C. Official Report*, vol. 827, 10 Dec. 1971, cols. 1687-96, speech by Mr Edmund Dell; cols. 1767-77 speech by Sir John Eden, Minister for Industry. The whole debate on a Friday Private Member's Motion is worth attention—unlike most of the major 'cut and thrust' debates on this subject.

as has been found in Northern Ireland where, as a result of the Cairncross Report, there is to be set up a Northern Ireland Finance Corporation.[1]

A state holding company has possibilities as a means of carrying out the functions of the Shipbuilding Industry Board which ended on 31 December 1971. On this date, the rights, liabilities and investments of the Board passed to the Department of Trade and Industry.

As well as grants which are once-for-all, the Board made loans. As of 31 December 1971, the following were outstanding and vested in the D.T.I., who inherited the responsibility of appointing one director to those marked with an asterisk.

Shipbuilder	Amount of loan Principal Outstanding £
Drypool Engineering & Drydock Co. Ltd	424,000
Appledore Shipbuilders Ltd	1,032,750
Robb Caledon Shipbuilders Ltd	400,000
*Harland & Wolff Ltd	8,000,000
*Yarrow (Shipbuilders) Ltd	1,185,000
Ryton Marine Ltd	99,950
Charles D. Holmes & Co. Ltd	85,244
*Scott Lithgow Ltd	3,800,000
Upper Clyde Shipbuilders Ltd (in liquidation)	3,520,000

Loans totalling some £3m were still being made between April and 31 December 1971—even though the Board was to end.[2] It would be surprising if government loans to shipbuilding were to end. The holding company solution would be a better means of working with this industry than direct to the D.T.I. itself. Indeed, a number of specialised such companies, working to rather than in the D.T.I., may prove to be the more logical and efficient development for industry as a whole. There could be, for example, a holding company for the aircraft industry with the responsibility for sponsorship and 'launching aid', as well as for ownership, e.g. Rolls-Royce; Short & Harland.

In all such industries where this solution is used it should be the 'advisory and executive filter between the Minister and private

[1] 'Review of Economic and Social Development in Northern Ireland', Cmnd 564 (Northern Ireland).
[2] H.C. Official Report, vol. 830, 7 Feb. 1971, col. 255.

industry',[1] and the vehicle by which other aid is given to industry. In the financial year 1970–1, for example, nearly £7m of grants were made to various shipbuilding firms.[2] A holding company could be used for the 'proper administration of such schemes as the cotton rationalisation plan'.[3] Whether one holding company or a number of smaller bodies, they could concern themselves with information, etc., and thus be allied with the appropriate Economic Development Committees; and with training, and thus have a link with the Industrial Training Boards.

A holding company, or companies, by their involvement in a variety of activities, could give a new impetus to regional development on the model of I.R.I., by placing socially necessary technological industry in the development and intermediate areas; there would be value in capital investment carried out against the prevailing commercial and industrial trend.

In the context of the existing public corporations and their possible reorganisation, it may be that the National Bus Company and the National Freight Corporation would be better administered in a holding company fashion.

Certainly the position of Cable & Wireless Ltd needs to be considered thus; it is a curious public corporation. As part of a telecommunication holding company it could be associated with firms that manufacture relevant equipment.

In all such changes thought would have to be given to parliamentary accountability. Before decisions are taken the views of the Select Committee on the Nationalised Industries should be sought.

National Shareholding Agency

Another approach to the problem of the existing haphazard system of state share ownership would be the setting up of a National Shareholding Agency.

A scheme was put forward by Jonathan Boswell in a Fabian research pamphlet in 1968. In this he suggested that such an agency could 'collect under one net the shares obtained for the

[1] Michael Posner, Richard Pryke, *New Public Enterprise*, Fabian Research Series 254, 1966, p. 14.
[2] 'Shipbuilding Industry Board Report and Accounts Year Ended 31 March 1971', H.C. 554, appendix A.
[3] Posner and Pryke, *op. cit.*, p. 14.

state as a by-product of industrial rationalisation'.[1] To this could be added the companies in which the public corporations and other type agencies have invested.

If this alone were done it would provide information which is now fragmented, and concentrate far more thought on the motives and philosophy behind such development. At the moment in some 'sponsoring' government department these seem not to be understood nor the nature of the firms responsible to them comprehended.

On this wider aspect Jonathan Boswell made other suggestions.[2] The agency could acquire shares in three other possible ways: (i) to oblige companies to issue some new form of 'community share', (ii) to buy shares on the Stock Exchange in the same manner as existing institutions, (iii) to take shares in payment of the new gift and wealth taxes.

The underlying philosophy is part of social democratic thought over the last 20 years; concerned less with the running of industry than with the redistribution of income and equality.[3]

The first suggestion is based on the developments in capitalist company organisation; the growth of managerial power and the declining influence of the shareholder and of 'risk' in large companies.

Other interesting proposals have been made over the years to deal with the same trend—that the return on ordinary, i.e. risk-bearing, shares should be limited in some large companies; that only a proportion of profits should be distributed. Both these proposals in effect ask for an extension of preference shareholding.

Associated with these ideas have been those for wider company accountability to the employee—another form of workers' participation—and to the wider community, with the right to participate in profits.[4] It is in this context that the 'community shareholding' idea of Boswell is made.

Such a concept would necessitate a radical change in company law. There is need too to reconsider this in the light of changes in capitalist organisation, for while it has technically changed

---

[1] Jonathan Boswell, *Can Labour Master the Private Sector?*, Fabian Research Series 271, Oct. 1968, pp. 28-9.
[2] *Ibid.*, pp. 28-9.
[3] See, e.g., *ibid.*, ch. 5, p. 25.
[4] See 'Further Reading', p. 230, below, for books, articles in this field.

over the last 100 years, its underlying philosophy has remained the same. In any such broad study 'the fundamental question should be: What are the modern conditions appropriate in our society on which private capital in a mixed economy can be allowed the privilege of incorporation with limited liability?'[1]

Company law changed to provide 'community' shareholding might be part of a new incomes policy. More preference-type shares with lower return, would ease the approach to the trade unions on wages and salaries. Insofar as this concept is more relevant to the large firms which can have an effect on prices, then prices as well as incomes policy could be taken into account.

It might also be appropriate to use company legislation to promote desirable social practices in industry, e.g. on recruitment, redundancy, collective bargaining, etc. At the least, the shareholding agency could provide not only the financial details of state holdings but also details of the existing social practices in the 'publicly' owned concerns.

The opportunity to reconsider the relevance of cooperative shareholding in certain industries and firms could be taken in any philosophical reconsideration of company law.

Boswell's remaining suggestions are redistributive in concept and are a reflection of the concern for the lack of such an effect from conventional public ownership. There is much in the argument for in this way the community could tap capital gains and obtain a share in the fruits of industrial expansion. Just as the public corporations—like large private industry—diversify into many different activities to obtain income for cash flow, etc., so the state as a shareholder could obtain a transfer income to help, for example, the expansion of the social services.

Nevertheless, the fate of the National Superannuation Fund Investment proposals should be recalled and change in this respect should be slow. What is urgent is the reconsideration of the law and in depth. Without this it would be so easy 'to jump from a Victorian primitivism to a new-fangled confusion'.[2]

The state shareholding form of organisation needs to be recognised as an unconventional part of the public sector. Whatever

---

[1] K. W. Wedderburn, *Company Law Reform*, Fabian Tract 363, Sept. 1965, p. 19.
[2] Boswell, *op. cit.*, p. 18.

the arguments are, concerning the nature of the firms in which equities are owned—the result is a type of public ownership.

It certainly needs more investigation, and as part of this it would be of value to look at the causes of the downfall of Rolls-Royce and the reasons for its rebirth as a state-owned company rather than as a conventional public corporation.

The Rolls-Royce model is not alone, for in the case of Govan Shipbuilders, the successors to U.C.S., a viability study as to its future by the merchant bankers, Hill, Samuel, has recommended that the firm should be wholly owned by the government because it is most unlikely that it 'can attract any private capital except perhaps a small amount on a purely emotional basis'.[1]

The case for its nationalisation as a public corporation is a strong one, as it is in shipbuilding generally; as it is in the case of Rolls-Royce. Nevertheless, whatever the argument in individual cases, the system of state shareholdings generally is likely to prove a growth form of public ownership.

In a basic respect it is of the essence of the mixed economy.

[1] 'Shipbuilding on the Upper Clyde', Report of Hill, Samuel & Co. Ltd, *Cmnd* 4918, 1972, p. 11.

Further Reading

A. Albu, *The Organisation of Industry*, New Fabian Essays, Turnstile Press, 1952.

A. Crosland, *The Future of Socialism*, Cape, 1956.

H. Crum Ewing, 'Better Law for Companies', *Crossbow*, April 1965, p. 50.

P. Derrick, *The Company and the Community*, Fabian Research Series 238, 1964.

M. Fogarty, 'Companies Beyond Jenkins', P.E.P., vol. XXXI, 486, Feb. 1965.

G. Goyder, *The Responsible Company*, Blackwell, 1961.

D. Jay, *Socialism and the New Society*, Longmans, 1961.

N. Ross, *The Democratic Firm*, Fabian Research Series 242, 1964.

Socialism and Managers, Fabian Tract 351, 1963.

T.U.C. *Economic Review 1968*, p. 66: 'Incomes Policy'; pp. 75-6: 'The Role of the Company'.

6 Conclusion: The Public Sector

The public sector—central government, local authorities and the public corporations—is a significant part of the national economy. Its work, as we have seen—over which the government has varying degrees of responsibility—encompasses a wide spectrum of activities.

Public expenditure, by the three parts of the defined public sector, and excluding debt interest, was estimated in 1970–1 to be of the order of £20,000m or some 45 per cent of the G.N.P.[1] The public sector owns about 45 per cent of the nation's capital assets and of the annual fixed investment.

In terms of landownership, and in the face of a dearth of statistics in this respect, the state appears to own over 5,000,000 acres of land—from playing fields to farmland and forests—out out of a total acreage of 56,000,000.[2]

In June 1970 the total employed labour force in the public sector was 6,300,000 or 25.1 per cent of the total. Within this group it employs some 60 per cent of the products of higher education; a significant number being scientists. Research and development is only profitable in the long run. It is a 'height of the economy' commanded by the state.

The number of organisations within the public sector are changing as government policy changes; the Land Commission and the Northern Pennines Development Board were set up under a Labour government and ended by its Conservative successor. In mid-1972 a Civil Aviation Authority took over the functions of the Air Registration Board, the Air Traffic Licensing Board and air traffic control functions of the Department of Trade and Industry. In terms of place in the public sector, the Post Office as a public corporation has replaced the civil service G.P.O.

[1] 'Public Expenditure 1969–70 to 1974–5', *Cmnd* 4578, table 1.3, p. 9.
[2] For information on landowning by government departments see *H.C. Official Report*, vol. 762, 2 April 1968, cols. 56-7.

The current classification of the public sector organisations, based though it is on the national accounts classification, is often not clear. For example, Letchworth Garden City Corporation is a public corporation, four of whose members are appointed by the Secretary of State for the Environment and whose borrowing powers are those of a local authority—yet because it is not accounted for in the Local Government Finance Statistics, it is not in the local government group nor in the public sector.[1] This is to be rectified.

Within the grant-aided organisation group there is Remploy Ltd, responsible to the Department of Employment, with 17 government-appointed directors and employing nearly 10,000 employees in 86 factories—yet allocated to the company sector because it only receives from the state a revenue subvention to make up the difference between total cost and revenue, together with a loan for capital investment.[2] The National Computing Centre, responsible to the Department of Trade and Industry, whose aim is to promote an increased and more efficient use of computers nationally, is allocated in the same way—presumably because just less than half its income comes from the state.[3]

Industrial Advisers to the Blind, responsible to the Department of Employment, with nine government directors and finance provided through the estimates, and the General Practice Finance Corporation which makes loans to general practitioners under firm direction from the Department of Health and Social Security, are allocated to the personal sector.

The question of the statistical allocation of Letchworth Corporation is perhaps an esoteric technical matter—but with the other examples, all subject to the P.A.C. and to the Expenditure Committee, there are good reasons for placing them in the central government group.

At the moment, for these and other similar examples, the real size and importance of the public sector both in expenditure and manpower is to some degree understated. It would be even greater

---

[1] For details of this Corporation see 'Special Report from the Select Committee on Nationalised Industries. The Committee's Order of Reference', H.C. 298, 1968, p. 50.
[2] 'Remploy. Report and Accounts for Year Ended 31 March 1971'.
[3] See National Computing Centre; Industrial Advisers to the Blind; General Practice Finance Corporation, 'Special Report from the Select Committee on Nationalised Industries', op. cit., pp. 54, 50 and 48, respectively.

if the state shareholding interests were also taken into account.

The development of the public sector has been politically motivated in Britain as in other parts of the world—but it crosses the political boundaries. In the U.S.A., for example, the state gets more and more involved in industry and in social expenditure, to the degree that the whole question of the method of state involvement—including local government reform—and accountability, is increasingly exercising the minds of politicians and administrators there.

The basic reason for the growth of a public sector is not political but to satisfy modern economic and social needs. The central and local government finds itself increasingly involved in the interstices of human existence. The public corporation meets the requirements of the twentieth century as the joint stock company satisfied the changing needs of the nineteenth-century industrial revolution. The joint stock company is still relevant today, but the growth of state shareholdings in some instances illustrates its inability to meet its old role.

The argument about public ownership in principle is deeply ingrained in our political life but what really matters in the public sector is to ask the questions that matter. What should be its structure and role? What new forms of public ownership are available? Have we anything to learn from the E.E.C. or Eastern Europe? How can accountability and management efficiency be improved throughout the public sector? What pricing policies should be followed and in what way should social needs be taken into account? What role can the trade unions, born of the capitalist system, play in this emerging unfamiliar field that they have politically supported? How should incomes policy apply in the public sector? Is this not the place to lead on the problem of the lower-paid worker? What is the relevance of workers' participation?

The questions that matter are asked by the Select Committee on Nationalised Industries, by the Public Accounts and Expenditure Committees and in the political journals. They are rarely asked or discussed in the partly political battle field; they ought to be; they could be.

This questioning approach does not imply perfection in the private sector. There are real and similar questions to ask there. It is not uniform in structure nor efficiency; what is appropriate for the large firm would be wrong for the small private limited company. In many private firms the method of investment taking is 'primitive' when compared with very large multinational companies or the state public corporations;[1] in others the approach to the trade unions is less historic but it is certainly nineteenth century.[2]

The extent of the public sector is greater than generally realised; it plays a major part in the mixed economy. It would be of value if more politicians realised this fact of life because the sector has bred its own non-Samuel Smiles attitudes and ethos to which they ought to respond—they are relevant, for example, to any approach to incomes policy. It would be of value also if more economists took the sector into account before formulating their basic economic theories.

The public sector is not static but, with changing forms and in changing directions, it is here to stay. It will provide a growing proportion of a more mixed economy.

---

[1] M. Peston, 'On the Nature and Extent of the Public Sector', *Three Banks Review*, Sept. 1965, p. 22.
[2] Jack Jones, 'How to Rebuild Industrial Relations', *New Statesman*, 18 Feb. 1972, p. 202.

INDEX

Civil Service College 51
  Department 51
Civil Service, Industrial 55ff.
  Non-Industrial 40ff.
  Pay, Management and account-
    ability problems 61
  recommendations for reorganisa-
    tion of 51
Clegg, Prof. H. *How to Run an
  Incomes Policy* 18
Clinical Research Centre 69
Clydebank 211
Coal 147, 180, 184, 189, 193
Combustibili Nucleari 72
Commonwealth Development Finance
  Co. 216
  War Graves Commission 73
Comptroller and Auditor General 76
Computer Agency, Central
Computer-aided Design Centre 24
Computers 24, 25, 26, 105, 208, 232
  Mergers Scheme 26
Concorde 32
Confederation of British Industries
  192
Conservative Government 15, 19,
  24, 25, 27, 28, 35, 92, 117
Cook, A. J. 127
Corporations, Public 123ff., 175ff.
  finance 177ff., 183-4, 191
  list of 125, 126
  objectives and performance 178ff.,
    192
  problems 191
  social cost 179
Countryside Commission 39, 76
Covent Garden Market Authority
  162, 182
Crawford Committee 124
Criminal Injuries Compensation
  Board 73
Crosland, C. A. R. *The Future of
  Socialism* 12
Crossman, Mr Richard 111
  Socialism and the New Despotism
  194
Crowther Commission 119
Customs and Excise 41

Dainton, Sir Frederick
Data Processing Service 153, 180
Data Recording Instrument Co. 208
Defence Estimates 62, 64
  expenditure 32
Defence, Ministry of 33, 42, 116
  establishments controlled by 48ff.
  Procurement, Minister of State for
    66
  range of activities, 57ff.

Dell, Mr Edmund 224
Development Areas 19
Distribution of Industry Act 19
Docks 83, 85, 89, 95, 128, 139, 164,
  180, 191
Drainage Boards 97

Eagle Star Insurance Co. 207
Economic Development Committee
  16, 226
  policy, British 14ff.
Economy, Mixed 10ff.
  Planned 11
Education Act (1944) 90
Education and Science, Department
  of 43, 69, 72, 87, 116
Education, local administration of 90,
  100, 103
Edwards, Sir George 32
Eisenhower, President (qu.) 33
Electricity Council and Boards 141,
  152, 156, 174, 176, 180, 190
Empire Test Pilots' School 48
Engineering Laboratory, National 45
Environment, Department of the 21,
  39, 41, 87, 104, 116, 171
  departments controlled by 46ff., 56,
    57, 60, 66, 85, 133, 139, 140,
    146, 150, 156, 163, 166
Eton Rural District Council 89
Expenditure Committee 77, 189
Explosives Research and Develop-
  ment Establishment 49

Fairfields (shipbuilding) 211
Fair Wages Resolution (1946) 61
Faith, N. *Squaring up to Yankee
  Imperialism* 13
Farms, experimental 50
Finance Corporation for Industry
  158, 216
Fire Authorities, Joint 83
  Brigades NJC 103
  Research Station 46
Fire Brigade Advisory Council, Cen-
  tral 118
Fishing research 46, 51, 74, 75
Foreign and Commonwealth Office
  72
Forest Products Research Laboratory
  46
Forestry Commission 73, 76, 77, 78
Friedman, Prof. Milton 15
Fulton Report on the Civil Service
  51

Gaitskell, Hugh 197
Galbraith, Prof. 34
Gas Council 143, 180, 190, 197
  Turbine Establishment, National
    48